THE SUPERHERO BLOCKBUSTER

THE SUPERHERO BLOCKBUSTER

ADAPTION, STYLE, AND MEANING

JAMES C. TAYLOR

UNIVERSITY PRESS OF MISSISSIPPI / JACKSON

The University Press of Mississippi is the scholarly publishing agency of the Mississippi Institutions of Higher Learning: Alcorn State University, Delta State University, Jackson State University, Mississippi State University, Mississippi University for Women, Mississippi Valley State University, University of Mississippi, and University of Southern Mississippi.

www.upress.state.ms.us

The University Press of Mississippi is a member of the Association of University Presses.

Copyright © 2025 by University Press of Mississippi
All rights reserved
Manufactured in the United States of America

∞

Publisher: University Press of Mississippi, Jackson, USA
Authorised GPSR Safety Representative: Easy Access System Europe - Mustamäe tee 50, 10621 Tallinn, Estonia, gpsr.requests@easproject.com

Library of Congress Cataloging-in-Publication Data

Names: Taylor, James C. (Teaching fellow in film and television studies), author.
Title: The superhero blockbuster : adaptation, style, and meaning / James C. Taylor.
Description: Jackson : University Press of Mississippi, 2025. | Includes bibliographical references and index.
Identifiers: LCCN 2024048635 (print) | LCCN 2024048636 (ebook) | ISBN 9781496856777 (hardback) | ISBN 9781496856784 (trade paperback) | ISBN 9781496856791 (epub) | ISBN 9781496856807 (epub) | ISBN 9781496856814 (pdf) | ISBN 9781496856821 (pdf)
Subjects: LCSH: Superhero films—History and criticism. | Comic strip characters in motion pictures.
Classification: LCC PN1995.9.S76 T39 2025 (print) | LCC PN1995.9.S76 (ebook) | DDC 791.43/75—dc23/eng/20241106
LC record available at https://lccn.loc.gov/2024048635
LC ebook record available at https://lccn.loc.gov/2024048636

British Library Cataloging-in-Publication Data available

For my wonderful sister Erica.
You once wrote me a book; it took me too long to return the favor.

CONTENTS

Acknowledgments ix

Introduction: Superhero Blockbusters as Adaptations 3

Chapter 1. Truth, Justice, and the Cinematic Way:
Superman: The Movie, the First Superhero Blockbuster 34

Chapter 2. Digital Power and Moral Responsibility:
Spider-Man and the Marvel Superhero in the Twenty-First Century 77

Chapter 3. Earth's Mightiest Superhero Blockbusters:
Networked Seriality in the Marvel Cinematic Universe 127

Chapter 4. The Strangest Continuity of All:
Alternate Timelines in Fox's X-Men Films 170

Conclusion: Crisis on the DC Extended Universe 214

Notes 237

Bibliography 243

Index 259

ACKNOWLEDGMENTS

I will forever be indebted to Catherine Constable and José Arroyo, whose knowledge and support are invaluable. My research would not have been possible without funding from the Arts and Humanities Research Council, to whom I give my sincerest thanks. I am also deeply grateful to James MacDowell and Lisa Purse, for their thoughtful and incisive feedback on the research.

Over the course of my studies, and in the subsequent years in which I expanded, reworked, and refined my research to develop it into this book, I have been fortunate to receive guidance, assistance, and friendship from many colleagues at the University of Warwick and beyond. This list includes (although is by no means limited to) Pablo Alvarez Murillo, Charlotte Brunsdon, Liam Burke, Hande Çayır, Matthew Denny, Jake Edwards, Ilana Emmett, Jessica Fowler, Ed Gallafent, Adam Gallimore, Ivan Girina, Joe Harrison, Tom Hemingway, Claire Jesson, Nike Jung, Catherine Lester, Julie Lobalzo-Wright, Tracey McVey, Drew Morton, Rachel Moseley, Georgia Mulligan, Joseph Oldham, Richard Perkins, Victor Perkins, Alastair Phillips, Patrick Pilkington, Ilaria Puliti, Isabel Rhodes, Vladimir Rosas Salazar, Josh Schulze, Zoë Shacklock, Charlotte Stevens, Rick Wallace, Marta Wasik, Owen Weetch, Leanne Weston, Helen Wheatley, and Josette Wolthuis. Thank you also to the undergraduate students at the University at Warwick who have engaged eagerly when discussing the superhero comics, films, and television shows that managed to find their way onto many of my modules.

Various aspects of this research have been presented at conferences over the years, with the Superhero Project and Association of Adaptation Studies in particular providing regular venues for me to talk about superhero adaptation. I am thankful to those conferences' organizers for granting me such opportunities and to the delegates for discussions that helped refine my ideas and sustain my enthusiasm for this research. A version of some of the material on digital imaging from chapter two of this book features in *Comics and Pop Culture: Adaptation from Panel to Frame*, edited by Barry

Keith Grant and Scott Henderson (2019). A version of chapter three was published in *The Journal of Cinema and Media Studies*; this material has since been revised and expanded. I am grateful to the editors of that volume and journal for their suggestions that helped develop my work and for the opportunities to share my research.

At the University Press of Mississippi, my deep gratitude goes to editors Craig W. Gill and Emily Bandy for their assistance and unwavering patience. It is due to them that this book is now a real tangible (and digital) object. For making that object look so striking, I thank Bruno Porto, who provided such spectacular cover art; every reader has my full permission to judge this book by its cover.

I am thankful to all my friends outside of academia who have put up with my academic endeavors, helped provide respite (in forms ranging from boozy holidays to long walks), and at times dared to go see superhero films with me.

Last, but by no means least, thank you to my family. To my parents, Linda and Mark, for always supporting my academic pursuits in every way possible. To my siblings Naomi and Robert—our distinct skills, ongoing adventures, and frequent bickering make us like a Marvel superhero team—and Simon and Erica, who will always be with us. To Ben and "the girls," Lotty and Thea, who with their boundless energy and creativity could have produced a hundred books in the time it took me to write this one. To Mel, for her photography skills. And, of course, thank you to two adorable Flerkens who kept me company and provided necessary distraction throughout the writing process: Kat, who was there for most of the project, and Jacob, who joined me for the final stretch.

THE SUPERHERO BLOCKBUSTER

INTRODUCTION

SUPERHERO BLOCKBUSTERS AS ADAPTATIONS

In one of *Deadpool 2*'s (David Leitch 2018) most spectacular scenes, the eponymous superhero (Ryan Reynolds) voices doubt that Domino's (Zazie Beetz) power of luck is even a superpower, while the on-screen action refutes him. Running down the road of a busy urban center, traffic fortuitously swerves and crashes around Domino, presenting a pathway for her through an elaborate chain of destruction that is presented in a single long take (constructed through much digital compositing and special effects). When toward the end of the shot Deadpool, speaking through his radio link with Domino, muses that her superpower is "hard to picture, it's certainly not very cinematic," the statement rings with irony. The preceding moments have clearly demonstrated that Domino's power can facilitate the kind of explosive spectacle central to how Hollywood blockbuster cinema conceptualizes the "cinematic." More generally, this shot exemplifies how core traits of the superhero genre—in this case, superpowers—prove ideal material for twenty-first-century blockbusters that readily incorporate sophisticated computer-generated imagery (CGI) to depict incredible feats. Deadpool's questioning of the cinematic quality of Domino's powers occurs as a car flips over her and the presentation of the action slows right down, the vehicle almost hovering for a moment before everything speeds up again and the car tumbles across the ground. This use of "speed ramping" (a technique where action is slowed and sped up within individual shots) goes beyond the cinematic; Dru Jeffries (2017, 43–50) identifies it as a strategy in comic book cinema whereby almost freezing the action at key moments gestures to the still compositions of comics panels and evokes the experience of reading a

A car flips over Domino in *Deadpool 2* (2018).

comic. Through style and form, the intersection between superhero comics and the Hollywood blockbuster is elucidated.

The characters' rooting in comics is even more explicitly attested after the shot finishes, when Deadpool wonders what comic book artist came up with Domino's powers, concluding it was "probably a guy who can't draw feet." The unnamed but (to comic book fans) clearly identified artist, Rob Liefeld, is a controversial figure in superhero comics. Deadpool's comment expresses a common but innocuous fan gripe with Liefeld's art style, while evading more incisive criticisms of Liefeld's presentation of anatomy that interrogate how Liefeld hyperbolizes hegemonic gender constructions in his hypermuscular men and hypersexualized women.[1] Domino's costume in *Deadpool 2*, tight leather with a low-cut top that bares much cleavage, somewhat conforms with the notoriously fetishistic costumes often given to female superheroes. Her power to manipulate probabilities to her favor is also in keeping with the kinds of powers typically granted female superheroes, which are "linked to traditional notions of female power, including manipulation, sexuality, and masquerade" (LeBel 2009, 65) and often treated with suspicion, in contrast to their male counterparts' celebrated displays of physical strength. Yet in other ways *Deadpool 2* challenges these traditions of representation. The destruction all around Domino as she runs down the road presents a markedly physical threat, and she demonstrates physical prowess as she dives into the armored truck she is chasing and easily bests the male driver in hand-to-hand combat. The film's presentation of Domino also intervenes in traditions of racial representation in superhero comics and Hollywood cinema. Typically depicted as an albino in comic books, having Domino played by a Black woman takes steps to redress the relative lack of Black characters in superhero narratives. In the scene under analysis, she is the only character from Deadpool's newly assembled team (besides Deadpool) who survives their disastrous approach to the city. Her survival subverts the well-worn trope in popular culture, from superhero comics to action cinema, of Black characters being dispensable. This evaluation of *Deadpool 2*'s racial subversion needs tempering, however, by acknowledging that she still conforms to the secondary role of "sidekick" often afforded Black characters in Hollywood action cinema (see Tasker 1993, 43–47).

This short analysis reveals some of the ways in which *Deadpool 2* adapts superhero conventions and gestures to the medium with which they are most associated—comics—while exhibiting the compatibility of these conventions with Hollywood blockbuster cinema. As superhero conventions and Hollywood blockbuster principles interlace, they prompt narrative and stylistic strategies that both continue and revise these two traditions. Through close textual analysis of these strategies, we can begin to unpick the film's layers of meaning, exploring for example how it positions itself in relation to comics and cinema, how it constructs humor and spectacle, and what sociopolitical ideas it expresses.

In many ways *Deadpool 2* is an easy candidate for this kind of analysis since the film adopts a parodic approach in which characters and style explicitly reflect on the traditions in which they are situated. Yet undertaking such a reading also allows one to probe the limits of *Deadpool 2*'s self-reflexivity by exposing ways in which the film is not as subversive as it proclaims. Despite how it presents itself, *Deadpool 2* is not an outlier to the superhero blockbuster boom, a cycle of superhero blockbusters that I see as beginning at the start of the twenty-first century with *X-Men* (Bryan Singer 2000) and *Spider-Man* (Sam Raimi 2002) and gaining an increasingly prominent position in Hollywood production over the following two decades.[2] The film performs comparable functions to other films in the cycle: continuing and developing the practices of superhero blockbusters, in part through intertextual interactions with other superhero texts. It is this book's contention that the kind of analysis sampled in this opening, which pays attention to issues of adaptation and style, can be used to rigorously examine the meanings of twenty-first-century superhero blockbusters.

While core elements of my approach can be applied to any superhero blockbuster, as evident in my first chapter when I examine the first superhero blockbuster, *Superman: The Movie* (Richard Donner 1978), my focus on the twenty-first-century boom in subsequent chapters allows me to expand my approach to cover crucial trends and developments in this cycle. Prominent qualities of these films that are central to their adaptive practices, such as the increasing use of CGI and complex modes of seriality based on those developed in superhero comic books, require us to add to our analytical toolboxes so that we are equipped to examine how these contribute to a film's meanings. In elaborating prominent qualities of the superhero blockbuster from its origins to its twenty-first-century boom, this book also outlines the ways in which superhero blockbusters participate in the development of Hollywood's blockbuster paradigm.

I am particularly interested in the *aesthetics* of superhero blockbusters' adaptive practices. I use this word in a commonly used sense in which aesthetics comprises the artistic construction of a text or object. In basic terms, aesthetics pertains to *form* and *style*. While form refers to the formal features of a text—in film, these can include shots, editing, and sound—style is a harder concept to pin down. In navigating some of the ways that the word has been defined, John Gibbs and Douglas Pye provide a useful basis for the concept: style "seems to refer to the 'how' rather than the 'what'" (2005, 9). The "what" of a text—its characters, plot, themes, etc.—can be presented in any number of ways that constitute its "how." Yet Gibbs and Pye problematize this schema. Adopting V. F. Perkins's elegant formulation from his foundational book on close analysis, *Film as Film* (1972), Gibbs and Pye assert that "'how' is 'what'" (10). Following Perkins, style is not a superficial adornment to the what, but rather determines the what. It is through style that meaning is shaped. Style is the chosen means through which an artist, be they a filmmaker or comics creator, utilize the forms available to them. The ways in which artists configure these forms express the text's meanings.

The forms available to an artist are determined by the medium in which they are working, while for those working in an established genre, the "what" of their texts is informed by that genre's conventions. To properly comprehend the adaptation of style and meaning from superhero comic books to blockbuster films, it is first necessary to clearly define these objects of study. Identifying key qualities of comic books, the superhero genre, and the Hollywood blockbuster, will establish the particularities of this book's objects of study as I understand them, and outline the need for greater scholarly attention to their aesthetics. I then spend the bulk of this introduction establishing a framework for analyzing the adaptation of style and meaning from superhero comic books to cinema. I examine formal relationships between comics and film form, outlining differences while identifying ways in which these can be somewhat, but not entirely, surmounted. Once I have established a model for conceptualizing the ways in which adaption between comics and cinema's distinct kinds of words and images can occur and may affect textual meaning, I combine this with concepts that understand adaptation as a process of material being exchanged not simply from one text to another, but across a whole network of texts. The framework that emerges enables examination of aesthetic and other exchanges as material is adapted between the vast networks of texts in superhero franchises. This theoretical framework underpins this book's analysis and is built on in subsequent chapters.

COMIC BOOKS

An understanding of the material qualities, modes of production, and cultural associations of different comics formats is important when analyzing comics. When formulating a dictionary-style definition for the medium, Scott McCloud notes "comics" as a noun that is "plural in form, used with a singular verb" (1994, 9). Following McCloud's identification of comics as the medium itself, the various kinds of comics—such as comic books, comic strips, and graphic novels—can be considered formats. Liam Burke employs this designation and lists some of the qualities that distinguish different formats as "length, layout, mode of presentation, and readership" (2015, 7). For example, one may summarize that comic books are periodicals of typically 20–40 pages with a traditionally young but increasingly specialist audience; comic strips are short comics told in one or a few rows of panels and are syndicated, traditionally in newspapers and magazines; graphic novels are longer, self-contained comics that are published as books and often intended for an adult audience. Although superheroes feature in comic strips and graphic novels, they are most commonly found in comic books. As will become apparent in my analysis, Hollywood blockbuster adaptations of superhero comic books adapt stylistic strategies, narrative models, and modes of seriality associated with the format.

Since the late 1930s, there has only been one period in which the superhero genre was not the dominant genre in comic books. Post–World War II, from roughly the mid-1940s to the mid-1950s, crime and horror comic books dominated the market. This trend incited a moral panic based on claims that are most notoriously crystallized in Fredric Wertham's 1954 study *Seduction of the Innocent*, a scathing denouncement of comic books which contended that they were causing juvenile delinquency. Although superhero comic books weathered the storm and in fact emerged rejuvenated with their competition from crime and horror comic books quashed, the inflaming of comic books' cultural stigma in this period continues to haunt discourse around comics.

Various strategies have been employed to salvage comics from its low cultural status. One was the development of the term "graphic novel" to describe longer self-contained works that fit comfortably in bookstores. The label seeks to elevate particular works from the disgraced medium by positioning them alongside the culturally respected novel. Ascribing the figure of an individual author—a culturally pervasive way to assign artistic worth to a text—has provided a key means for exalting graphic novels. Many of the most revered graphic novels, such as Art Spiegelman's *Maus: A Survivor's Tale* (1986), Chris Ware's *Jimmy Corrigan: The Smartest Kid on Earth* (2000), and Alison Bechdel's *Fun Home: A Family Tragicomic* (2006) are created by individuals who both write and draw the works. This celebration of individual creation further situates graphic novels in opposition to superhero comic books, which, despite certain creators gaining auteur status, are generally associated with corporate brands. The majority of superhero comic books are produced by at least two people, a writer and an artist, with most featuring other collaborators such as inkers, colorists, and letterers. The most popular superheroes have had hundreds of different creators work on them throughout their publication history and are owned not by creators but by publishers, the most prominent of which are part of media conglomerates. Strategies for celebrating certain comics as works of art situate these in opposition to superhero comic books, which are instead positioned as corporate products that lack individual identity.

Discourses that seek to assert the artistic worth of certain kinds of comics thus stymie aesthetic analysis of superhero comics by discrediting them as artistically bankrupt. While there are increasingly more academic studies of superhero comic books (see, for example, Reynolds 1992; Klock 2002; Hatfield, Heer, and Worcester 2013), their status as genre works leads to many studies favoring frameworks offered by genre studies. Genre criticism helps elucidate both the superhero genre's conventions and capacity for variation.

THE SUPERHERO GENRE

The superhero genre is a well-established tradition that predates the first superhero blockbuster by forty years. Widely agreed as beginning with Superman's June 1938 debut in *Action Comics* #1, the superhero genre proliferated rapidly in comics and was soon adapted into a range of media.[3] Peter Coogan formulates an oft-quoted definition of the superhero genre based around the figure the superhero:

> A heroic character with a selfless, pro-social mission; with superpowers—extraordinary abilities, advanced technology, or highly developed physical, mental, or mystical skills; who has a superhero identity embodied in a codename and iconic costume, which typically express his biography, character, powers, or origin (transformation from ordinary person to superhero); and who is generically distinct, i.e. can be distinguished from characters of related genres (fantasy, science fiction, detective, etc.) by a preponderance of generic conventions. Often superheroes have dual identities, the ordinary one of which is usually a closely guarded secret. (2006, 30)

The three "primary conventions" that Coogan elaborates on are powers, mission, and identity. He argues that the unique ways that these traits combine differentiate the superhero from other heroic figures. Coogan's definition begins to indicate the potential for variation within the genre's conventions. For example, superpowers can be biological, technological, or magical.

Genre criticism provides tools to examine conventional features and their scope for variation. Identifying developmental stages is one means of mapping and appreciating variation in genres. Thomas Schatz identifies four stages of generic evolution. He argues that each Hollywood genre will have

> an *experimental* stage, during which its conventions are isolated and established, a *classic* stage, in which the conventions reach their "equilibrium" and are mutually understood by artist and audience, an age of *refinement*, during which certain formal and stylistic details embellish the form, and finally a *baroque* (or "mannerist" or "self-reflexive") stage, when the form and its embellishments are accented to the point where they themselves become the "substance" or "content" of the work. (1981, 37–38, emphasis in original)

Each stage reworks or reframes a genre's underpinning formula. Narrative and aesthetic structures evolve as the primary interest of texts in a genre shifts from telling stories to formalist self-reflection. Thus, applying developmental stages reveals that the centrality of formula to genre does not cause stagnation, but rather provides a pliable framework though which development and change is implemented.

Coogan (2006) demonstrates that Schatz's stages of generic evolution can be mapped onto the ages that have been applied to superhero comics by fans and critics. These ages track discernable shifts in the genre's "nexus of concerns, storytelling techniques, marketing strategies, styles of art and writing, and approaches to genre conventions" (193). Although the ages are subject to continued contestation, Coogan (193–94) identifies them as: Golden Age (1938–1956), Silver Age (1956–1971), Bronze Age (1971–1980), Iron Age (1980–1987 for DC Comics, 1980–2000 for Marvel Comics), and Renaissance Age, which we are currently in. The first four of these correspond to Schatz's stages. Coogan posits that the texts produced in the Renaissance Age comprise a fifth stage that indicates Schatz's four stages have been completed. Coogan sees the Renaissance as an era of reconstruction, in which the conventions that were deconstructed in the Iron Age are "reestablished in ways that incorporate an understanding of the genre's completed cycle" (198). The superhero genre has been through all the shifts that Schatz outlines and reached a stage where the genre's narrative and formal structures are reconstituted to deliver familiar pleasures alongside a knowing appreciation of the structures themselves. Schatz's stages help illuminate the changes that the superhero genre has gone through.

While applying stages of evolution to a genre enables an appreciation of variation, the practice also limits this appreciation. Steve Neale (2000, 200) demonstrates that imposing a neat, predictable model of linear development on all genres denies more heterogeneous strands of dialogue between texts. Coogan's adherence to Schatz's model causes him to repress significant qualities of texts when those qualities do not fit with the age in which the text was produced. For example, Coogan proposes that "Captain Marvel and Plastic Man best exemplify the Golden Age with their simpler and more humorous approach to superheroics" (2006, 205). However, as demonstrated in Art Spiegelman and Chip Kidd's (2001) auteurist appraisal of Jack Cole's *Plastic Man*, the series's self-reflexively plays with superhero conventions. Applying stages thus risks overlooking the unique qualities of particular texts. Elsewhere, Coogan (2006, 200) does note the parodic tone of *Plastic Man*. He also provides earlier examples of parody in the Golden Age as evidence that the superhero genre's conventions were widely accepted from early on (196–97). Such occurrences disrupt Schatz's model, which states parody occurs at the end of the second stage. Coogan rationalizes this rupture by suggesting that mini cycles operate within ages, and thus each age is marked by parodies of its output (197). The need for such qualifications reveals that genres do not cleanly adhere to linear developmental models. The designation of ages to superhero comic books is useful to the extent that it helps identify broad trends, but it is also crucial that one be attuned to individual qualities of texts.

This book does not purport to offer an all-encompassing study of the superhero genre. The depth of analysis that I seek necessitates sacrificing certain kinds of breadth. While I am attentive to the various media that feature in a superhero franchise's textual network, my analysis privileges comics and films so as to attain a nuanced understanding of ways in which aesthetic and narrative strategies developed in superhero comic books are adapted into cinema. The analytical framework that I formulate will be developed through close analysis of key superhero blockbusters. These films, while making important contributions to the superhero genre, also participate in a well-established filmmaking paradigm.

THE HOLLYWOOD BLOCKBUSTER

It is widely agreed that *Jaws* (Steven Spielberg 1975) initiated the Hollywood blockbuster as we understand it today, during the "postclassical" era of Hollywood filmmaking typically termed "New Hollywood." While films referred to as blockbusters, which were produced for massive budgets and emphasized spectacle, had been produced in Hollywood for decades prior to the 1970s (see Hall 2002), *Jaws* established a significant new filmmaking paradigm. *Jaws* and its sequels exhibit some of the key qualities associated with the contemporary Hollywood blockbuster: an emphasis on special effects spectacle, an increased commitment to serializing big-budget features, and a concerted effort to maximize the merchandising and licensing potential of a film property. These traits have been targeted in discourse that positions blockbusters as artistically degraded.

A feature shared by superhero comic books and blockbuster cinema is that disparaging discourse positions the kinds of spectacle central to both as averse to narrative and character complexity, suggesting that their meanings are shallow. The prevalence of elaborate special effects sequences in blockbusters has intensified as digital imaging has become more sophisticated and ubiquitous in the filmmaking paradigm. The potential to view blockbuster spectacle as a return to Tom Gunning's (1986) conceptualization of a "cinema of attractions," which favors visual excitement over storytelling, has been surveyed by Jeffrey A. Brown (2016, 27–28) in relation to superhero blockbusters. Brown joins scholars like Geoff King (2000) in challenging the simplistic opposition of spectacle and narrative, while others, such as Lisa Purse (2013, 57–69) and James N. Gilmore (2014), analyze the expressive potential of digital imaging in superhero blockbusters. Yvonne Tasker (1993) and Purse (2011) have also demonstrated that examination of the sociopolitical meanings of action blockbusters requires close attention to style and form, for example by looking at how bodies, performance, and characterization shape the films' ideas about gender and race.

That blockbusters are designed to spawn sequels, spin-offs, and merchandise has led many scholars to situate them firmly on the commerce side of an art/commerce binary. Schatz brands the New Hollywood blockbusters "multi-purpose entertainment machines" (1993, 9–10) geared at churning out products and harnessing all available ancillary revenue sources. Schatz relates this fragmentation in industrial organization, where different branches of a conglomerate and licensees produce different texts and products for a blockbuster property, to narrative and aesthetic fragmentation. For Schatz, blockbusters exhibit episodic narratives in which different fragments and intertextual gestures within the film direct audiences outward to related texts and merchandise. Catherine Constable demonstrates that despite many scholars having challenged Schatz's conceptualization, "It is widely circulated as a summary of the key aesthetic features of the films of New Hollywood" (2015, 25).

The fragmentary qualities commonly ascribed to the New Hollywood blockbuster present obstacles to close textual analysis. Traditional close reading in film criticism typically emphasizes individual films' internal cohesiveness, in which "the meanings which are contained most securely within a film are those formed at the deepest level of interrelation and synthesis" (Perkins 1972, 117). Historically, the narratively self-contained classical Hollywood film received the most attention from this school. As Constable outlines when mapping Schatz's conceptualization of New Hollywood in a table that contrasts popular understandings of the classical and the postclassical, the classical quality of "integrated, organic whole" is upended by the "fragmented/open ended/intertextual" (2015, 25) nature of the postclassical. By being in stark opposition to the integrated wholeness of the classical Hollywood film, the fragmentation associated with the postclassical blockbuster thwarts Perkins's search for meanings produced through the interrelation and synthesis of a film's expressive elements.

Interpretation of narratively self-contained classical Hollywood films certainly benefits from being attuned to the ways in which the films accrue meaning by reaching outside of their diegetic worlds, as when they harness stars' personas or genre conventions. However, discussions of postclassical Hollywood and serialized films reveal other modes of intertextuality that contribute to meaning. Noël Carroll explores the prevalence of allusions to film history in New Hollywood cinema, which directors use to "make comments on the fictional worlds of their films" (1982, 52). In relation to serialization, Carolyn Jess-Cooke argues that film sequels intrinsically prompt audiences to read across texts in a reflective manner: "The sequel is essentially a response to a previous work, a rereading and rewriting of an 'original' that additionally calls upon an audience to reread and rewrite their memories of a previous text" (2009, 12–13). In this simultaneous engagement with present and past texts, audiences observe a dialogue between sequel and predecessor through which both texts' meanings are (re)formed.

Attention to intertextuality is thus crucial when undertaking close textual analysis of Hollywood blockbusters. The adaptive strategies of superhero blockbusters add complex modes of intertextuality to those outlined above. To equip oneself to analyze these intertextual strategies, it is vital to develop an approach that illuminates the aesthetics of superhero blockbusters' modes of adaptation.

CONCEPTUALIZING COMICS TO FILM ADAPTATION

There is a developing body of scholarship examining the aesthetics of comic book cinema (which I take to include, but not be limited to, superhero blockbusters).[4] Key entries include the last two chapters of Burke's *The Comic Book Film Adaptation* (2015), Drew Morton's *Panel to the Screen* (2016), and Jeffries's *Comic Book Film Style* (2017). Despite differing positions on how the films' strategies relate to Hollywood's stylistic conventions, these works are united in their contention that aesthetics is a prime site for understanding the impact that comic book films have had on contemporary Hollywood cinema. Burke, Morton, and Jeffries are committed to interrogating formal relationships between comics and cinema. However, while at points these scholars note ways in which formal interactions between media shape a text's meanings, their approaches largely preclude sustained attention to relations between style, intertextuality, and meaning.

In their studies of stylistic relations between comics and film, Morton and Jeffries jettison adaptation theory in favor of Jay David Bolter and Richard Grusin's (2000) concept of remediation. This concept focuses on intermediality (simply put, interactions between media) rather than intertextuality (interactions between texts). Bolter and Grusin conceptualize remediation to describe the ongoing process in which all active media in a society are engaged in dialogue with one another. Remediation can also manifest as a specific aesthetic strategy: "the representation of one medium in another" (Bolter and Grusin 2000, 45). Morton and Jeffries undertake instructive work examining the range of ways in which film form relates to and can seek to emulate comics form. Yet remediation focuses on form and largely overlooks content, rarely observing the ways in which the stylization of a text's form shapes and is inseparable from its meaning.

This separation of style and content is interlocked with attempts to distinguish remediation from adaptation that are founded on a limited understanding of theories of adaptation. Bolter and Grusin argue that in Hollywood film adaptations of classic novels, "the content has been borrowed, but the medium has not been appropriated or quoted" (44). This position suggests that, in opposition to remediation's concern with form, adaptation purely concerns content. Many studies of adaptation, however, situate formal interactions as a core area of interest. Regarding intermedial quotations, Thomas Leitch identifies an "obsession with authors, books, and words" (2008, 112) as a key motif through which adaptations often signal their status as adaptations to audiences: "Every filmgoer is familiar with the credits that appear as the magically turning pages of a book, a trope that aims to give the adaptation the authority of a book itself" (113). The key distinction between studies of remediation and adaptation is therefore that *remediation is concerned with form*, while *adaptation can be concerned with both form and content.*

I wish to develop a framework that explores how superhero blockbusters' adaptation of stylistic and narrative strategies developed in comic books shapes their meanings. A nuanced understanding of the relationship between form and content is crucial when examining adaptation between the distinct but related forms of comics and film.

FORM AND CONTENT

Much detailed work has been done examining the formal relations between comics and film, from early writings by Francis Lacassin (1972) and Pascal Lefèvre (2007) to the more recent work of Burke, Morton, and Jeffries. It is not my intention to reexamine these formal relations at length. For now, I wish to establish some analytical tools for examining what may happen to content when adapted between the formal systems of comics and film.

Medium-specific approaches to adaptation foreground issues of form. Proponents of medium-specificity seek to overcome the limitations of fidelity criticism, which has haunted adaptation studies since its genesis and is in many ways reductive. Approaches that claim or imply that an adaptation's duty is to be as faithful as possible to its announced source text provide a restrictive framework for analysis that does not allow an adaptation any degree of creativity. Meanwhile, fidelity is a very slippery concept: are we to assess fidelity on grounds of faithfulness to plot, characterization, style, ideology, the elusive notion of text's "spirit," etc. (Stam 2000, 57–58)? Conversely, medium-specific theories of adaptation hold that "an adaptation should be faithful not so much to the source text, but rather to the essence of the medium of expression. This 'medium-specificity' approach assumes that every medium is inherently 'good at' certain things and 'bad at' others" (58). Inherent differences between media necessitate changes when a text is adapted from one medium to another. If fidelity criticism presupposes that content can freely transfer between different forms, medium-specificity suggests that content is bound to form, so when the form changes through adaptation, the content must also change to suit the new medium.

George Bluestone's foundational *Novels into Film* (1957) develops a medium-specific approach to adaptation that establishes binaries between novels and film in which the novel's expressive capacities are presented as superior. Kamilla Elliott traces how Bluestone adopts categorical distinctions that Gotthold Ephraim Lessing (1766) developed for charting differences between painting and poetry to apply to films and novels. Following Lessing, Bluestone designates "the novel as conceptual, linguistic, discursive, symbolic, and inspiring mental imagery, with time as its formative principal, and the film as perceptual, visual, presentational, literal, and given to visual images, with space as its formative principle" (Elliott 2003, 11). Bluestone thus maintains Lessing's binary logic, in which the opposition between words and images is underpinned by binaries of conceptual/perceptual and temporal/spatial. For Bluestone (1957, 46–47), as a novel's words present concepts to be processed by mental processes, they can evoke thoughts, memories, and dreams. Conversely, images are perceived by the eye and thus operate in a more basic, materialistic realm. While presenting cinema's spatiality as limiting, Bluestone also sees it as restricted temporally: "The novel has three tenses; the film has only one" (48). The conceptual and temporal properties of words enable, while the perceptual and spatial properties of images restrict, expression.

Many of these ideas circulating medium-specific discussions of formal binaries between novels and film recur or are reframed in discussions of comics and film form. While comics form is distinct from that of novels in significant ways, there are also shared physical and conceptual qualities in how the two media relate to film form. Elliott's *Rethinking the Novel/Film Debate* (2003) can help elucidate these, examining relations between the forms of two media—illustrated Victorian novels and film—which, like comics and film, use related but distinct kinds of words and images. Elliott argues that Bluestone's transferal of arguments pertaining to poetry and painting over to discussions of novel and film is reductive. The presence of different types of illustrations in many Victorian novels, while almost all films feature words of some kind (such as dialogue and intertitles), means that "the designation of novels as 'words' and of films as 'images' is neither empirically nor logically

Superman torments gangsters in a car in *Action Comics* #1 (1938).

sustainable" (14). Comics feature even more varied combinations of words and images than illustrated Victorian novels. As such, if binaries that stem from the division of words and images emerge in discussions of comics and film, we should ask why they are there and how sustainable they are.

Lefèvre offers a medium-specific approach to comics to film adaptation that identifies fundamental formal binaries. Lefèvre's "four main problems in the adaptation of comics into film" are:

> (1) the deletion/addition process that occurs with rewriting primary comics texts for film; (2) the unique characteristics of page layout and film screen; and (3) the dilemmas of translating drawings to photography; and (4) the importance of sound in film compared to the "silence" of comics. (2007, 3–4)

The first of these is primarily concerned with narrative and the remaining three "problems" pertain to form. These three erect binaries of page layout/film frame, drawn images/photographic images, and silence/sound or, more pertinently, written words/spoken words. Lefèvre's binaries allow for comics and film to both feature words and images, but they still reframe key terms from the word/image binary that can be traced from Lessing to Bluestone, namely temporal/spatial and conceptual/perceptual.

Spatiotemporal properties are a central concern of the page layout/film frame binary. Comics create meaning not just in individual images, but through the juxtaposition of multiple images on the space of the page. The ways in which panels are laid out on a page can complement or add to the meaning conveyed in individual panels and can also indicate the temporal flow of the images. For example, a page from Superman's first comic book adventure in *Action Comics* #1 on which Superman torments gangsters in a car presents the moment the superhero smashes the car against a rock in the largest panel on the page, taking up a whole row at the page's center. The width of the panel encourages the reader to pause momentarily on this act, taking it in over a greater period of time than the rest of the panels on the page, which are narrower and include less visual and written information. These strategies emphasize the significance of this climactic peak in the action. Cinema cannot completely replicate these strategies as films typically present one image at a time, in frames of the same size that traditionally replace one another twenty-four times a second. Henry John Pratt explains this distinction:

> Films are (partially) constituted by images that succeed each other in actual time but appear to the viewer in the same actual space. Comics are (partially) constituted by images that succeed each other in actual space but appear to the reader at the same actual time. (2012, 150).

Time is the agent of change and progression in film; space is the agent of change and progression in comics.

It is significant that, in discourses on adaptation, films are generally considered spatial in relation to novels, but temporal in relation to comics. Structural traits of media can therefore be assigned differently depending on the perspective from which they are viewed, while a medium such as film demonstrably has both spatial and temporal properties. Even examinations of comics and film that designate the former as spatial and the latter as temporal assign spatiotemporal qualities to both media through the assertion that comics use space to manage time while film uses time to manage space. Thus, neither medium is solely spatial or solely temporal. Both forge complex relations between space and time. The presence of both temporal and spatial qualities in film means that, although its composition may be fundamentally different than comics, film can construct spatiotemporal configurations that recall those of comics. An example of such a strategy is speed ramping, as explained in my opening analysis of *Deadpool 2*, wherein, comparably to the wide panel of Superman smashing the car in *Action Comics* #1, slowed footage places emphasis on particular actions performed by superpowered characters.

The drawn images/photographic images binary reworks the conceptual/perceptual binary. Lefèvre designates drawn images as subjective and photographic images as objective.

> A drawn image offers a specific view on reality and the creator's subjectivity of this reality is built into the work.... A photographic image has, by its optic nature alone, a quite different visual ontology.... Although photos can also be manipulated by using special software such as Photoshop, generally the viewer still accords more realism to a photo than to a stylized drawing. (8–9)

For Lefèvre, the subjective qualities of drawn images and objective qualities of photographic images cause audiences to comprehend them differently. Since audiences do not expect drawn images to be realistic, they are more likely to accept certain content, such as hyperbolic violence, when drawn rather than when presented in a photographic medium. Perceived ontological distinctions between drawn and photographic images therefore suggest that certain content cannot easily transition from comics to film. I will return to these debates about subjectivity, realism, and image ontology in more detail in chapter two, when exploring strategies through which digital imagery is integrated into live-action superhero blockbusters.

Interestingly, the logic that underpins the drawn images/photographic images binary exposes the instability of the binary that presents images as perceptual and words as conceptual. Following Lefèvre, drawn images represent the unique worldview of a particular artist, offering a glimpse into their mind. As such, drawn images express interiority and a certain amount of conceptual processing is required for readers to fully understand drawn images. McCloud's study of the pictorial vocabulary of comics reveals the ability for images in comics to be stylized in ways that require different levels of perceptual and conceptual processing. McCloud (1994, 49) initially categorizes images as "received" information that one only needs to see to understand and words as "perceived" information that requires specialized knowledge to mentally decode, effectively erecting the perceptual/conceptual binary. This binary is unpicked, however, in McCloud's diagram that "represents the total pictorial vocabulary of comics or of *any* of the visual arts" (51, emphasis in original). The three points that mark out the parameters on this triangular diagram are "reality," which pertains to photorealistic images; "meaning," where written words convey meaning through alphanumeric icons that require knowledge of language to decode; and "the picture plane," where images are abstracted from reality and meaning. In populating the space between these points with examples of comics art, McCloud reveals these different modes of image as existing on a continuum rather than as discrete categories. Drawn images can be stylized in ways that require different levels of conceptual and perceptual processing. In also including words on the diagram, McCloud demonstrates that "when pictures are more abstracted from 'reality,' they require greater levels of perception, more like words . . . when words are bolder, more direct, they require lower levels of perception and are received faster, more like pictures" (49). By outlining how realistic, iconic, and abstract qualities can be blended and balanced in images, McCloud provides tools for dismantling both the word/image and drawn/photographic image binaries. McCloud demonstrates that realistic and more heavily stylized images, and images and words, although often held as oppositions, actually exist on a shared plane in which each can adopt qualities of the other. This stylistic pliability should be considered alongside McCloud's assertion that the range of pictorial vocabulary his diagram depicts is available to "*any* of the visual arts," suggesting that no content is unavailable to a particular kind of image, so long as the image is appropriately stylized.

Emerging from the silence/sound binary, the key distinctions typically outlined between written words in comics and spoken words in film are that the former are spatial, iconic, and only imply tone of voice, while the latter are immaterial and delivered aurally with specific intonation. Written words take

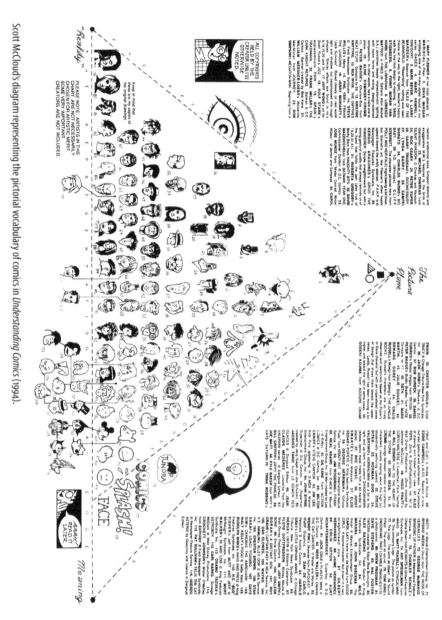

Scott McCloud's diagram representing the pictorial vocabulary of comics in *Understanding Comics* (1994).

unique iconic forms in comics, suggesting intonation through factors such as style of writing, line thickness, and shape of speech balloon (Burke 2015, 199–200). Despite these variables making the form of written words in comics more expressive than words in a novel, where the font is typically uniformly formatted throughout, the reader must still imagine what a character's voice sounds like, unlike in film (Lefèvre 2007, 11). A parallel is evident between the written/spoken word and word/image binaries, as in each written words are conceptual information processed by the brain, while the opposing element is perceived by a sensory organ, ear and eye respectively.

Lefèvre argues that the different forms dialogue takes in comics and film again determine content.

> The texts in speech balloons are generally not suited for film dialogue and they need some rewriting. Superhero comics, for example, often use very stylistic and bombastic dialogue; a literal screen translation may emphasize such dialogue's artificial nature to the point of unintentional camp. (11)

To support this argument, Lefèvre quotes comics creator Stan Lee on the decision to not have monstrous superhero Hulk talk when adapted from comics to television series *The Incredible Hulk* (CBS 1977–1982): "In the comics, when the Hulk talked—he'd go, 'Me Hulk! Me smash! Hulk Kill!' That type of thing. Well, that would have been corny as hell on the screen" (11–12). As with the opposition between drawn and photographic images, the issue is one of stylization. Dialogue that seems more realistic is purportedly required when actors utter words. However, the ability for actors to alter their intonation is effectively a kind of vocal stylization. Rather than choosing an iconic form for words that suggests intonation in a particular way, as comics do, film actors choose a specific vocal register. For example, in Marvel Studios' blockbusters, Hulk increasingly talks. Actor Mark Ruffalo changes his intonation to reflect Hulk's changing psychology: for the primal Hulk in *Thor: Ragnarok* (Taika Waititi 2017) Ruffalo growls out broken English, while for the highly intelligent Hulk in *Avengers: Endgame* (Anthony Russo and Joseph Russo 2019) Ruffalo lucidly articulates his thoughts. Different vocal stylization facilitates the realization of different Hulks on screen.

The above interrogation of purported formal binaries separating comics and film exposes the instability of these binaries. Conceptual/perceptual and temporal/spatial divisions that uphold the word/image binary recur at the foundations of formal binaries used to separate comics and film. The contradictory ways that these qualities are applied to media by different binaries suggests that, rather than maintaining oppositions, both sides can be at play at once in forms and media. Visual and aural elements and the means through which they are presented in comics and film can be both conceptual and perceptual, and temporal and spatial. While these shared qualities of comics and film aid adaptation, the qualities' unique configurations in each media pose obstacles. Existing literature on comics and film form explores how these obstacles necessitate "aesthetic compromise" (Morton 2016, 6) for films to recall comics, or prompt aesthetic strategies that find "equivalences" (Burke 2015, 174–81) between the media's formal systems that facilitate the transferal of content. From these positions, content is either not a concern or is able to be transferred between media once comparable formal configurations are found. Elliott (2003) offers a more nuanced discussion of the relationship between form and content. Elliott formulates a useful theoretical framework for understanding how conceptual and perceptual, and temporal and spatial, qualities interact in words and images, which illuminates how obstacles between related but distinct formal systems may engender transformations in content in the process of adaptation.

In comparable ways to those I have outlined above, Elliott (2003) dismantles binaries that medium-specific approaches deem to separate media. In her interrogation of the word/image binary, Elliott finds that "in illustrated novels and worded films, pictures can operate according to the features and functions traditionally assigned to words, and words can function according to the features and functions conventionally assigned to pictures" (16). For example, illustrations in books and intertitles in silent films can have comparable temporal functions. The fact that illustrations in novels and intertitles in film are both frequently criticized for disrupting narrative progression reveals that both can freeze temporal flow (18). Conversely, certain images in novels and intertitles in silent films function as agents of temporal progression (19–23). Furthermore, Elliott argues not just for words and images performing comparable functions but reveals that they can hybridize in complex ways in media that contain both.

Elliott uses the demonstrable interplay between forms within media as the foundation of a theoretical model for observing exchanges between forms in different media as content is adapted from one to the other. Elliott proposes the analogy of a looking glass, in which each medium and text acts as a mirror that, while able to reflect other media and texts, will necessarily perform inversions that alter the content (209–41). Specific qualities of media are acknowledged, but relations between these qualities enable content to be adapted, albeit in an altered form. The looking glass allusion stems from Elliott's study of Lewis Carroll and John Tenniel's *Alice's Adventures in Wonderland* (1865) and *Through the Looking Glass, and What Alice Found There* (1871). In *Through the Looking Glass*, a looking glass leads to a fantastical world that is constantly inverting reality. The books play with the formal features of words and images, swapping their traditional functions

AND A LONG TALE.   37

so that her idea of the tale was something like this:——"Fury said to
    a mouse, That
        he met
          in the
           house,
        'Let us
        both go
      to law:
    I will
  prosecute
you.—
  Come, I'll
    take no
     denial;
      We must
        have a
          trial:
            For
          really
          this
           morning
             I've
           nothing
         to do.'
        Said the
       mouse to
      the cur,
      'Such a
       trial,
      dear sir,
     With no
   jury or
judge,
   would be
    wasting
      our breath.'
       'I'll be
       judge,
     I'll be
   jury,'
  Said
  cunning
    old Fury;
     'I'll try
      the whole
       cause,
       and
      condemn
     you
    to
     death.'"

The mouse's tail/tale in *Alice's Adventures in Wonderland* (1865).

and calling attention to their form. In so doing the form becomes the content, while simultaneously narrative content shapes form.

The episode in *Alice's Adventures in Wonderland* where a mouse tells Alice his tale exemplifies these exchanges. The pun on tail/tale is evoked by the words telling the tale being arranged on the page in the shape of a tail. Elliott analyzes as follows.

> The tail *is* a tale and the tale *is* a tail, pressing the two toward union. The words are the picture and the picture is the words. In a parody of the dogma that makes form and content indivisible, the tail as form is one with the tale as content. However, the tail as form holds the tale as content even as the tale forms the tail, so that one cannot confidently determine which is the form and which is the content in the union. As in facing looking glasses, the tale forms the tail which forms the tail which forms the tale endlessly, turning form and content relations topsy-turvy, *ad infinitum*. (227, emphasis in original)

Elliott's analysis is appropriately difficult to articulate, reading like something of a tongue twister. The repetition and constant switching between tail and tale, and form and content, derails attempts to form fixed relationships between them. This confusion illustrates that, through the application of looking glass logic, word and image, and form and content, are revealed as inverted reflections of each other. Form and content each inform, but neither wholly determines, the other.

To demonstrate the applications of the looking glass analogy to adaptation, Elliott explores ways in which Disney's *Alice in Wonderland* (Clyde Geronimi, Wilfred Jackson, and Hamilton Luske 1951) creates puns that reflect the novel's interplay between words and images, and form and content, through devices that harness cinematic forms (224–32). Formal qualities of film that novels do not have can affect meaning. For example, the written description of the bread and butterfly in *Through the Looking Glass* prompts the mental image of a butterfly constructed from bread and butter, while the illustration of a single bread and butterfly gestures to the play on words. Disney's *Alice* uses cinema's capacity to present movement to modify the image's gesture to the verbal pun: a swarm of bread and butterflies "fly together to form a loaf" (231). Different forms and media can therefore evoke comparable content, but changing the forms will reshape meaning. The looking glass analogy thus "yokes the pictorial and the verbal in cognition without erasing all differentiations between them and opens a space between form and content that nevertheless maintains their bond" (185). Both comparisons and differences between forms are acknowledged, while the ways these forms shape and are shaped by content are illuminated, revealing dynamic interconnectivity between form and content.

Observing ways that different forms can inflect meaning illuminates alterations that content undergoes when adapted between media that use related but not identical forms, such as comics and film. In Elliott's looking glass model of adaptation, content is not unaltered when adapted between forms, nor does it necessarily radically change; rather, content undergoes degrees of transformation. As such, "The film is not translation or copy, but rather metamorphoses the novel and is, in turn, metamorphosed by it" (229). Elliott's notion of metamorphosis occurring in the exchanges between source text and adaptation provides an instructive way to frame transformations that the adaptation process engenders. In this model, an adaptation does not reproduce the source to the best of its ability, nor does it create something entirely new. Instead, content metamorphoses as it is exchanged between two integrally joined texts with related (but not identical) formal properties.

This model and the term metamorphosis are highly suited to the study of superhero adaptation, not just due to formal comparisons between comics and film but also because the idea of metamorphosis appropriately reflects the various kinds of transformation that superheroes undergo. The most obvious diegetic example of this is the transformation from one identity to another, for example by a change of costume, biological mutation, or magical spell. As will be seen in chapter one, the different identities held by a superhero character are always integrally linked, informing and inverting each other. Another aspect my analysis will explore is the range of transformations superheroes undergo through modes of serialization and multiplication that occur over the course of decades. In comic books alone, superheroes are passed between different creative teams and often have numerous parallel incarnations existing at once. These transformations proliferate further with adaptations into other media. The metamorphosis of superheroes spans texts, time, and media.

The multifaceted intertextual exchanges inherent to superheroes as they transform across creative teams, incarnations, and media necessitate an expansion of Elliott's looking glass model of adaptation. Elliott mobilizes her model to examine adaptation between texts on a one-to-one basis, looking at metamorphosis occurring between one book and one film. Superheroes exist in complex networks of texts. While Elliott dismantles structural divisions between texts, approaches to adaptation that explicitly harness poststructuralist theory illuminate the myriad routes along which intertextual transformation occurs as superhero blockbusters adapt such vast textual networks.

POSTSTRUCTURALIST THEORIES OF ADAPTATION

Adaptation scholars who harness poststructuralist theory illuminate an ongoing process in which multiple texts and other elements interact with one another. In a foundational essay, Robert Stam (2000) discusses this model of adaptation as "intertextual dialogism." Adaptation in this sense "is less an attempted resuscitation of an originary word than a turn in an ongoing dialogical process" (64). In applying Mikhail Bakhtin's concept of dialogism to adaptation studies, Stam outlines how each adaptation, like any cultural text or utterance, is shaped through a continuous process of dialogic exchange. Each text builds on and pieces together elements from a nebulous array of texts while itself being part of this textual network and informing subsequent production. A new adaptation will be informed by previous adaptations of the "source" text while also finding other intertexts. Stam expands this network of exchange beyond the textual: "In the broadest sense, intertextual dialogism refers to the infinite and open-ended possibilities generated by all the discursive practices of a culture, the entire matrix of communicative utterances within which the artistic text is situated" (64). Each text interacts not just with preceding and contemporary texts, but with surrounding cultural contexts and trends.

Burke (2015, 19–20) and Will Brooker (2012, 65–66) note that comic book creative practices provide an exemplary demonstration of such ongoing intertextual dialogue. Superheroes are passed from creative team to creative team over the course of decades. A new creative team selects elements (such as characters, themes, and iconography) from previous comics, then combines and reworks these, channeling them through contemporary contexts and trends, to produce a story intended to be both fresh and familiar. Superhero comics are formed through a process of dialogic exchange and newer versions can become fans' preferred incarnations, adding elements that come to define the character. For example, very few fans nowadays would consider the Superman from his first published comic book story in *Action Comics* #1, who could not fly or see through walls, as the definitive Superman. Furthermore, the creators of this first Superman comic, Jerry Siegel and Joe Shuster, were themselves taking cues from other texts. Ian Gordon identifies characteristics of contemporaneous comic strips that inform Siegel and Shuster's Superman (2017, 99), while Coogan (2006, 116–74) and Aldo J. Regalado (2015, 17–77) undertake deeper surveys of the literary and other antecedents to superhero comics. The Superman story of *Action Comics* #1 was another utterance in an ongoing dialogic exchange, albeit one that refocused and enlivened the conversation, manifesting a franchise and genre.

Scholars writing on intertextuality and adaptation in the superhero genre have adopted various names to conceptualize the textual networks that superheroes inhabit. Jim Collins (1991) terms the textual network that comprises Batman's history an *array*. Following Collins, Angela Ndalianis (2009a) adopts the word array and engages with Bakhtin to elucidate the dialogic exchanges between specific Superman texts and other texts within and outside of the Superman array. Brooker, situating his study of Batman firmly in poststructuralist theory, derives the model of a *matrix* to frame the superhero's multiplicities, arguing that "all Batman texts enter a matrix of cross-platform product" (2012, 219). Martin Zeller-Jacques (2012) and Matt Yockey (2017) adopt Sarah Cardwell's conceptualization of a *meta-text* to frame how popular superheroes exist beyond any single text and instead comprise an "ever changing, ever developing" (Cardwell 2002, 14) cultural understanding which each text featuring a character draws from and contributes to. Richard Berger (2008), upon harnessing poststructuralist theory to examine interactions between Superman texts, arrives at the word *assemblage*. Gordon explores Superman as a multifaceted construct, deploying familiar language as he asserts that "Superman is in and of itself a rich paratext involving audiences, industry, and an *array* of texts and artifacts, and the meaning of the character lies in a constant process of negotiating this *assemblage*" (2017, 87, my emphasis). These words serve comparable purposes; array, matrix, meta-text, and assemblage are all used to conceptualize the network of ongoing dialogic exchanges that form the cultural perception of a superhero property.

Rather than choosing one of these words over the others, or devising another specialist term, I use a more widely familiar word to comparable effect: *franchise*. When framed appropriately, franchise captures the breadth and mutability of the network of texts concerning a specific superhero property alongside the forces shaping this network. Even popular understandings of the word suggest these qualities, ensuring that a reader picking up an individual chapter of this book will have a basic understanding of this central piece of terminology.

When applied to media, the word franchising has been deployed quite loosely to describe a range of textual configurations. Multiplication across texts and officially sanctioned paratexts (merchandise, product tie-ins, etc.) is central to each use of the term, with Daniel Herbert outlining how "within the logic of a franchise, a specific intellectual property gets manifested as multiple consumer products, from movies and television programs to books, comic books, toys, video games, clothing, and so on" (2017, 13). My understanding of what constitutes a media franchise follows Derek Johnson's usage of the term in *Media Franchising: Creative License and Collaboration in the Culture Industries* (2013). Johnson discusses media franchises as comprising all the different texts and products produced from their given intellectual properties. While Johnson examines the "network of industrial relations" (29) through which an intellectual property is franchised as it is multiplied via the company or conglomerate that owns it along with companies to whom they license the property, I explore the textual networks that are produced from this process. In this book, a media franchise is therefore defined as an intellectual property (like DC's Wonder Woman or Marvel's Spider-Man) that features in multiple texts and paratexts that need not fit into the same narrative continuity. The Superman franchise, for instance, includes all the different iterations of Superman that have been produced in various media since the character's 1938 comic book debut.

Adaptation is a means through which multiplication occurs in a franchise. Clare Parody identifies adaptation as

> fundamentally sympathetic to the aims and protocols of franchise storytelling. It is an efficient way of getting maximum use out of a fictional creation . . . its pleasures of re-visioning, re-versioning, and revisiting, meanwhile, resonate strongly with the balance of familiarity and novelty so crucial to the appeal of franchise fiction. (2011, 211).

This interplay between familiarity and variation, a quality shared by franchising, adaptation, and genre, guides the continual reworking of superheroes from incarnation to incarnation. Underpinned by textual exchanges, multiplicity, and expansion, my understanding of media franchising usefully frames the intertextual dialogism within a superhero property. The word franchise thus captures the composition of a superhero property's ever-expanding textual network.

Furthermore, franchising's industrial connotations indicate how producers try to control and contain a franchise's multiplicities, promoting certain texts and interpretations of characters over others. In his study of media franchising, Johnson (2013) emphasizes the interplay between textuality and industry as creativity is mediated by industrial structures. Johnson also situates interactions between producers and audiences central to franchising. Probing this relationship further, Johnson (197–231) and Kyle Meikle (2019, 49–91) explore the extent to which fan activity and fan productions can maintain franchises while potentially expanding them beyond limits imposed by producers. The composition of a franchise is negotiated by textuality, producers, and audiences.

This process of negotiation indicates the competitive quality of a media franchise's composition. Leitch sees a new adaptation within a franchise as engaged in combative relations with other iterations: "All adaptations of any canonical fictional franchise . . . do not want to be faithful to any particular members of the franchise. They do not even want to be faithful to the franchise in general. What they want is to become canonical members of the franchise themselves." (2007, 230). Each new iteration of a property tussles with other iterations as it makes a bid for centrality in the franchise. Despite the competition between texts, Collins argues that in popular culture "earlier texts do not simply disappear or become kitsch, but persist in their original forms as well as diverse reactivations that continue to be a source of fascination for audiences, providing pleasure in the present and forming a fundamental part of cultural memory" (1991, 171). Audience memory of past incarnations and recognition of intertextual dialogue is vital to maintaining the scope of a superhero franchise. All iterations continue to inform the franchise so long as these iterations exist in cultural memory. Collins's notion of reactivation also indicates that new incarnations are not simply hostile to all other versions but through intertextual strategies like allusion can remind audiences of older texts.

Combining Elliott's analytical tools with poststructuralist theories of adaptation equips me to examine the aesthetic qualities of textual dialogue as superheroes are adapted between media. In general, existing work that applies poststructuralist theory to superhero franchises lacks close attention to the role style and form play in the process of intertextual negotiation.[5] For example, Brooker's (2012) analysis of the *Dark Knight* trilogy of Batman films (Christopher Nolan 2005, 2008, and 2012) traces the transformations of a superhero's meanings as they traverse texts and contexts yet disregards aesthetic interactions between Batman comics and films. For Brooker (48–74), any visual links between Batman comics and *Batman Begins* (2005) are either inconsequential quotations or superficially constructed by paratexts, in neither case contributing anything substantial to the film's meanings. Elliott's looking glass model of adaptation helps illuminate the aesthetic dimension of the dialogic exchanges that occur across a superhero franchise. Applying Elliott's analytical tools to theories of adaptation that illuminate dialogic exchanges across a superhero franchise facilitates exploration of aesthetic interactions between a network of intersecting texts in different media, and how these interactions shape a text's meanings.

THE SUPERHERO BLOCKBUSTERS UNDER ANALYSIS

This book considers superhero blockbusters' adaptative practices in relation to contexts that have facilitated the superhero genre's expansion into blockbuster cinema. Burke (2015, 23–83) attributes what he calls the "golden age of comic book filmmaking"—a designation that incorporates the superhero blockbuster boom—to a set of sociopolitical, technological, and industrial factors: post-9/11 sociopolitical discourses, the increasing sophistication of CGI, the organization of Hollywood studios into conglomerates geared toward the cultivation of media franchises, and a new generation of filmmakers and producers who themselves are comic book fans. I explore the impact of the first three of these on the aesthetics of superhero blockbusters' adaptive practices at key points throughout the book. The issue of filmmakers and producers being comic book fans will echo through my analysis in the sense that the modes of dialogue between texts and media that I analyze testify to creative forces well versed in superhero comic books. However, it is my contention that superhero texts are best understood when situated in the networks of texts with which they are in dialogue. Awareness of how a creator's relationship with the material filters a particular text's interactions with these networks can be useful, but I do not wish to privilege an individual creator's influence over the array of creative forces and textual interactions that shape a superhero blockbuster.

Each chapter of this book examines a different superhero or superhero team while exploring distinct aspects of adaptation. While aesthetic interactions within a superhero franchise provide the foundation of my analysis, as the chapters progress I develop my framework by introducing new concepts that help understand the ways in which the superhero blockbusters under analysis engage with sociopolitical, technological, and industrial contexts. Furthermore, I illuminate the role that aesthetics play in the adaptation of key narrative strategies from superhero comic books into cinema.

I am specifically concerned with "live-action" superhero blockbusters: films that are presented as being primarily set in real spaces with real actors that are filmed using photographic processes, despite often featuring large amounts of digital animation. The particular representational qualities of live-action superhero blockbusters are a continuing concern of my chapters. The ways in which physical spaces and bodies are presented, and instances in which they are manipulated by and interact with digital imaging, are key elements to examine when assessing these films' meanings.

The superhero blockbusters selected as my case studies exemplify popular character models and storytelling strategies within the wider genre. They feature franchises owned by the two biggest publishers of superhero comics (DC Comics and Marvel Comics) and cover the four studios that have most prominently produced superhero blockbusters (DC Studios/Warner Bros., Columbia Pictures/Sony, Marvel Studios/Disney, and 20th Century Fox). Each chapter surveys aspects of superhero history, such as the development of specific franchises, narrative strategies, and tropes, introduces pertinent contexts and useful concepts, while providing detailed close textual analysis of its chosen superhero blockbusters that elucidates complexities of meaning. To accommodate this necessary breadth and depth, each chapter is granted ample length. A set of analytical tools for examining superhero blockbusters develops across the chapters, along with understanding of the ways in which superhero blockbusters exemplify and contribute to Hollywood's blockbuster paradigm.

The first chapter demonstrates the use of the analytical framework established in this introduction through analysis of *Superman: The Movie* and situates the superhero blockbuster in the context of 1970s Hollywood's emerging blockbuster paradigm. I begin by mapping the development of DC's longest-running superhero across texts in various media produced in the forty years preceding *The Movie*'s release, exploring how Superman's identifying motifs develop as they are adapted between forms and media. I then examine the ways in which *The Movie*'s stylistic strategies adapt, and position the film in relation to, these preexisting Superman texts, in doing so making a bid for centrality in the Superman franchise. The film's cinematic significance is probed through exploring how it exemplifies contemporary Hollywood blockbuster practices of spectacle and genre hybridity, while demonstrating how these qualities are harnessed to situate its iteration of Superman in relation to previous versions. This first chapter illuminates *Superman: The Movie*'s adaptive strategies and how these shape Superman's meanings while forging a place for the superhero blockbuster alongside other superhero texts and within Hollywood.

The second chapter jumps to the beginning of the superhero blockbuster boom, focusing on a key series that led the cycle: the Columbia Pictures/Sony-produced *Spider-Man* trilogy (Sam Raimi 2002, 2004, and 2007). These films are discussed in relation to the increasing use of digital filmmaking technologies in Hollywood and the post-9/11 sociopolitical climate. I outline the ways in which digital imaging in live-action cinema problematizes debates about differences between comics' drawn images and cinema's photographic images. I build these observations into a discussion of the challenges and expressive opportunities that digital imaging presents to superhero blockbusters. The appearance, movement, and narrative function of digital imaging in the *Spider-Man* trilogy are examined in analysis of the superhero's and his supervillains' bodies. In my exploration of the trilogy's sociopolitical engagement, I move from analysis of bodies to space. I consider how the relationship between New York's external spaces, its citizens, and Spider-Man is expressed, and what this reveals about the films' engagement with contemporary sociopolitical discourses on New York and America's identity. This reading of sociopolitical meaning develops as I analyze the nostalgic stylization of internal spaces. A nostalgic retreat into the past has been identified as one form of immediate response to 9/11 that is prominent in certain 2000s superhero blockbusters (Burke 2015, 27–30). While this tendency is often discussed as conservative withdrawal, my analysis reveals greater complexity of meaning in the *Spider-Man* trilogy's coding of spaces to different eras. Throughout the chapter, my analysis is attuned to how meaning is created both within individual films and across the trilogy, instigating an exploration of how seriality is implicated in the superhero blockbuster's adaptive practices.

Chapter three turns to Marvel Studios' Marvel Cinematic Universe (MCU). Through focusing on *The Avengers* (Joss Whedon 2012) while casting a wider eye over other MCU texts, I explore the MCU's adaptation of the model of seriality developed in superhero comic books in which multiple series interconnect to form a shared fictional universe. I begin by surveying narrative and aesthetic strategies through which a fictional universe's breadth is managed in superhero comics. I then sketch the composition of the MCU, considering the range of texts and paratexts in its diegetic network, from comic books and television shows to licensed tie-in promotions, and outline the extent to which these shape the universe's meanings. After this broader survey, I undertake deep analysis of *The Avengers* to explore the ways in which ensemble films adapt comic book strategies for managing the universe and how these adapted strategies shape the films' and universe's meanings. This exploration continues in my survey of MCU texts produced after *The Avengers*. I provide more sustained analysis of *Captain Marvel* (Anna Boden and Ryan Fleck 2019) and *Avengers: Endgame* to examine the extent to which the masculinized structures that govern the MCU are upended in its first film led by a woman, and whether such potential shifts in the universe's underpinning structures are maintained in the ensemble film in which its first overarching story, the "Infinity Saga," culminates. The chapter demonstrates that the shared universe mode of seriality is not just of industrial interest; the intertextual strategies through which it is pursued inflect a text's meanings in significant ways.

If the MCU films endeavor to maintain a tightly interwoven fictional construct, the fourth chapter discusses 20th Century Fox's more loosely structured X-Men films. The first X-Men film sparked the superhero blockbuster boom in 2000, and over the course of two decades, sequels and spin-offs adapted the pluralities of superhero comics onto the big screen. This chapter focuses on a key narrative strategy that developed in superhero comic books for both enlivening and managing the fragmentation of superhero universes: the alternate timeline. I begin by outlining the history of alternate timelines in superhero comic books, reflecting on the various forms that these can take and the different uses to which they have been put, and establish the crucial role of style in mapping an alternate timeline. My subsequent film analysis focuses on *X-Men: Days of Future Past* (Bryan Singer 2014)—the first superhero blockbuster to feature an alternate timeline—and *Logan* (James Mangold 2017). I explore how in their adaptation of alternate timeline tropes, these films' fracturing of Fox's X-Men films' spatial, temporal, and narrative continuity facilitates a process of (re)negotiating the franchise's sociopolitical meanings, particularly in terms of gender and race. I analyze how elements of cinematic construction discussed in previous chapters, including bodies, spaces, and genre conventions, are configured in distinct ways to envision *Days of Future Past*'s and *Logan*'s alternate futures. My analysis also considers how other recent trends in twenty-first-century blockbuster filmmaking—namely the use of international story settings and 3D presentation—are harnessed or rejected in the films' efforts to distinguish their timelines.

I conclude by applying the analytical tools developed across my chapters to DC Studios' cinematic universe, the DC Extended Universe (DCEU). Applying my approach to a set of superhero blockbusters that are distinct in composition from those analyzed in the preceding chapters allows me to demonstrate the suppleness of the framework that this book constructs. My analysis includes examination of the ways in which the Superman franchise is rearranged and the universe is established in *Man of Steel* (Zack Snyder 2013) and *Batman v Superman: Dawn of Justice* (Zack Snyder 2016). In inverse to the MCU, the DCEU was primarily constructed in ensemble films like *Batman v Superman* and *Justice League* (Zack Snyder 2017) before segmenting off into solo films, so it is important to consider the ways in which this different structure impacts its meanings, and how solo films like *Wonder Woman* (Patty Jenkins 2017) and *Black Adam* (Jaume Collet-Serra 2022) negotiate its underpinning gendered and racial structures. The universe's fragmentation led to it ultimately being reformed via the use of alternate timeline tropes in *The Flash* (Andrés Muschietti 2023), paving the way for a new cinematic universe. Analyzing *The Flash* provides an opportunity to explore the use of alternate timeline tropes to both reset narrative continuity and revisit past incarnations of DC characters. As superhero blockbusters forge new futures, they continue to look to the past, affirming the need for analytical tools that illuminate their adaptive practices.

CHAPTER 1

TRUTH, JUSTICE, AND THE CINEMATIC WAY

SUPERMAN: THE MOVIE, THE FIRST SUPERHERO BLOCKBUSTER

The teaser trailer for *Superman: The Movie* comprises a long take from the perspective of a camera flying through clouds toward a glowing sunset. It is only once the Superman logo is presented near the end of the trailer that it is indicated that this enigmatic shot emulates Superman's point-of-view as he soars through the sky. The footage is not from the film but rather promises the kind of spectacular experience that it will offer. Swelling orchestral music and names of Hollywood stars bursting from the fourth wall before gliding into the distance accompany the footage to underscore this promise. The rousing sounds and images suggest that this film will eclipse all other Superman texts. Yet the presentation of the instantly recognizable "S" logo at the end of the trailer, followed by the name Superman in a swooshing font familiar from many previous Superman texts, reveals that the film is not severing ties with past incarnations. As indicated by and initiated in this trailer, *The Movie*'s process of adaptation entails asserting cinematic superiority while weaving together and reframing previous incarnations of a character that had proliferated in thousands of texts and multiple media in the preceding forty years. In seeking to launch Superman, and by extension the superhero genre, into blockbuster cinema, *The Movie* performs a complex negotiation of the Superman franchise and cinematic form.

In this chapter I demonstrate the use of the framework developed in this book's introduction for analyzing superhero blockbusters' process of adaptation. The tantalizing footage in *The Movie*'s teaser trailer reflects the film's famous tagline, which promises that "you will believe a man can fly," revealing the potential that Elliott's analytical tools elucidate for images and words to convey comparable meaning. To explore the applications of these tools in examining the adaptation of material across the whole network of texts that make up a superhero franchise, I undertake an analysis of Superman texts that takes three stages. Firstly, I look at Superman texts produced in the forty years spanning the character's first comic book adventure to *The Movie*'s release. This analysis focuses on aesthetic interactions between Superman texts as the character was adapted between media that have different formal configurations. I then analyze *The Movie*'s adaptive strategies. I explore how through its adaptive strategies the film positions itself in relation to both the preestablished network of Superman texts and emerging practices in Hollywood blockbuster production, thus contributing to the development of the Superman franchise and Hollywood's blockbuster paradigm. The impact that *The Movie* had on the Superman franchise is examined in the final section of my analysis, in which I survey Superman texts produced since *The Movie*'s release.

In undertaking a broad survey of the history of Superman while closely analyzing the first blockbuster film adaptation's stylistic and narrative strategies, I explore textual strategies through which the competitive tussling between incarnations within a superhero franchise is enacted. I identify aesthetic means utilized by different versions of Superman to negotiate and organize the Superman franchise, while maintaining awareness of industrial and cultural factors. My analysis illuminates textual interactions that occur across constantly expanding networks of superhero texts, the affects these interactions have on textual meaning, and the role blockbuster adaptations can play in shaping these networks.

SUPERMAN'S PREBLOCKBUSTER YEARS

Surveying Superman texts produced in the forty years that spanned the character's comic book debut to his first Hollywood blockbuster adventure allows one to chart the defining features and breadth of the franchise that *The Movie* both adapts and expands. I undertake this exploration in two parts. Firstly, I utilize Elliott's analytical tools to investigate ways in which Superman's identifying features metamorphose as they are reflected between forms and media. I then map the range of roles that Superman and his civilian identity Clark Kent adopt by examining aesthetic strategies and other factors that shape the identities.

Superman smashes a car on the cover of *Action Comics* #1 (1938).

ESTABLISHING SUPERMAN IN WORDS, IMAGES, AND SOUNDS

Gordon discusses Superman as "a process, rather than as a static, fixed phenomenon" (2017, 3). Within a few years of Superman's 1938 comic book debut, this process was already spanning various media. Alongside multiple comic book series and a newspaper strip (1939–1966), other incarnations included: radio serial *The Adventures of Superman* (WOR/MBS/ABC 1940–1951); a series of animated theatrical shorts, the first nine produced by Fleischer Studios (1941–1942) and a subsequent eight when Fleischer were reformed as Famous Studios (1942–1943); novelization *The Adventures of Superman* (Lowther and Shuster 1942); two film serials, *Superman* (Spencer Gordon Bennet, Thomas Carr 1948) and *Atom Man vs. Superman* (Spencer Gordon Bennet 1950); and television series *Adventures of Superman* (first run syndication 1952–1958).[1] The Superman franchise developed through exchanges between these incarnations, as content was reflected between different kinds of images, words, and sounds. It is beyond the scope of this chapter to undertake detailed analysis of all these incarnations. Analyzing strategies and tropes used to introduce Superman at the beginning of texts reveals how the superhero's core traits were established. Tracing how these strategies and tropes emerge from and are exchanged between key incarnations enables one to track their impact on the franchise. The incarnations included in this analysis span a range of media that allow me to examine interactions between different but related formal configurations. My analysis charts the importance of aesthetic exchanges between texts in developing meanings that circulate the franchise.

Superman was introduced to the world on the now-iconic cover of *Action Comics* #1.[2] Shuster's art presents the key moment from the story in which Superman, placed at the cover's center, smashes a car into a rock. Grant Morrison observes,

> Aside from the bold Deco *whoosh* of the *Action Comics* logo, the date (June 1938), the issue (no. 1), and the price (10 cents), there is no copy and not a single mention of the name *Superman*. Additional words would have been superfluous. The message was succinct: Action was what mattered. What a hero did counted far more than the things he said, and from the beginning, Superman was in constant motion. (2011, 5–6, emphasis in original).

Superman's visual qualities—his actions and costume—are foregrounded above all else, immediately establishing key traits of the superhero's iconography and mentality. These qualities continue to be foregrounded throughout the Superman story inside *Action Comics* #1. Action sequences showcase Superman's extraordinary physical abilities, while his brightly colored costume provides the most eye-catching element on pages.

Despite the significance and endurance of Superman's iconography, visual signifiers are by no means the only elements that define Superman.

Catchphrases, conversational exchanges, and worded descriptions can be just as familiar. These can be reflected between written and spoken forms in different incarnations. I use the term "worded identifiers" to describe the various kinds of worded motif that perform the same identifying function as iconography.

The first page of the Superman story in *Action Comics* #1 communicates Superman's abilities and mission through a combination of words and images. The descriptions of most of Superman's powers are complemented by pictorial demonstrations, such as an image of the character jumping over a skyscraper depicting his ability to "hurdle a twenty-story building," and one of him racing a locomotive showcasing his capacity to "run faster than an express train." This page also features the first usage of the enduring worded identifier that names Superman a "champion of the oppressed." Written descriptions of Superman's powers that compare him to skyscrapers and trains, along with images of Superman leaping skyscrapers and racing trains, are peppered throughout early Superman comics. Superman comic book stories published in the few years following the superhero's debut often open with a caption that reiterates his abilities and dedication to liberating the oppressed. A popular wording used in multiple stories from this era is

> Leaping over skyscrapers, running faster than an express train, springing great distances and heights, lifting and smashing tremendous weights, possessing an impenetrable skin—these are the amazing attributes which Superman, savior of the helpless and oppressed, avails himself of as he battles the forces of evil and injustice![3]

These captions are accompanied by pictorial demonstrations of one of Superman's abilities. Early Superman comics thus established both worded and pictorial identifying motifs that convey the same information.

Morrison outlines these motifs' resonance in Depression-era America:

> If the dystopian nightmare visions of the age foresaw a dehumanized, mechanized world, Superman offered another possibility: an image of a fiercely human tomorrow that delivered the spectacle of triumphant individualism exercising its sovereignty over the implacable forces of industrial oppression. (2011, 7)

Superman can be read as a conqueror of industrialization. He can also be read as embodying modernity's promise to raise humanity ever higher, propel us ever faster. Dan Hassler-Forest outlines this dichotomy, stating that superheroes "represent not only a fantasy of overcoming the obvious limitations of the human body within the physically and mentally overpowering vertical landscapes of the modern metropolis; they can also be read as the literal embodiments of modernist aspirations" (2012, 174). The worded and pictorial motifs outlined above collaborate to connote this weighing of the fears and aspirations of industrialization. These concerns were reiterated as central themes of Superman, while embedding a discourse on urban life into the figure of the superhero.

Superman incarnations in other media do not just reflect worded identifiers established in comics, but also contribute their own to the franchise. The radio serial's opening sequence features a conversation between awestruck onlookers:

"Up in the sky, look!"

"It's a bird!"
"It's a plane!"
"It's Superman!"

This exchange was adopted in the openings of the Fleischer/Famous Studios cartoons and television series. The famed exchange is also reflected into comics. For example, in *Superman* #276 (June 1974) a crowd utters the words, only for a passerby to say to the fourth wall "Hunh. More tourists who come from all over the world just to catch a glimpse of the superguy!" While in this period Superman comics were being modernized, for instance by Clark's traditional job as newspaper reporter being updated to television news anchor, this self-reflexive statement reveals that the comics still defined themselves in relation to other incarnations. However, branding characters who utter the exchange as "tourists" positions texts in which this exchange was a core motif as outdated and only offering a "glimpse" of Superman. This framing of the worded identifier seeks to push older incarnations to the periphery of the franchise.

When this worded identifier introduces the radio serial, Fleischer/Famous Studios cartoons, and television series, it is preceded by the sound of wind whistling that signifies Superman's flight. The sound can be slowed or faded to indicate Superman's progress. This device metamorphoses motion lines, the pictorial signifiers that trace Superman's flight in comic books, into an aural motif. The specific qualities of each facilitate different effects. While the direction in which a motion line points indicates Superman's exact trajectory, the fading in and out of the sound cannot be so precise, only roughly suggesting Superman's position in relation to the action. However, the sound can signal that Superman is approaching a scene, whereas motion lines generally work best when he is already in, or leaving, a panel.

While images, lines of dialogue, and sounds can signify Superman on their own, combinations of all three in screen adaptations provide powerful evocations of the superhero. Similar to the summaries of Superman's abilities provided in early comics, after the "up in the sky . . . " exchange in the opening of the Fleischer Studios cartoons, the narrator announces, "Faster than a speeding bullet! More powerful than a locomotive! Able to leap tall buildings in a single bound!"[4] Images and sounds emphasize Superman's alignment with modernity's technological achievements. The metallic burst of a gun being fired and a bullet shooting across the screen follow the first proclamation; a medium shot of a train racing along, pistons pumping, complements the second; an image of Superman leaping a towering skyscraper accompanies the third. The gunshot and train provide hard mechanical sounds to enhance the juxtaposition of Superman and industrialization. The dialogue and sounds were clearly deemed powerful enough by themselves to be introduced to the opening of the radio serial in 1942 upon the show's moving to the Mutual Broadcasting System (MBS). This new radio serial opening also added a few vital words that have endured as the most famous worded identifier for Superman. Previously, in the radio serial and Fleischer/Famous Studios cartoons Superman stood for "truth and justice." In the year following the attack on Pearl Harbor that prompted the United States to formally enter World War II, the radio serial added a new element that was firmly rooted in sociopolitical surroundings: Superman now fought for "truth, justice, and the American way."

The full opening to the radio serial now initiated with the "faster than a speeding bullet . . . " declaration, proceeded to the "up in the sky . . . " exchange, before stating,

> Yes, it's Superman, strange visitor from another world, who came to Earth with powers and abilities far beyond those of mortal men. Superman, who can change the course of mighty rivers, bend steel in his bare hands, and who, disguised as Clark Kent, mild-mannered reporter for a great metropolitan newspaper, fights a never-ending battle for truth, justice, and the American way.

The television series reproduces this introduction almost verbatim and sets it to images, some of which rework those featured in previous screen incarnations.[5] On "faster than a speeding bullet" a hand points a gun at the viewer, then turns ninety degrees and fires a bullet across the screen. On "more powerful than a locomotive," a train races toward the fourth wall, before a close-up on its wheels is shown. On "able to leap tall buildings in a single bound," the camera tilts up a skyscraper to reveal its imposing height.[6] This sequence metamorphoses the opening of the Fleischer/Famous Studios cartoons by recreating it in live action and altering the framing. Each shot places the viewer in a position of vulnerability: in the sight of a gun, the path of a train, or at the base of a towering skyscraper. The proceeding shot of Superman flying through the clouds, accompanied by the familiar sound of whirling wind, announces his ability to overcome modernity's threatening creations. His powerful status is reinforced in a high-angled shot of onlookers performing the "up in the sky . . . " routine. As with the Fleischer/Famous Studios cartoons, an image of Superman is then shown, chest puffed out and fists on hips, which dissolves into one of Clark. Whereas the cartoons' opening ends with Clark, the television series cross-fades back to Superman on the word "justice." Superman now stands in his heroic stance with a US flag waving behind him, visually aligning Superman with the American way.

Superman's core motifs can be iconic, worded, or aural. Motifs accumulate, combine, and metamorphose as they are reflected between incarnations and media. The recurrence of motifs can affirm the position in the franchise of incarnations to previously use them, while specific ways in which motifs are deployed and reworked can seek to rearrange the franchise while metamorphosing key themes. The differing deployments of these motifs and themes contributes to the development of a range of characteristics and potential roles for Superman and Clark.

DISMANTLING THE CLARK KENT/SUPERMAN BINARY

Superheroes have been discussed as both static icons and fluid palimpsests. In his influential 1962 essay "The Myth of Superman," translated into English in 1972, Umberto Eco argues that a superhero has fixed traits that are reiterated from text to text. Following Eco, Matt Yockey argues that the Clark/Superman duality functions as an inflexible binary that helps maintain the character's stasis: "Both Superman and Clark Kent can never change because they are fixed contrasts to one another. Superman is defined by what he is not, Clark Kent, and vice versa" (2008, 27). Vanessa Russell outlines the traits attributed to each identity in this binary:

> The figure of the reporter is a dialectical construct, a dry, dull, mild persona who exists in opposition to Superman, the supercharged champion of the underdog and vigilante seeker of justice. There is no Hegelian synthesis in Superman: Kent does not take on heroic characteristics without first changing into a cape and tights, and Superman

does not take on Kent's "fear-struck" or "meek" characteristics without first donning the clothes of the working journalist. (2009, 216)

Clark is the meek journalist, Superman the heroic vigilante. Yockey and Russell assert that there is no overlap between these traits; different outfits delineate discrete identities. Poststructuralist thinking, however, provides a means to dismantle apparent binaries.

Brooker (2012) uses the model of a spectrum, derived from Duncan Falconer's (2008) conceptualization of the "Prismatic Age" of comics, to illuminate the range of characteristics a superhero can adopt across their incarnations. Falconer argues that the Prismatic Age started in mid- to late 1990s superhero comic books. The prism analogy offers a potent image of light being refracted into all the colors on the spectrum, and through doing so "captures the sense of alternates, analogues and parallel iterations of characters that frequently recurred in these stories" (Brooker 2012, 165). This prism analogy presents seemingly opposed incarnations, such as the camp Batman of television series *Batman* (ABC 1966–1968) and the brooding vigilante of cinema's *Dark Knight* trilogy, not as binaries but as different points on a shared spectrum. Brooker also uses the spectrum model to dismantle another commonly perceived binary in the superhero genre: superhero and supervillain. Applying the model to a reading of Batman and Joker, Brooker demonstrates that "the relationship between Batman and Joker is not so much an opposition as a spectrum; they do not occupy opposite sides, but different points on the rainbow range of light thrown by a prism" (176). In different texts Batman and Joker can possess similar traits and be resituated in relation to each other. This model of a spectrum is therefore equipped to explore the range of roles a superhero can adopt by placing them in relation to a figure often perceived as their binary opposite.

Interactions between Clark and Superman on their shared spectrum reveal the possibilities of both identities. I now look at different elements that affect Clark's and Superman's positioning in relation to each other. Surveying firstly the identities' characteristics, then strategies for presenting the transformation between identities, and finally looking at industrial and sociopolitical factors, I analyze some notable instances of these elements repositioning the identities on a spectrum.

In *Action Comics* #1, Clark and Superman are constructed as a binary that is upheld in subsequent early Superman comics. In this first Superman story Clark plays the timid weakling, with fellow reporter and future love interest Lois Lane venomously branding him "a spineless, unbearable coward."[7] Clark is rarely dominant in compositions and is typically placed in a

Superman meets Lois Lane in *Action Comics* #1 (1938).

submissive position when sharing a panel with Lois. Twice in the story Lois is in the foreground of panels with her back to Clark, refusing to face him. As such, "meek" became the primary adjective used to describe Clark in early Superman comics, in opposition to the foregrounding of Superman's immense physical strength.[8] Superman's interactions with Lois exhibit his intimidating physical qualities. The two meet properly in a panel where they stand opposite each other. His claim that "you needn't be afraid of me. I won't harm you." is undermined by him leaning forward, looming over her, forcing her downward into the panel's corner, causing a compositional imbalance that stresses his dominance. Distinct speech patterns also separate the identities, communicated not just by differences between what they say, but also their dialogue's presentation. Clark's dialogue, mainly when talking to Lois, is often interspersed with grammatical ellipses and nervous tics such as "er" to convey stuttering. Bold font is used more commonly in Superman's dialogue, expressing his confidence. Pictorial and worded devices in *Action Comics* #1 consistently express the Clark/Superman binary as weakness/strong masculinity.

George Reeves as Superman in the opening sequence of *Adventures of Superman* (1952).

George Reeves as Clark Kent in the opening sequence of *Adventures of Superman* (1952).

Screen and radio incarnations express the relationship between Clark and Superman in different ways. The Fleischer/Famous Studios cartoons harness animation's ability to present movement. Superman's characterization is conveyed predominantly through physical feats, his extraordinary abilities showcased in elaborate battles in which he races and leaps fluidly around the screen.[9] These acrobatics distinguish him from the grounded Clark. The cartoons feature minimal dialogue, particularly for Superman, who only speaks a few lines in two of the seventeen cartoons: *The Arctic Giant* (Dave Fleischer 1942) and *The Magnetic Telescope* (Dave Fleischer 1942). When Superman does speak, voice actor Bud Collyer uses a far deeper voice than Clark's. Collyer uses the same vocal distinction to differentiate the identities in the radio serial, while Kirk Alyn similarly gives Superman a deeper voice than Clark in the film serials. This technique is an aural reflection of grammatical and iconic devices used to separate the identities in comic books' written words.

Despite the seeming establishment of this vocal distinction, George Reeves, in the television series, uses the same gentle but authoritative tone for both identities.[10] As the first actors to play Clark/Superman in live-action adaptations, however, Alyn and Reeves could use other elements of performance to reposition the identities on their spectrum. Alyn's Clark is far from a coward, staying composed in chapter seven of the first serial while being held at gunpoint. He is also very action-orientated, for instance tackling and restraining an assassin in chapter three of *Atom Man vs. Superman*. Alyn's energetic heroics as both Clark and Superman draw the two identities into close alignment. Reeves's Clark on occasion demonstrates proficiency in physical combat and is generally assertive yet is also very gentle. This gentleness is evident from every episode's opening sequence, when the image of Superman standing with his chest puffed out, fists on hips, dissolves into one of Clark, who stands less imposingly, arms hanging by his sides. These postures resonate throughout the episodes. Clark often leans casually on desks. Superman enters scenes by smashing through walls with his barrel chest before either assuming the assured stance with fists on hips or standing poised for action, feet apart and arms raised. Reeves's postures affirm Clark's mild nature while conveying Superman's heroic vitality.

Clark is therefore not always meek. Indeed, the opening sequences for the radio serial, Fleischer/Famous Studios cartoons, and television series instead introduce him as "mild-mannered." These mild-mannered Clarks are more respected within the diegesis than their early comic book counterpart, often exuding authority that more closely binds them to Superman.

While Clark and Superman's characteristics can vary significantly, in terms of appearance Superman's vivid red and blue costume provides a stark contrast to Clark's typically grey suits. In superhero fiction, the outfits worn by superhero and civilian identities conventionally uphold a binary whereby "the superhero costume constructs uniqueness, while the civilian wardrobe constructs normality" (Brownie and Graydon 2016, 71). Yet the presentation

Clark/Superman midway through the transformation between identities in *Action Comics* #1 (1938).

of a character's transformation from one identity to another can uphold or unpick this binary by revealing either distinctions or overlaps between identities. Even though *Action Comics* #1 presents the binary at its starkest, the opposition is destabilized in a panel that isolates a moment midway through the transformation, Clark's shirt half covering Superman's costume. This literal overlap presents the identities as two sides of the same man.

In comics, the transformation has been presented in a range of other ways, both between and within panels. Elsewhere in *Action Comics* #1, Clark transforms into Superman in a gutter between panels and rows. The panel at the end of a row depicts Clark exiting to the right, his left elbow already out of the panel. Superman enters the next row from the left of the first panel, led by his left elbow. The consistency of stance presents the transition from one panel and identity to the next as a single, continuous action, expressing a clear link between identities. Comparable fluidity is created in a single panel that depicts the transformation in *Superman* #233 (January 1971). Clark is to the left of the rectangular panel, running around a corner while loosening his tie. He is proceeded by four more figures that depict different stages in the transformation, their overlapping copresence indicating the speed at which this well-rehearsed action takes place. Momentum is enhanced by motion lines flowing from one figure to the next, affirming the connection between identities. Both these examples use strategies for presenting movement in comics to present a dynamic flow between identities.

Worded devices can also create a smooth transition between identities. While Collyer's distinct voices for Clark and Superman clearly separate them in the radio serial and Fleischer/Famous Studios cartoons, this strategy also creates a link between identities when the shift occurs midsentence. As Larry Tye describes,

> Collyer drew on his training as a crooner to underscore the difference between Clark and Superman, playing the former in a tenor that oozed milquetoast, then dropping several pitches midsentence to a gravelly baritone that was just right for the world's strongest man, yet making clear that both voices came from the same man. (2012, 86–87)

The worded identifier "this looks like a job for Superman" exemplifies this shift in vocal register. The first five words are spoken in Clark's gentler tone, and on "for Superman" Collyer's voice dramatically drops into the superhero's deep pitch. Aurally signaling the shift between identities in a single sentence creates a closer connection between the identities than the grammatical and iconic vocal segregation in early comic book stories.

While the tonal shift during "this looks like a job for Superman" is the central way the radio serial signifies Clark's transformation into Superman, the Fleischer/Famous Studios cartoons combine it with an iconic motif. Clark utters the catchphrase aloud before entering a concealed location. The audience witness the hidden transformation in silhouette, as the outline of the figure changing clothes through a window or as a shadow on a wall.

Clark transforms into Superman in a gutter between panels and rows in *Action Comics* #1 (1938).

Clark's transformation into Superman is presented as overlapping figures in a single panel in *Superman* #233 (1971).

Seconds later Superman emerges. This shadow play is consistent with the cartoons' expressionistic stylization and emphasis on flowing movement, while granting the transformation an air of mystery. Spoken words and motion create a link between identities, but the visual element's abstraction maintains the largely mute superhero's mystique.

Rather than seeking elaborate ways to directly present the super-fast transformation, early live-action adaptations, namely the serials and television series, conceal the transformation in an edit. In the serials Alyn announces, "This looks like a job for Superman," complete with tonal dip, then runs behind an object, upon which the filmmakers cut away. The television series forgoes the worded identifier. Instead, Reeves takes off his hat and/or glasses and loosens his tie while running to a concealed location. The repetition of this "traditional off-with-the-glasses routine" (Grossman 1976, 70) exchanges the worded identifier for a performative motif, albeit one that does not offer a sense of fluid transition between identities. In both the film serials and television series, Superman emerges in a subsequent shot, either moments later or in a different scene. Having the transformation occur in an edit metamorphoses the strategy from comics in which the transformation happens in the gutter between panels. Since comics panels are spatially juxtaposed, compositional strategies can create a clear link between identities. The temporal replacement of one shot with another in film and television editing elicits more visual dislocation between Clark and Superman.

The lack of elaborate special effects to depict the transformation in the serials and television series can be linked to budgetary constraints. These constraints intersect with formats and genre preferences to produce unique narrative formations that influence the identities' depiction. The quick-witted heroics of Alyn's Clark and Superman, which puts the identities on somewhat equal footing, is in keeping with contemporaneous film serials, in which the action-adventure genre thrived despite miniscule budgets.[11] Such low-budget action-adventure entails Clark/Superman countering human criminals or human-like antagonists, in contrast to the fantastic monsters that Superman alone fights in the lavishly produced Fleischer cartoons, where animation also alleviates limitations on the kind of action that can be easily portrayed. While the Superman film serials are filled with tightly budgeted fights and death traps, the television series's low budget[12] likely contributed to Superman's spectacular feats being mostly reserved for each episode's climactic last few minutes. Gary Grossman also attributes Clark's greater screen time to the conventions of televisual narrative structure:

> With less than a half hour to work with, exposition and ultimate resolution of conflict were only a commercial away from one another. There had to be a new reason each week for Lois, Jimmy or Perry White to be terrorized. It was Clark Kent who engineered their salvation, making the exciting switch to Superman only for the actual heroics. (1977, 55)

Episodes of the television series typically revolve around a criminal investigation, the stakes heightening when one of Clark's friends is placed in danger. Clark, in his role as investigative reporter, solves the case before Superman apprehends the villain. In the television series, a combination of budget and format contribute to a relation between identities where Clark provides the brains and Superman the brawn.

The ongoing dialogue between Superman texts and changing sociopolitical contexts can also contribute to Clark and Superman being positioned very differently on their spectrum from incarnation to incarnation. Gordon (2017, 52–53) argues for another factor explaining the greater presence of Clark in the television series; placing emphasis on Clark at the workplace conformed to the US government's postwar efforts to assert stable workplaces with dedicated employees as a social norm. While the television series's gently assertive Clark's successful investigations suggest that dedication to the working world helps remedy threats to society, the meek Clark of early Superman comics stories needs to transform into the brash Superman to be effective in Depression-era America. Illuminating dialogue with other popular entertainment informed by this context, Bradford W. Wright describes this early comic book Superman as "a tough and cynical wise guy, similar to the hard-boiled detectives like Sam Spade who also became popular during the Depression years" (2001, 9). This early Superman's hard-boiled masculinity responds to the crisis of masculinity in the Depression, prompted by many men being emasculated upon losing their jobs (Regalado 2015, 82–83). In these early comic book adventures Superman frequently fought for those who had been neglected by the establishment, liberating workers from corporate and government corruption as a "champion of the oppressed."[13]

Gordon identifies three key factors that drove a shift from Superman's role as a champion of America's disenfranchised to "a symbol of more general American cultural values" (2017, 18). These are: America's entry into World War II, social fears about comics that bubbled up in the early 1940s and incited moral panic in the early 1950s, and Superman's commercial success. The Famous Studios cartoons offer an early example of a jarring shift in Superman's sociopolitical role, with multiple shorts explicitly functioning as US war propaganda. For example, Superman is pitted against crassly caricatured Japanese saboteurs in *Japoteurs* (Seymour Kneitel 1942) and aids US secret agents in *Secret Agent* (Seymour Kneitel 1943). After the war, to appease charges of comics causing juvenile delinquency, comics publishers introduced a self-imposed system of censorship called the Comics Code. The Code mandated that the law and family values be upheld in comic books (Regalado 2015, 162–64). While directly shaping comic book portrayals of Superman, these strictures also informed incarnations in other media. The hand Superman's commercial success and subsequent implication in consumerism played in pushing Clark and Superman into more wholesome roles can be seen most overtly in the overall lightening of the television series's tone from season one to two, which Jake Rossen (2008, 30) attributes in part to Kellogg's signing on as sponsor on condition that the tone was softened.

The "American way" that Superman embodies, however, did not cleanly transition from promoting the nation's war effort to maintaining values of family and consumerism. Tensions in how Superman texts conceptualize the American way emerge in the postwar period. Certain Superman stories from this period demonstrate allegiance to the US government through direct collaboration with governmental bodies. For instance, television series episode "Stamp Day for Superman" (1954) was made in cooperation with the United States Treasury Department and shown in schools to promote savings bonds, while Superman performs missions for President John F. Kennedy in two 1960s comic book stories.[14] Elsewhere, a famous storyline from the radio serial, "Clan of the Fiery Cross" (1946), pits Clark/Superman and the staff of Clark's newspaper, the *Daily Planet*, against the eponymous clan— a surrogate for the Ku Klux Klan—who are terrorizing a Chinese family. Tye (2012, 83) suggests that, due to racial segregation in America at the time of production, sponsor Kellogg's would have been uneasy about the persecuted family being African American, but the writers were able to explore racial discrimination through an Asian family. Throughout the story, Clark/Superman and his friends assert that racial equality is integral to America. In the final episode, when handing out trophies to the Chinese family's son's baseball team, Perry White (Julian Noa), editor of the *Daily Planet*, states, "You've proved that youngsters of different races and creeds can work and play together successfully, in the American way." By promoting racial equality prior to the Civil Rights Act of 1964, the "American way" in this instance does not represent unequivocal allegiance to US law, but rather the values for which America *should* stand. Despite becoming a totem of national identity during World War II, once the war finished Superman's earlier role as champion of those oppressed by the US establishment continued to inform his new status as emblem for the "American way." In Superman texts, the "American way" worded identifier can have different meanings depending on the way in which it is deployed.

In the Superman franchise's first few decades Clark adopted a variety of roles, from meek coward to shrewd investigative reporter, and Superman ranged from champion of the oppressed to protector of the US government. A permeability exists between the two identities, with traits of each appearing in the other. Different narrative configurations, often influenced by a medium's properties, can resituate the identities in terms of dominance. Stylistic and narrative strategies apply different shades to Clark and Superman to reposition them on their shared spectrum. These shades at times contrast one another to imbue the identities with somewhat contradictory qualities. For example, with Reeves's Clark/Superman in the television series, intonation draws the identities closer together, while their distinct postures push them apart, and the brains/brawn distinction gives both distinct heroic qualities. Any representation of Clark/Superman is a composite, formed through combining a variety of differently shaded factors. Between the incarnations I have discussed there are a whole range of Clarks and Supermen, mapping a vivid spectrum of possibility for the character.

NEVER-ENDING INTERTEXTUAL DIALOGUE

Superman does not develop along a simple chronological trajectory. Each incarnation engages in nonlinear intertextual dialogue with previous and contemporaneous incarnations. Looking at aesthetic interactions between texts and the ways traits of Clark/Superman from past incarnations recur or are reconfigured in later incarnations attests to Collins's (1991, 171) argument that texts can never be dispelled from a superhero franchise.

Diegetically redistributing past incarnations became a narrative strategy undertaken by DC in the 1960s. *Flash* #123 (September 1961) establishes a parallel universe inhabited by the Golden Age incarnations of DC's superheroes, setting a clear diegetic distinction between DC's past and present superheroes via the concept of a multiverse. It was designated that the Silver Age superheroes inhabit Earth-One, the Golden Age ones Earth-Two, with other universes subsequently introduced. Team ups between Silver Age superhero team the Justice League of America and Golden Age team the Justice Society of America soon became an annual tradition.[15] Different incarnations were officially situated as alternates existing together in a multiverse in which they could meet up, literalizing the dialogic interactions between incarnations. The designation of numbers that effectively ranks the Earths also reflects efforts to hierarchically arrange incarnations in a franchise.

Comic book story "Superman Takes a Wife!" from *Action Comics* #484 (June 1978), is set on Earth-Two and demonstrates the continuing circulation of earlier incarnations in the Superman franchise. The story resurrects details from very early Superman comic books, such as the newspaper Clark works for being the *Daily Star*. Motifs from other incarnations are also prominent. The opening page deploys the introduction from the radio serial and television series, starting "Superman—strange visitor from another planet..." This familiar description is disrupted when "and who, disguised as Clark Kent, mild-mannered reporter for a great metropolitan newspaper" is followed by "long ago decided there was one woman in the world he loved so deeply that he had to have her by his side." The stark alteration to the worded identifier announces a desire to liberally reconfigure familiar traits, a freedom permitted by the story being set in what is designated a secondary universe. Other elements from earlier incarnations in "Superman Takes a Wife!" include the use of the "up in the sky..." worded identifier twice, an onlooker commenting on a whistling sound as Superman approaches, and Superman defeating bank robbing robots that distinctly recall the eponymous creations of Fleischer Studios cartoon *The Mechanical Monsters* (Dave Fleischer 1941). The story concerns a magic spell erasing the Superman identity, leaving Clark oblivious to his superpowered alter ego. Clark then becomes heroic, cracking down on organized crime, brawling with gangsters, and successfully romancing Lois. Positioning Clark as a tough crusader draws him closer to Superman while recalling the hard-edged aspects of Alyn and Reeves's Clarks. This tougher Clark is thus rooted not just in the Superman of Golden Age comic books, but also screen portrayals of Clark.

Narrative details, the redeployment of motifs, and Clark's demeanor in "Superman Takes a Wife!" straddle incarnations of Superman in various media from the thirties, forties, and fifties. This story, published in 1978 months prior to *Superman: The Movie*'s domestic release in December, reveals that all these incarnations were still present in the Superman franchise when Superman was on the verge of being launched into his first blockbuster film. Although these incarnations were decentered through being officially placed in a secondary universe, motifs originating in them were still familiar and available to be reflected into new incarnations. *The Movie* had this whole network of incarnations, featuring a vivid spectrum of roles for Clark and Superman, on which to draw as it made a bid for centrality in the Superman franchise.

SUPERMAN: THE MOVIE

The following analysis explores strategies through which *Superman: The Movie* is positioned in relation to other Superman incarnations and the context of 1970s Hollywood. The connections that an incarnation of Superman forms with other incarnations in its presentation of Clark/Superman are a key means through which its positioning within the Superman franchise is asserted. I therefore begin by analyzing the ways in which the film positions the Clark and Superman identities on their spectrum of possible roles. I proceed to look at how *The Movie*'s cinematic qualities are foregrounded to position it as a spectacular new envisioning of Superman's mythology. Finally, I outline some of the ways in which *The Movie* contributed to the development of Hollywood's emerging blockbuster paradigm and proved the superhero genre's suitability to this filmmaking model. Each piece of analysis outlines the ways in which the film's strategies of adaptation metamorphose elements of previous Superman texts and seek to rearrange the Superman franchise.

CLARK/SUPERMAN/REEVE

Casting an unknown actor, Christopher Reeve, as Clark/Superman enabled *The Movie* to freely select traits from the Clark/Superman spectrum without having a Hollywood star's persona influencing audience perceptions. The ways in which Reeve's Clark/Superman reconfigures traits from past incarnations signals reverence for certain earlier texts while forging the film a unique space in the franchise.

Reeve's Clark is introduced in the same sequence as the city of Metropolis and the *Daily Planet* offices. A shot from within the offices is presented through a camera lens that searches the space. Upon arriving at Lois (Margot Kidder) the focus fluctuates, building anticipation until this new version of a famous character is in sharp focus in close-up, tossing her hair and smiling for the camera. The reverse shot grants Jimmy Olsen (Marc McClure), the holder of the camera, a similarly typical introductory shot, his bowtie rooting him firmly in his dominant image in the franchise. Perry (Jackie Cooper) gets a comparable medium shot as Lois enters his office. Clark is conspicuous by his absence and retains a degree of invisibility even once introduced. Rather than having an introductory shot, Clark emerges as the camera follows Perry to his desk. Perry offhandedly introduces Lois to Clark, who rises from a seat situated below the frame and reaches out to shake

Lois smiles for the camera in *Superman: The Movie* (1978).

Clark comedically strains to open a bottle in *Superman: The Movie* (1978).

Lois's hand, only to be ignored. The camera does not isolate and foreground Clark, who must find his own way into the frame. Clark proceeds to glance around uneasily, shifting his eyebrows and pushing his glasses back with his finger, a gesture that George Reeves's Clark uses to assert genteel assuredness, but when performed by Christopher Reeve in this chain of fumbling gestures seems more like a nervous tic. Reeve's Clark's inability to demand the camera's full attention and his unassured gestures establish the identity as awkward and timid.

Although Reeve's Clark has a meekness comparable to his early comic book incarnation, other elements of his cinematic presentation metamorphose the identity's characterization. Tye claims that Reeve based his performance on a young Cary Grant: "shy, vulnerable, and charmingly klutzy" (2012, 198). Reeve's Clark is like the physically animated but psychologically fumbling Grant of *Bringing Up Baby* (Howard Hawks 1938), rather than Grant's verbally animated and self-assured newspaperman in *His Girl*

Friday (Howard Hawks 1940). After Clark fails to introduce himself, Lois and Perry engage in quick-fire discussion, their rapid vocal tempos recalling those of Grant and Rosalind Russell's sharp-witted journalists in *His Girl Friday*. Clark is sidelined during this exchange, comedically straining to open a bottle before spraying the contents over himself. Reeve's Clark's stuttering reflects the Clark of early comic books while his nasal intonation links him with incarnations whose voices are pitched higher than Superman's. This combination makes Reeve's Clark's intonation more boyish than that of any previous screen incarnation, wavering as if his voice is breaking. His full suit, tie, and trilby recreate a look that is rooted in Golden Age comic books and recurs in the Fleischer/Famous Studios cartoons, film serials, and television series, but in 1970s comics had been replaced with more contemporary fashions.[16] *The Movie*'s Clark harkens back to the 1930s and 1940s through combining traits from previous incarnations with performative elements that emulate a screen icon from classical Hollywood. Yet while Golden Age comic books present Clark as deplorably weak, Reeve's Clark's qualities connote wholesomeness. These connotations are evident in Lois's pleasant astonishment and affectionate smile upon hearing that Clark sends half his weekly paycheck to his mother.

Further metamorphosis of familiar strategies and characterization is evident upon Clark's first full transformation into Superman. As Lois hangs in peril from a skyscraper rooftop following a disastrous helicopter launch, from down on the street Clark initiates the transformation. Running toward the fourth wall, Clark pulls open his shirt to reveal the iconic "S" symbol on the superhero costume underneath, which fills the frame by the end of the shot, transitioning from a momentary midpoint between identities to an iconic Superman symbol. In the next shot, Clark enters a revolving door, whizzes it around, and reemerges fully clad as Superman. The motion blur in the spinning doors metamorphoses the motion lines that certain comics use to present the transformation in a single panel, creating a comparable sense of speed that is complemented by cinema's temporarily directly presenting, rather than evoking, the action's rapidity. Clark/Superman's abstracted transformation, witnessed as a blur through moving glass, also recalls the silhouette motif from the Fleischer/Famous Studios cartoons. The whirling sound of the doors augments the denotation of speed, while building toward the aural identifier of Superman's flight. As Superman takes flight a sharper whooshing noise than in previous incarnations signifies greater velocity. Numerous strategies from previous incarnations are thus reworked and combined to create a

Superman meets Lois in *Superman: The Movie* (1978).

smooth transition from one identity to the other in one continuous action. Although each strategy has antecedents, their fresh metamorphosis grants the transformation from Clark to Superman a fluidity and air of spectacle not before seen in live action.

Reeve's Clark's mild nature is retained in Superman's gentleness. After Lois falls from the skyscraper, Superman catches her, and they are framed face-to-face. While offering a literal reflection of the panel that depicted their meeting in *Action Comics* #1 through having the characters occupying opposite sides, the effect is also modified. The shot's composition is much more balanced than in the panel. Although Superman is still inches taller than Lois he does not encroach on her side of the frame. Instead of offering grimaces and threats, he smiles and assures "easy Miss, I've got you." When they land, Superman is shot from a low angle, Lois a high one, encapsulating his power, but rather than retreat in fear Lois gazes in wonder as Superman jokes about flying being the safest form of travel. He then enigmatically introduces himself as "a friend" and flies away. By acting with warmth and humility, Reeve's Superman is drawn into close proximity to his mild-mannered Clark.

Reeve's Clark/Superman harkens back to the era of the character's early adventures and forges links with a range of previous incarnations, yet also claims his own place on the Clark/Superman spectrum. While eliciting nostalgia for the 1930s and 1940s, Reeve's Clark/Superman is shaded in ways that pointedly distinguish him from the meek Clark and hypermasculine Superman of early comic books. Reeve's Clark takes characteristics from mild-mannered incarnations and resituates these as wholesome. His Superman, rather than appearing as Clark's opposite, takes on traits from Clark, upon which they come to emblematize heroism. Superman becomes mild-mannered!

The Movie's efforts to avoid explicit politicization further place its superhero at odds with the Golden Age "champion of the oppressed." The 1970s US's fractured sociopolitical landscape, following social movements of the 1960s and widespread disillusion with the government's handling of the Vietnam War and Watergate scandal, is only alluded to once. When Superman utters the famous worded identifier, telling Lois that he is "here to fight for truth, justice, and the American way," she laughs in disbelief and retorts, "You're gonna end up fighting every elected official in this country." Superman chuckles slightly and responds, "Surely you don't really mean that Lois?" before sincerely assuring her that he never lies. Considering Reeve's Superman's characterization, it could be argued that the values he embodies of warmth, empathy, and honesty are being promoted as the heroic qualities for which the "American way" *should* stand, but which have been lost. Conversely, it could be argued that Reeve's Superman functions as a reassuring representation of the US establishment to placate society's unrest. In this reading, Superman maps a rose-tinted construction of America's past onto the present, thus obscuring contemporary concerns. Such conflicting readings of how nostalgia can be mobilized in superhero blockbusters will be examined in greater depth in the next chapter. The significant thing to note for now is what Reeve's Superman's lack of explicit politicization contributes to the film's reorganization of the Superman franchise. The loving recreation of elements from past incarnations at once draws *The Movie* into alignment with these texts while contributing to its distinct meanings. Nostalgia for past incarnations engenders a lack of the kind of direct engagement in contemporary sociopolitical issues that some of those incarnations exhibit. This pattern of evoking previous incarnations while in the same move diverting from them manifests in a range of other ways throughout the film, being pointedly evident in assertions of superior spectacle.

LAUNCHING INTO THE CINEMATIC

The Movie begins with a black and white image of curtains, which open to reveal a 4:3 frame on which the title "June 1938" appears before an image of a comic titled *Action Comics*, thus paying homage to Superman's comic book genesis. Yet the image on the comic's cover is not the iconic picture of Superman smashing the car from *Action Comics* #1. Instead, the cover features a rocket blasting away from an exploding planet. This alteration indicates an interest not just in the character within the rocket, but in the

SUPERMAN: THE MOVIE, THE FIRST SUPERHERO BLOCKBUSTER   59

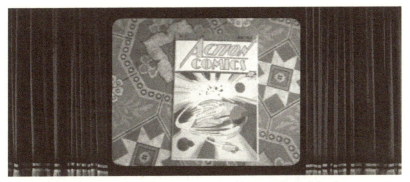

A comic titled *Action Comics* is shown in the opening moments of *Superman: The Movie* (1978).

wider fictional universe that had developed since Superman launched into comic books. As the sequence progresses, various strategies indicate that the filmmakers do not simply intend a reverential tour of this universe but promise a spectacular reenvisioning of Superman's mythology.

A motif deployed throughout *The Movie* to assert spectacle picks up and refines a strategy from the teaser trailer. The motif, in which movements of characters and the camera penetrate the depth of cinematic space, initiates in this opening sequence. As the camera draws forward, accompanied by a child's narration, the child's hand opens the comic, and the camera zeroes in on a panel showing the *Daily Planet* offices. The image then dissolves into a black-and-white shot of these offices (as represented by a somewhat unrefined model). The camera proceeds to move beyond the globe atop these offices, glides upward past the moon and into space. Vivid blue credits soar toward the screen and the curtains framing the images open fully, elongating the 4:3 frame to the 2.35:1 widescreen aspect ratio. This strategy is borrowed from *This Is Cinerama* (Michael Todd, Michael Todd Jr., Walter Thompson, Fred Rickey 1952), which begins in 4:3 and black and white with Lowell Thomas introducing the eponymous widescreen system. Upon Thomas's declaring, "This is Cinerama," the boxed monochrome image is consigned to the past as it changes to a widescreen color image that connotes the future of cinematic spectacle, as affirmed in the proceeding sequence where the camera is attached to a rollercoaster cart as it rushes forward, thus adding depth to the image's width and color. Burke (2015, 292) and Morton (2016, 48) identify how *The Movie*'s shifts from representations of previous media in which Superman has featured into widescreen images proclaim that

Superman has transcended these other media.[17] By passing though media in which Superman has previously featured, over a globe, and upward into space, the movement quite literally announces that the film is going beyond the world envisioned in earlier incarnations. In underscoring spatial depth, the camera's forward penetration also grants this cinematic reenvisioning of Superman's universe a dimension that the movement indicates as missing from the flat comic book page that is left behind.

The linking of spatial depth with cinematic spectacle continues in the credits. "Alexander Salkind Presents" glides in from the back of the frame before the letters burst toward the fourth wall. Marlon Brando's name follows. Brando was arguably the biggest star in Hollywood at the time following high profile roles in films like *The Godfather* (Francis Ford Coppola 1972), for which he won an Oscar, and *Last Tango in Paris* (Bernardo Bertolucci 1972), for which he was nominated for an Oscar. Brando's role in *The Movie*, along with his highly publicized salary of "$3.7 million and a percentage of the gross" (Rossen 2008, 66), gained the film much exposure prior to release while setting new precedents for Hollywood stars' pay. Credits for the film's next most bankable star, Gene Hackman, and director Richard Donner come next. Star presence is an established form of Hollywood spectacle (King 2002, 181). As the names of Brando and Hackman burst forward, these Hollywood stars are juxtaposed against cosmic stars that recede into the vastness of space. These complementary forms of spectacle suggest that the film will be grand in every respect. The sequence's trajectories are subsequently inverted, with credits receding back from the fourth wall and cosmic stars moving toward it, as if the audience is being propelled forward through the cosmos. The disorientating reversal of direction suggests that this journey leads to unknown territory, while the sense of rapid momentum denotes a great distance being covered. The sequence's stylistic strategies proclaim that the spatial dimension of cinema along with stunning special effects technologies enable this fantastic journey to a strange star system, while promising further spectacle through the names of film stars soon to feature and the motion gesturing to Superman's flight.

The opening journey concludes at Superman's home planet, Krypton. As the camera glides toward a white dome atop a shimmering city, Brando's authoritative voice announces, "This is no fantasy, no careless product of wild imagination." While Brando, playing Superman's father Jor-El, is referring to the charges held against criminals Zod (Terence Stamp), Ursa (Sarah Douglas), and Non (Jack O'Halloran), the words also assert the film's status. We have traveled from the juvenile origins of the comic book hero to a universe that is no longer mere "wild imagination" but is lavishly realized in cinema and carries the weight of Brando's solemn intonation.

SOARING THROUGH CINEMATIC SPACE

While used to showcase *The Movie*'s universe, trajectories through the depth of cinematic space are also used to present the extraordinary ways in which the eponymous hero inhabits this universe. The film redeploys the motif of head-on propulsion most prominently in the presentation of Superman's flight. Besides offering spectacle, this strategy expresses the superhero's relationship to urban surroundings when Superman flies through Metropolis.

Scott Bukatman's (2003) discussion of kaleidoscopic perception helps situate *The Movie*'s emphasis on penetration through the depth of cinematic space and other stylistic strategies deployed in its flight sequences in broader cinematic and cultural frameworks. Kaleidoscopic perception describes ways in which human perception adapts to modernity's fragmented and ephemeral phenomena. Bukatman identifies the kaleidoscopic effects sequence as an aesthetic strategy that expresses kaleidoscopic perception, as featured in science fiction films such as *2001: A Space Odyssey* (Stanley Kubrick 1968) and *Altered States* (Ken Russell 1980). "The archetypal kaleidoscopic effects sequence . . . features a first-person camera engaged in a relentless movement of forward penetration, distortions of the visual field, and a distended sense of time" (117). This aptly describes the opening credit sequence for *The Movie* along with a later sequence in which Clark's psyche is guided through Krypton's history and Jor-El's teachings, represented as a first-person journey through stars and celestial phenomena.

Presentations of Superman's flight in Metropolis deploy comparable strategies to convey the kaleidoscopic qualities of the modern city. Zoran Perisic devised the technique for realizing *The Movie*'s flight sequences. Perisic

> put zoom lenses on both the camera and the projector so that the projected image, as seen by the camera, never changed size. Superman, who was in front of that image, appeared to come closer or move farther away—and to be performing aerial maneuvers when the camera/projector rig rotated—when in fact he was standing still. (Tye 2012, 197)

Motion is evident in complementary zooms of the camera and projected image, and in the camera's rotations, while Reeve swerves and banks. These alternating layers of movement recall the view down a kaleidoscope. This presentation of Superman's flight encapsulates many elements of the "combination of delirium, kinesis, and immersion . . . the headlong rush, the rapid montage, and the bodily address" (2003, 3) that Bukatman attributes to kaleidoscopic perception. Bukatman aligns these qualities with the giddy experiences of urban life:

Superman flies with his chest parallel to the bottom of the frame in *Superman: The Movie* (1978).

City lights appear in the background as Superman seemingly drifts upward in *Superman: The Movie* (1978).

> Kaleidoscopic perception was fundamental to the rhetorics that surrounded the modern metropolis. . . . The city was presented as a chaotic tumult of activity and sensory bombardment, sometimes to damn it, other times to celebrate it, but always to heighten its transformative power. Kaleidoscopic perception served to turn the fear of instability into the thrill of topsy-turveydom. (3)

The city's sensory overload is at once disconcerting, transformative, and thrilling. Kaleidoscopic perception therefore provides a powerful means for expressing the superhero's embodiment of urban fears and aspirations.

Superman's flight in *The Movie* goes beyond the metaphorical representation of urban experience through kaleidoscopic stylistics that Bukatman describes. When Superman flies away after saving Lois and revealing himself to Metropolis, actual urban phenomena—city lights and skyscrapers—are

SUPERMAN: THE MOVIE, THE FIRST SUPERHERO BLOCKBUSTER   63

Superman rolls clockwise and the city's skyline rotates counterclockwise in *Superman: The Movie* (1978).

Kaleidoscopic rotations conclude once Superman and Metropolis settle upright in *Superman: The Movie* (1978).

integrated into kaleidoscopic presentational strategies. As Superman enjoys his aerial freedom, a shot that showcases the superhero's flight begins with him gliding into the frame from the bottom-right, framed head-on with his back parallel to the right side of the frame. His body then rolls 90 degrees so that his chest is parallel to the bottom of the frame, while he curls into roughly the frame's center. The navy night sky behind Superman is filled with the lights of Metropolis in the distance as he seemingly drifts upward. The spectacle of Superman's flight distracts from the fact that the city's skyline is upside down. Superman then rolls clockwise, and the city's inversion is made clear by the disorientation caused when, once he has turned about 270 degrees, the skyline rotates counterclockwise. The rotations continue until both Superman and Metropolis settle upright. The destabilizing rotations of the city and Superman evoke the multitude of rotations in a kaleidoscope. Presenting flight in this way imbues Metropolis with the same unbounded

Superman flies toward the camera and smiles at the audience in the final shot of *Superman: The Movie* (1978).

freedom as Superman enjoys, encapsulating Bukatman's assertion that "the superhero city is a place of weightlessness, a site that exists, at least in part, in playful defiance of the spirit of gravity" (188).

The Movie grants a photographic representation of Metropolis ("played" by New York) dynamism through kaleidoscopic rotations that draw superhero and city together in complementary kinesis. This technique metamorphoses devices used in previous incarnations to express Superman's spatial freedom and conquering of urban space. While spatial cues in comics can map Superman's trajectories across panels and pages, and convey his ability to freely navigate space as, for instance, he races locomotives and leaps skyscrapers, *The Movie* achieves this effect through a multitude of movements within a single shot. If certain other incarnations of Superman invite a reading of the city as an oppressive force that Superman surmounts, *The Movie*'s kaleidoscope presentation of Metropolis transforms the city into a fairground of glimmering delights.

Throughout *The Movie*, extravagant exhibition of movement and depth through deployment of head-on propulsion showcases the film's ability to construct, and Superman's power to move uninhibitedly though, a vividly realized universe. This motif continues through to the final shot.[18] Superman is shown curving gracefully around the Earth then toward the camera, smiling to the audience as he passes.[19] The motif has taken the audience to alien planets, rearticulated Superman's relation to urban space, and now conveys his acknowledgment of the world beyond the fourth wall. *The Movie*'s proclamation of superiority over previous incarnations is achieved through heightened spectacle that seeks to involve viewers in the diegesis while simultaneously showcasing its special effects. This showcasing is a key feature of blockbuster films, which "feature spectacular on-screen events that often include expensive displays of the latest in special effects technologies" (King 2002, 50). Through the deployment of spectacle, *The Movie* does not just bid for centrality in the Superman franchise, but also exhibits its credentials as blockbuster cinema at a time when Hollywood's filmmaking practices were changing.

THE NEW HOLLYWOOD ADVENTURES OF SUPERMAN

The Movie established both Superman and the superhero genre as viable material for blockbusters in the changing political economy of 1970s New Hollywood. As outlined in this book's introduction, three core traits of Hollywood's blockbuster paradigm that emerged in the late-1970s are an emphasis on special effects spectacle, a shift in strategies of textual expansion to the serialization of big-budget features, and an intensified pursuit of paratextual expansion through merchandising and licensing. While I have analyzed uses of spectacle above, it is instructive to note some of the contributions that *The Movie* made to the development of the blockbuster paradigm in terms of textual and paratextual expansion, before focusing on how the film deploys the New Hollywood blockbuster's approach to genre.

Stuart Henderson identifies *The Movie* as a significant turning point in the history of sequel production, "at which the blockbuster philosophy and increased conglomeration of the previous twenty years officially converged with the production-line approach of the B-Movie" (2014, 56). As New Hollywood's blockbuster paradigm was taking shape, *Jaws*' self-contained narrative spawned sequels, and Star Wars was conceived as part of a series, but *The Movie* integrated a commitment to serialization into its production, with scripts for two films written, and set to be filmed, at the same time. This strategy was theoretically economic—for instance, all the filming on a specific set for both films could be done in one block—but various problems led to the eventual abandonment of shooting the sequel until after the first film had been released (see Tye 2012, 189–205; Rossen 2008, 56–117; Mankiewicz and Crane 2012, 188–220). In what can be seen as a reaction to these issues, future blockbuster productions that employ a comparable model generally shoot sequels back-to-back after the first film's commercial success is ensured.[20] This inbuilt serialization contributes at the level of narrative to what Schatz (1993) sees as an inherent fragmentation in blockbusters. For example, after standing trial and being imprisoned in *The Movie*'s opening act, Zod, Ursa, and Non do not feature for the rest of the film, instead being introduced so that they can return as the sequel's main villains.

Schatz sees the diversification of media conglomerates from the 1970s onward as central to the blockbuster paradigm's logic of fragmentation. This diversification facilitates lucrative merchandising and licensing across the different arms of a media conglomerate and between companies. Films based on existing properties are favored as they are "presold": they already have a media presence and audience. Studio Warner Brothers found in Superman an ideal franchise to multiply across texts and paratexts. Tom Shone argues that *The Movie*

> marked the first wholly successful instance of blockbuster synergy, with every arm of the Warner Brothers conglomerate successfully feeding the next: Warner Brothers television showed short films about the making of the film; Warner Brothers records released John Williams's soundtrack album; Warner Brothers books released eight titles; and DC comics, acquired by Warners ten years previously, brought out twenty-eight comic books; while another Warners subsidiary, Atari, brought out a Superman pinball machine. (2004, 99)

As properties that already exist in numerous texts, media, and products and have, over the course of decades, built multigenerational audiences, superhero franchises are primed for conglomerated Hollywood studios to multiply further with a blockbuster at the epicenter of expansion. *The Movie* provided a merchandising and licensing blueprint for subsequent blockbusters and demonstrated how ideally superhero properties lend themselves to the commercial strategies of blockbuster cinema.

The generic qualities of superheroes further lend them to blockbuster treatment. Sheldon Hall, in tracing the New Hollywood blockbuster's genealogy, observes that

> the most common genres for recent blockbusters have been fantasy, science fiction and occasionally horror, but most often action-adventure films the collective generic origins of which lie in the matinee serials, B-movies and exploitation movies which once seemed least amenable to blockbuster treatment. (2002, 23)

New Hollywood blockbusters favor genres previously associated with low-budget, low-brow films, like the superhero genre which, prior to 1978, Hollywood had primarily used in film serials.[21] While these favored genres had proved rife for serialization in low-budget productions, Hall attributes their subsequent blockbuster treatment to studios striving to sell blockbusters to young audiences, who were the most common audiences for serials. These genres can also broaden blockbuster audiences by appealing to the nostalgia of older audiences who would have enjoyed serials in their youth (Schatz 1993, 23).

Schatz (23) argues that audience appeal is further widened by the lively genre hybridity in New Hollywood blockbusters engendering a "purposeful incoherence" that opens up films to multiple interpretative strategies. The inherent multiplicities of superheroes, who across the networks of texts that make up their franchises accommodate diverse genre elements, again predisposes them to the New Hollywood blockbuster paradigm. My analysis of early Superman texts revealed that incarnations in media other than comics are often shaped by genres and formats that are popular in their chosen medium. To explore the functions that the kind of frenzied genre hybridity deployed in New Hollywood blockbusters performs in *The Movie*, I now look at two sequences that both in isolation and together offer interesting combinations of genres.

The film's spectacular finale, in which Superman races around the San Andreas Fault attending to catastrophes caused by an earthquake, offers a typical action-oriented premise for a superhero text. In this case tropes of the disaster movie, a genre popular in early-1970s Hollywood that served as a precursor to the New Hollywood blockbuster, frame the action. Ken Feil summarizes the formula of 1970s disaster movies as, "A powerful natural force isolates the characters, challenges their survival, and motivates a string of spectacular adventures and effects displays" (2005, xv). The San Andreas Fault sequence changes the space in which these events transpire from the confining structures like skyscrapers or boats in disaster movies to broad desert land. In expanding the terrain over which the disaster occurs, *The Movie* reconfigures disaster movie conventions to showcase Superman's flight, speed, and strength. The disaster movie's "dual threats of technological and natural catastrophe" (14) are evident in how the earthquake is instigated by a missile launched through supervillain Lex Luthor's (Gene Hackman) machinations and triggers an array of technological hazards, such as electric cables whipping around at power stations and lengths of train track collapsing. Superman's status as champion of industrialization is enforced when he shuts off the power station's electricity and replaces the collapsed train track with his own outstretched body. Disaster movie conventions thus facilitate the rearticulation of key tropes from the Superman franchise.

These heroic feats present Superman as a figure of action, whose fluid movements recall the kinesis of the Fleischer Studios cartoons' Superman. The immense anguish that Lois's death puts Reeve's Superman through, however, distinguishes him from the purely action-orientated Fleischer Superman. As Superman arrives at the scene of Lois's death the onslaught of rapidly edited shots and cacophonous sounds ceases, and the music slows to a melancholic tune. Superman lifts Lois's body while fighting back tears. This generic shift from disaster movie to romantic tragedy illuminates a different side of Superman, refocusing from the unstoppable man of steel to the lonely figure repeatedly denied contentment with the woman he loves. Generic coding shifts again into a science fiction scenario as Superman fires upward, out into space and circles Earth so fast that it rotates backward, thereby reversing the flow of time. Science fiction is another genre common to Superman adventures, often prominent in Silver Age Superman comics (see Tye 2012, 169–73), an era in which the superhero also gained the ability to travel through time.

King (2002, 197–201) observes that cinematic spectacle can take different forms, which can be deployed alongside one another in blockbusters to appeal to different audiences. Superman's heroic feats and reversal of time appeal to fans of disaster films and science fiction, which are traditionally perceived as masculine genres, while his emotional anguish at Lois's death appeals to fans of romantic tragedy, traditionally considered to be feminine. Despite appealing to different audiences, the segues between genres within a single sequence do not fragment Superman, but rather articulate aspects of the identity that are already in dialogue with one another on his character spectrum. The effect of this combination of genre conventions that appeal to different audiences is therefore far from the incoherence that Schatz suggests. Various genres' conventions metamorphose familiar traits of Superman to present a superhero who is completed by his multiple facets.

Romance is even more pronounced in the earlier sequence in which Superman takes Lois flying over Metropolis, which deploys conventions of another genre that traditionally attracts female spectatorship: the musical. This generic framework may seem at odds with the action-adventure associated with superhero texts. Yet closer study reveals the extent to which the sequence complements many of the film's strategies and its presentation of Superman. This sequence occurs after Lois interviews Superman on her rooftop in a scene filled with romantic flirtation. The rooftop offers a respite from urban modernity; it is many stories above the city streets, the hustle and bustle of which are not even audible, and laden in green plants. This space acts comparably to Northrop Frye's conceptualization of "the green world," a forest space with magical properties that allows characters in Shakespeare's comedies to transcend social constrictions and is analogous to "the dream world that we create out of our own desires" (1973, 183). In this environment gender inequalities begin to resolve, with Lois taking charge

Superman and Lois break the cloud surface in *Superman: The Movie* (1978).

Superman is framed in the foreground during *Superman: The Movie*'s (1978) romantic flight sequence.

and directing her questions to a somewhat coy Superman, and romance blooms. These features are accentuated as Lois and Superman rise further above the strictures of the city through flight. Bukatman identifies strong relations between urban musicals and superhero comics: "The city is refigured as a playground in the two genres that permit the most strikingly unfettered access to urban space, genres that license the suspension of the physical laws that govern time and space" (2003, 7). Characters in both genres enjoy liberated movement around urban space. As Superman takes Lois flying, the structures of urban space are transcended completely, left behind under a floor of clouds.

Transcending the physical and social structures of the city enacts a move toward the utopianism that Richard Dyer (2002, 19–35) locates in musicals. Dyer argues that entertainment generally does not present models of utopian worlds: "Rather the utopianism is contained in the feelings it embodies" (20). He pays particular attention to ways that these feelings are conveyed

Lois is framed in the foreground during *Superman: The Movie*'s (1978) romantic flight sequence.

The composition is balanced as Superman and Lois glide toward the camera in *Superman: The Movie* (1978).

by nonrepresentational signs, such as "colour, texture, movement, rhythm, melody, camerawork" (20). When Superman and Lois break the cloud surface, the moonlight reflecting off the white clouds acts as a nonrepresentational sign that grants the sequence a romantic utopianism. As they glide along, a shot presents Superman's profile in the foreground to frame right and Lois in the background to the left as she loosens her grip on his arm, gaining confidence. This is proceeded by a reverse shot with Lois in the foreground as Superman smiles. The film switches between these angles until Lois's arms are fully outstretched, and the couple are shown head-on in long shot, gliding toward the camera. Rhythmic editing that grants both characters equal screen time builds to a shot in which Superman and Lois inhabit equal sides of the frame, while other nonrepresentational signs along with the characters' actions further contribute to the expression of equality and romance.

As Lois and Superman embrace while the camera circles their aerial slow dance, Lois's interior monologue begins to play in voiceover, reciting the romantic song "Can You Read My Mind?"[22] While in comics a reader would literally read Lois's thought balloons, in this musical number the ruminative inflection of Kidder's voice, along with her performance of enchantment, express the loving musings of her mind. The dance continues as Lois and Superman stretch out and glide toward the camera once again, although this time on opposite sides of the frame than in the earlier shot: Lois on the right, Superman on the left. The equal status of the two is such that they can freely swap positions. Lois then rises above Superman, seemingly gaining his ability to fly, before he balances the choreography by rising above her. In this utopian escape, even the roles that distinguish the characters dissolve as Lois effectively gains Superman's powers.

This sequence's presentation evokes utopianism in a general sense, while also expressing more specific meanings that refine the characterization of Lois and Superman. The broad sense of freedom-through-flight aligns with Bukatman's argument that utopianism is embodied by a superhero's unrestricted movements, and as such, "Utopia is less a place, a fixed site, than a trajectory. Actually, it's a field of possible, and multiple, trajectories" (2003, 125). However, utopia is not only figured as movement and flight in this sequence; the particular ways these phenomena are presented also evoke Dyer's conceptualization of utopia as a feeling. Movement is just one element of cinematic construction that combines with rhythmic editing, shot composition, music, and delivery of dialogue to communicate the feelings of utopianism. The qualities of these representational strategies refine the sense of utopianism even further so that it is not just evoked as general feelings, but also expresses, and is expressed by, Superman and Lois's feelings. The deployment of musical conventions in this sequence augments sensations that the musical and superhero genre share, while metamorphosing a key feature of the Superman franchise: the relationship between Lois and Superman.

The specific kind of utopianism conveyed in the scene is also motivated by the film's positioning of Superman on his character spectrum. Dyer argues that utopianism in musicals only provides solutions to specific needs and "effectively denies the legitimacy of other needs and inadequacies, and especially of class, patriarchal and sexual struggles" (2002, 27). This aerial dance differs in that it takes steps to dismantle gender inequality through the equal presentation of Lois and Superman in rhythmic edits and balanced compositions. The film's presentation of Superman as gentle, caring, and romantic, and of Lois as a determined yet kind-hearted reporter, provide the foundations for this equality, which are then reinforced through the deployment of Hollywood musical conventions.

Throughout *The Movie*, utopianism-through-movement is evoked using the head-on propulsion motif, while interactions between Lois and Clark/Superman contribute to a romantic narrative. As such, although the dance routine is signified, through rising above the cloud surface, as occurring in a discrete space, with unique generic coding, the sequence in fact continues and develops motifs and themes that permeate the film. Conventions of Hollywood musicals amplify and metamorphose traits of other Superman texts and the superhero genre. *The Movie* demonstrates that the New Hollywood blockbuster's genre hybridity can be used to harness points of overlap between genres to create meaning and foster narrative cohesion. Conventions of Hollywood genres that share concerns with the superhero genre help facilitate Superman's transition into blockbuster cinema. Deploying forms of spectacle associated with different cinematic genres is also a strategy for multiplying the film's splendor to further assert a position of centrality in the Superman franchise.

SUPERMAN AFTER *THE MOVIE*

The extent to which *The Movie* was successful in its bid for centrality in the Superman franchise can be gauged by tracing its impact on subsequent Superman texts. Sequels *Superman II* (Richard Lester and Richard Donner [uncredited] 1980), *Superman III* (Richard Lester 1983), and *Superman IV: The Quest for Peace* (Sidney J. Furie 1987), along with an attempt to expand the universe in *Supergirl* (Jeannot Szwarc 1984), reinforced many of the first film's motifs but experienced diminishing box office receipts and critical reception. After *Superman IV*, attempts to bring the franchise back to cinema screens would fail until *Superman Returns* (Bryan Singer 2006). Yet throughout this unstable cinematic period Superman retained a prominent presence in other media, particularly comics and television.

In 1986, as the film series was waning, *The Man of Steel* #1 (October 1986) "rebooted" the comic book Superman by restarting the character's narrative continuity. The "Special Collector's Edition" cover of this first issue recreates a momentary but iconic image from *The Movie*'s first transformation scene, in which the frame is filled with a close-up on Clark/Superman's chest as he pulls his shirt open to reveal the "S" symbol. While the cover indicates the film's centrality to the Superman franchise and suggests its influence on the comic, as this new incarnation of Superman developed into the 1990s, it was torn between different poles that can be broadly framed as "dark and gritty" and "light and romantic," echoing a central opposition Brooker (2012, 104) identifies in the Batman franchise between dark and camp texts. These poles are represented by the two biggest Superman comic book events of the 1990s: the "Death of Superman" storyline (December 1992–January 1993)[23] and Clark and Lois's marriage in *Superman: The Wedding Album* (December 1996). Superman's highly publicized death and subsequent return, initially machine-gun-toting and dressed in black, channels the trend for dark and violent superhero comic books that permeated the 1990s. Conversely, Clark and Lois's marriage and related stories focusing on their relationship are in dialogue with the era's most prominent screen incarnation, *Lois and Clark: The New Adventures of Superman* (ABC 1993–1997). Indeed, the couple's marriage in comics and the television series was engineered to coincide for audiences.

Lois and Clark accentuates the romantic elements of the Superman franchise that *The Movie* also amplified. Superman's (Dean Cain) first encounter with Lois (Teri Hatcher) in the show's pilot establishes their relationship on the same terms as in *The Movie*: Lois looks at Superman in awe as he coolly swallows a miniature bomb and proceeds to smile warmly. In the next scene, as Lois looks on captivated, Superman repeats a famous line from the film, introducing himself to a girl as "a friend." Through characterization and direct allusion, this sequence anchors the show's Superman and his relationship with Lois in *The Movie*. Other elements of the show metamorphose this relationship. Lois's characterization resonates with the contemporary postfeminist sensibility. Matthew Freeman examines how the show's representation of Lois negotiates postfeminism's contradictory "amalgamation of feminine and feminist—incorporating the broader understanding of the feminist struggle to achieve career dominance while markedly displaying a feminine sensibility that clearly wishes to get her noticed by a special super man" (2013, 194). These qualities recall while reframing *The Movie*'s Lois. The show's episodic televisual format, meanwhile, like the 1950s television series, places emphasis on journalistic investigation but has Lois more actively involved in this process, thus granting her a more central narrative role than she has in the film.

Superman's early twenty-first-century screen incarnations are also deeply reverential for *The Movie*. Television show *Smallville* (WB/CW 2001–2011) explores Clark's (Tom Welling) teenage years. The show's numerous allusions to *The Movie* culminate in the series finale's coda, set in the future when Clark has assumed a job at the *Daily Planet*. Throughout the sequence, John Williams's score from *The Movie* builds, overwhelming the soundtrack as Clark runs toward the camera while opening his shirt to reveal his Superman costume underneath so that the "S" logo fills the screen before cutting to the credits, the first few of which are projected forward in blue bursts. In deploying aural and iconic motifs from *The Movie*, *Smallville* suggests that its Clark has become

The Movie's Superman. If *Smallville* is loosely positioned as a prequel, *Returns* is more directly positioned as a sequel to the first two Reeve films. *Returns* anchors itself in *The Movie* in its opening moments, replaying some of Brando's lines before reproducing the rush through cosmic space and whooshing blue credit motifs from *The Movie*'s opening titles, with added digitally rendered celestial bodies to enhance the spectacle. Alongside numerous further allusions to the first two Reeve films, *Returns* inserts itself into their narrative continuity by referencing the newspaper headline "I Spent the Night with Superman" from *The Movie* as an artifact of its diegetic past.[24] Again, points of intertextual connection enshrine a central position for *The Movie* in the Superman franchise.

Smallville and *Returns*' most significant inflections to *The Movie*'s portrayal of Clark/Superman and the world he inhabits pertain to tone and gender representation. *Smallville* and *Returns* focalize distinct representations of masculinity. Rebecca Feasey situates *Smallville* in the context of teen television drama, demonstrating how the show uses science fiction conventions to explore teen television's recurrent concerns of "difference, otherness and alienation" (2008, 48). In reconfiguring the Superman franchise's romantic dimension around adolescent longing, *Smallville* explores a Clark whose fear of his developing powers (a metaphor for puberty) prompts anxiety over sexual relations (54–55). Concurrently, Feasey argues that this Clark is more in touch with his emotional "feminine" side (50).

Returns shifts the focus to a brooding adult Superman (Brandon Routh). The film's somber tone and representation of Superman are commonly discussed as a reaction to the attacks of 9/11 (see, for example, DiPaolo 2011, 166–67; Hassler-Forest 2012, 57–67). *Returns*' discourse on masculinity can be read in relation to its conflicted position; reverent for the Reeve films while expressing post-9/11 anxiety, the film is caught in a struggle between the light and dark poles of the Superman franchise. The "I Spent the Night with Superman" headline gains new resonance through the revelation that Clark/Superman fathered a son with Lois (Kate Bosworth). Gordon (2017, 86) observes that through this plot *Returns* develops *The Movie*'s discourse on fathers and sons, the film ending with Superman reciting to his sleeping son the same wisdom Jor-El shares with Superman in *The Movie*. For Hassler-Forest (2012, 67), this nostalgic rooting in *The Movie*'s patriarchal discourse echoes the George W. Bush administration's post-9/11 promotion of a return to neoconservative family values to strengthen America's inherent heroism. *Returns*' channeling of post-9/11 sentiment transforms *The Movie*'s portrayal of Superman, eschewing the mild-mannered in favor of the morose and amplifying a patriarchal worldview at the expense of the first film's utopic expressions of gender equality.

After the commercial underperformance of *Returns*, 2013's *Man of Steel* "rebooted" the cinematic Superman and, alongside follow up *Batman v Superman*, restructured the Superman franchise around the dark pole. I will return to these films in this book's conclusion when discussing the DCEU. Despite *Man of Steel* and *Batman v Superman*'s efforts to rearrange the *Superman* franchise around a dark set of texts that foreground violent and vengeful masculinity, certain other Superman texts in the 2010s pushed against these currents. In comics, after DC restarted their narrative continuity in 2011, in 2016 they reverted to the continuity that initiated in 1986, thus bringing back the married Clark and Lois along with their son, Jonathon. *Superman: Lois and Clark* (December 2015–July 2016), the miniseries in which this iteration of the characters returns, shares its attention between the three family members and the portrayal of Lois foregrounds her skills as an investigative reporter. Miniseries *Lois Lane* vol. 2 (September 2019–September 2020) continues this emphasis on Lois's conscientious and tenacious reporting. The series offers a fairly direct critique of the Donald Trump administration, thematizing concerns about the internment of immigrants and threats to the freedom of the press in contemporary America. *Lois Lane* refocuses the thematic concerns of contemporaneous dark Superman texts while striking dark tonal notes, its artwork steeped in thick shading, to characterize the sociopolitical context it interrogates.

Television series *Supergirl* (CBS/CW 2015–2021) also interrogates the Trump administration, looking at issues of gender, race, and immigration, but enacts this exploration through a lighter lens that reflects its eponymous superheroine's (Melissa Benoist) optimism. The show is steeped in allusions to lighter Superman texts, including *The Movie*. Like Reeve's Superman, Benoist's Supergirl presents an affable demeanor and, despite the show's critical edge, exhibits faith that the US is at its heart truthful and just. In the episode "Fallout" (2018) Supergirl breaks up a clash between anti-alien and pro-alien demonstrators outside the White House (the show using aliens to allegorize racial tensions) while clutching an American flag, providing a visual evocation of the American way as diplomacy.

The Movie's lasting impact on the Superman franchise is evident in how, in the forty years since its release, other incarnations have frequently drawn the film back to a position of centrality. Motifs from *The Movie*, along with tonal qualities and its characterization of Superman, recur in many subsequent incarnations, although the process of metamorphosis continues as these elements are refracted through different media, formats, trends, and sociopolitical contexts. In the above survey there was not space to fully sketch out the array of intertextual gestures in each incarnation. The incarnations that I have discussed as reverential to *The Movie* also establish direct links to many other incarnations, arranging the franchise around a group of interconnected texts. I have outlined ways in which *The Movie* is placed central to this group. It is not simply the case, however, that *The Movie* has maintained an unchallenged position of centrality in the franchise. Other incarnations seek to decenter *The Movie*. The organization of the Superman franchise is itself a never-ending battle as texts jostle for centrality. Yet the dark and light poles that emerged in the decades following *The Movie* are not binaries. Elements of dark and light can intermingle in different ways from text to text, this dialogue contributing to the emergence of fresh ways to approach Superman, feeding the franchise's continuing expansion.

My analysis of Superman texts has demonstrated the use of an analytical framework equipped to examine the aesthetics of adaptation in a superhero franchise. Comics and cinema, along with other media in which superheroes appear, use comparable but not identical forms. In illuminating how stylistic and narrative strategies metamorphose as they are adapted across texts, media, and incarnations in the Superman franchise, my framework reveals the ways in which such transformations shape textual meaning.

In a superhero franchise, the shifting network of intertextual exchanges forms the "source" that any new incarnation adapts and enters. A new text metamorphoses qualities of other texts within this network, while also being shaped through dialogue with texts outside of the franchise, along with cultural contexts and filmmaking trends. Many of the motifs and strategies that I have identified in *The Movie* as emerging through these processes exhibit an interesting tension, expressing affection and nostalgia for previous Superman incarnations while simultaneously asserting superiority over them. It is significant that, while the analytical frameworks I have adopted reject binary and hierarchical logics, industrial forces and texts themselves continue to assert hierarchies, with a medium's formal and representational capacities mobilized in these assertions.

The reworking of strategies and motifs from *The Movie* in twenty-first-century Superman blockbusters indicates not just the film's enduring hand in shaping the Superman franchise, but also its impact on superhero and blockbuster cinema. After establishing the superhero genre as ideal material for Hollywood blockbusters and exemplifying New Hollywood's blockbuster filmmaking paradigm, *The Movie*'s legacy is clearly apparent in the twenty-first-century superhero blockbuster boom. The proceeding chapters pick up and delve deeper into many of the issues discussed in this chapter, from special effects spectacle and Hollywood stars to seriality and gender representation in twenty-first-century superhero blockbusters.

CHAPTER 2

DIGITAL POWER AND MORAL RESPONSIBILITY

Spider-Man and the Marvel Superhero
in the Twenty-First Century

Just over twenty years after *Action Comics* #1 began the superhero genre, Marvel helped reinvigorate it. Similarly, just over twenty years after *Superman: The Movie* propelled the first superhero into blockbuster cinema, the first blockbuster adaptations of Marvel superheroes were released, instigating the twenty-first-century superhero blockbuster boom. The commercial success of blockbuster *Spider-Man*, which was the top-grossing domestic release of 2002, and its sequels, was central to this cycle.[1] The increasing prominence of digital imaging in Hollywood production and the attacks on the World Trade Center on September 11, 2001, are two contexts that are frequently deemed instrumental to the production and popularity of twenty-first-century superhero blockbusters.[2] This chapter explores how the *Spider-Man* trilogy's adaptive strategies harness digital filmmaking technologies and engage with the twenty-first-century sociopolitical climate.[3]

I begin by outlining the ways in which Marvel reworked superhero conventions in the 1960s, demonstrating this fresh approach to the superhero through analysis of Spider-Man's comic book debut. My proceeding analysis of the *Spider-Man* trilogy starts by examining the ways in which the films use digital filmmaking technologies to metamorphose Spider-Man's traits. To consider the opportunities that computer-generated imagery (CGI) affords live-action adaptations of superhero comics, I explore ontological relations between drawn, photographic, and digital images. This discussion goes beyond merely thinking through CGI's capacity to recreate fantastic comic book imagery; instead, it illuminates how the perceptual and conceptual qualities of CGI can be harnessed to adapt thematic tensions in superhero comic books. I explore the *Spider-Man* trilogy's uses of CGI through analysis of the superhero's and his supervillains' bodies.

I move from analysis of bodies to an examination of space, which reveals ways in which the *Spider-Man* trilogy communicates sociopolitical meanings. The films' use of CGI continues to be of concern as I explore the sociopolitical ideas that are articulated in the presentation of New York's external spaces. This exploration develops as I analyze the nostalgic stylization of the first film's internal spaces, paying particular attention to what roles these spaces present to Peter Parker/Spider-Man (Tobey Maguire). My analysis of the *Spider-Man* trilogy concludes by expanding this discussion of character roles and sociopolitical values over the second and third films. I consider the sequels' repositioning of Peter/Spider-Man on his spectrum of possible roles along with the trilogy's presentation of Mary Jane Watson (Kirsten Dunst). This discussion picks up a concern that recurs throughout the chapter with how serialization can complement superhero blockbusters' adaptive practices.

The chapter ends by surveying the ways in which the strategies and meanings found in the *Spider-Man* trilogy are developed in subsequent live-action Spider-Man blockbusters, namely *The Amazing Spider-Man* (Marc Webb 2012) and sequel *The Amazing Spider-Man 2* (Marc Webb 2014), and the later integration of Spider-Man into the MCU in *Spider-Man: Homecoming* (Jon Watts 2017), *Spider-Man: Far from Home* (Jon Watts 2019), and *Spider-Man: No Way Home* (Jon Watts 2021). The three blockbuster iterations of Spider-Man represent Marvel's most iconic superhero traversing the first two decades of the superhero blockbuster boom, being shaped by and shaping this filmmaking cycle.

THE MARVEL SUPERHERO

Spider-Man was not the first of Marvel's Silver Age superheroes but is typically seen as "the unquestioned flagship character of Marvel Comics" (Weiner and Peaslee 2012, 4). In discussing 1960s Spider-Man comics, Wright suggests that "it is difficult to overstate the impact of these early Spider-Man comic books on the subsequent development of the industry. The young, flawed, and brooding antihero became the most widely imitated archetype in the superhero genre since the appearance of Superman" (2001, 212). The fresh approach to superheroes undertaken in Silver Age

Marvel comics and exemplified by Spider-Man has thus been compared in significance to Superman's debut.

Wright (180–225) identifies three key contexts that shaped Marvel's comics, and facilitated their success, in the 1960s: the Comics Code, the Vietnam War, and the shifting role of youth culture in America. The Comics Code forced many publishers of crime and horror comics to cease production, leaving a gap in the market for comics that could offer appealing stories within the Code's restrictions. Meanwhile, America's actions in Vietnam were dividing the nation's opinion, and a significant group that were speaking out against the government's decisions were America's youth, who were burgeoning as an "economic, social, and political force" (200). Wright argues that in the late 1950s to early 1960s, DC's superheroes conformed to establishment values (184–87). DC's approach left space for Marvel to tell superhero stories that spoke more directly to the disillusionment felt by many of America's youth. In channeling this disillusionment, Marvel's superheroes "displayed self-doubt and anxiety.... A regular trope was the perception of heroic powers not as gifts, but as a curse or unbearable responsibility" (Flanagan, McKenny, and Livingstone 2016, 7). Marvel's 1960s comics refocused superhero narratives to explore not just superheroes' powers, but also their weaknesses.

Teenager Peter Parker's adolescent anxieties were particularly relatable to young readers. Prior to Spider-Man, adolescent superheroes had typically only been sidekicks, like Batman's Robin.[4] Young readers were explicitly encouraged to project themselves onto Marvel's character, with the caption that ends *The Amazing Spider-Man* #9 (February 1964) stating "next issue: more fascinating details about the life and adventures of the world's most amazing teen-ager—Spider-Man—the super-hero who could be— you!" Spider-Man is pitted against the adult establishment through being repeatedly persecuted by the media and police. Peter Lee argues that early Spider-Man comics, rather than simply presenting adults as wrong, explore "the intergenerational tension in the 1960s between the emerging counterculture and the 'establishment'" (2012, 29). 1960s Spider-Man comics express adolescent unease with the sociopolitical climate while not wholeheartedly criticizing it, enabling them to operate within the Comics Code's regulations.

Analysis of Spider-Man's comic book debut further elucidates ways that the character remolded superhero conventions. Points of intersection with and departure from Superman are evident from the very first glimpse of Spider-Man on the cover of *Amazing Fantasy* #15 (August 1962), the comic in which he debuted. The image shows Spider-Man swinging through the air, chest thrust out, a criminal squirming under one arm. As with Superman smashing the car on *Action Comics* #1, Spider-Man's abilities are

Spider-Man swings through the air on the cover of *Amazing Fantasy* #15 (1962).

foregrounded. Yet the heroic image is not the only element to which our attention is drawn. Unlike *Action Comics* #1, this cover features speech balloons that offer a different perspective on the character. Spider-Man exclaims, "Though the world may mock Peter Parker, the timid teen-ager ... it will soon marvel at the awesome 'might' of Spider-Man!" These words hint at hubris, while indicating anxieties that the bombastic costume conceals.

Another disjoint exists between the image and the comic book's interior art. The cover is drawn in bold lines by Jack Kirby, who depicts muscular heroes in kinetic compositions. The Spider-Man story's interior art is drawn by Steve Ditko, who utilizes thinner lines and frailer figures. On the story's opening splash page (a single or double page that acts as a complete panel unto itself) a lanky Peter stands apart from peers who mock him. Behind Peter is a panel within the panel, containing a silhouette of an assertive figure, a web, and a spider. The heroically poised silhouette's head is in the center of the web, which the spider descends toward. While all three of these omens bear down on Peter, promising greatness yet foreboding danger, they also form a chain in which the silhouetted hero is itself prey to the spider. This composition suggests that even the heroic identity looming in Peter's future will suffer under the weight of his powers. The opening glimpses of Spider-Man and Peter in *Amazing Fantasy* #15 juxtapose contrasting styles and signs to evoke tensions such as hero and victim, power and burden, that the character is caught between.

Whereas the opening page of Superman's first comic book adventure exhibited his abilities, the first page of Spider-Man's foregrounds Peter's problems. This continues as Spider-Man's origin unravels over eleven pages. Peter initially uses his powers to help himself and those he cares for, shunning the world that shunned him, by attaining wealth through televised displays of his abilities. However, his refusal to stop a robber is punished in a cruel act of fate when the same robber kills his Uncle Ben. As such Peter learns, in the final panel of his first adventure, a maxim that became his most resonant worded identifier: "With great power there must also come—great responsibility!"

Following *Amazing Fantasy* #15, Peter/Spider-Man's adventures continue in *The Amazing Spider-Man*, which launched in 1962. As the series develops Peter becomes much less socially ostracized. High school concerns are also overcome when Peter graduates in *The Amazing Spider-Man* #28 (September 1965). However, Peter's anxieties do not recede with these developments but change as he struggles to juggle his social life and new responsibilities with superheroics.

The various facets of Spider-Man multiplied further as more incarnations were created. Beyond comics, Spider-Man has appeared in media including

Peter Parker stands apart from peers who mock him on the opening splash page of "Spider-Man!" in *Amazing Fantasy* #15 (1962).

music LPs, videogames, television, and cinema. The ways in which 1960s Spider-Man comic books reconfigure superhero conventions continue to be deployed and reworked as Spider-Man is adapted into other media and interacts with changing cultural contexts. In the 2000s, digital filmmaking technologies provided new tools with which to metamorphose these conventions.

THE DIGITALLY RENDERED SUPERHERO

The majority of Spider-Man's screen adaptations, from animated *Spider-Man* (ABC 1967–1970) to Japanese live-action television series *Supaidāman* (TV Tokyo 1978–1979), parade the character's iconography in their opening title sequences through devices such as close-ups on his mask and logo, and having credits appear over a web motif. The opening of blockbuster *Spider-Man* functions similarly. A virtual camera soars and swerves around digitally rendered space comprised of spider webs, glimpses of Spider-Man and supervillain Green Goblin, and New York.[5] The rapid propulsion through this phantasmagorical environment exhibits traits of Bukatman's kaleidoscopic effects sequence, discussed in the previous chapter. The rush through space that opened *Superman: The Movie* is therefore recalled but transformed through the virtual camera's twisting movements. From the very opening of *Spider-Man 1*, digital technology is foregrounded as a key means for reworking the Spider-Man franchise and superhero blockbuster in spectacular new ways.

REALISM AND EXPRESSIVITY

The particular ontological qualities of digital images, in relation to those of photographic and drawn images, arguably influence their reception and construction. As noted in this book's introduction, Lefèvre (2007) deems photographic images objective and realistic and drawn images as subjective and stylized. This distinction is rooted in the nature of an image's production. André Bazin (2005, 12–14) argues that the photographic image is objective due to being produced through an automatic process that occurs without human intervention. Lev Manovich (2001, 295) situates digitally constructed images in the subjective category, arguing that, due to their being manually constructed by human artists, they have less in common with traditional photographs than with painting. Like drawn images, CGI does not reproduce profilmic material ("a figure, object or scene that actually was in front of a camera in the real world" [Purse 2013, 6]) but is rather the product of human

Drawn skyscrapers merge into a photographic representation of New York in *Giant-Size Astonishing X-Men* #1 (2008).

imagination. The fact that many modern films are shot on digital cameras, and comics drawn using digital processes, eliminates material distinctions between image types: each is formed from intangible numerical data. The different methods of production, however, and the ontological qualities they affix, largely remain. Digital photography still captures profilmic phenomena with a camera, digital techniques for creating comics art typically emulate traditional drawing methods whereby the artist forms lines and shapes on a two-dimensional surface, while CGI entails rendering three-dimensional objects and space.

The perceived realism of the photographic image is often credited to its indexicality. As Stephen Prince (1996, 28–29) surveys, a pervasive school of film theory places this quality of indexicality central to discourses of realism in cinema. In traditional analogue photography, the photography process imprints an indexical representation of profilmic material onto celluloid. A photograph is an index of that which was captured, comparable to how a footprint is an index of the foot that left it. The photographic image in cinema thus possesses a direct causal relationship with the reality that was photographed. Following this logic, a drawn image or digitally constructed image cannot be realistic, since they inherently lack the quality of indexicality. If photographic images represent reality, drawn images and digitally rendered images are equipped to deal with fantasy; the opposition of photographic images as perceptual and drawn images as conceptual is imposed, with the digital image aligned with the conceptual.

The instability of this opposition between image types is exposed when one acknowledges that the image types do not simply exist in isolation. The ability to combine different kinds of images in a single medium enables ontologically complex composites that are rich in meaning. The practice of compositing different profilmic elements together, or with artificial elements, to provide an illusion of indexicality, when in fact a camera did not capture the finished shot in one take, was accomplished using analogue methods from the early days of cinema (Purse 2013, 4–5). The history and nature of compositing undermines the separation of celluloid photography and digital images, revealing that both can offer a hybrid indexicality (5–6). For example, the compositing process in the *Spider-Man* trilogy means that photographic representations of New York are interspersed in, and mapped onto, a digital construct of the city.[6] A variety of digital, profilmic, and digital/profilmic hybrid bodies populate this space. The films' composite New York welds indexical representations of profilmic material with digitally rendered phenomena.

While images in comics are generally constructed from scratch, drawn and photographic elements can be combined, as is evident in John Cassaday's splash page depicting Spider-Man in *Giant-Size Astonishing X-Men* #1 (July 2008). In the foreground, Spider-Man is drawn in an acrobatic pose above the roofs of skyscrapers. In the background, the drawn skyscrapers merge into a photographic representation of New York. The geometric precision of the drawn skyscrapers enables them to segue into the photographic ones, while the diagonal angle in which Spider-Man's body is positioned matches the tilted perspective from which the skyscrapers are presented.

The intermingling of artificial and photographic elements in the *Spider-Man* trilogy and Cassaday's panel evokes the figure of the superhero's dichotomous relation to modernity. The ontological disjunction between Spider-Man's drawn or digitally rendered body and Manhattan's indexical qualities situate hero and city as oppositions. Spider-Man's superhumanly acrobatic form allows him to freely traverse, and thus conquer, the oppressive structures of industrialization. Conversely, stylistic continuities between body and cityscape, such as seamless segues between artificial and indexical elements, present them as reciprocal realizations of modernity's promises fulfilled. Jason Bainbridge (2010) discusses the centrality of New York to the Marvel universe, arguing that Spider-Man in particular has a symbiotic bond with New York. Bainbridge presents Cassaday's panel to demonstrate this bond. The comparable compositing process used to synthesize superhero and city in the film trilogy rearticulates this prominent theme from the Spider-Man franchise. Image compositing can thus produce compositions in which the combination of photographic images commonly perceived to be objective with subjective kinds of image enriches conceptual meaning.

While the above analysis demonstrates that maintaining elements of ontological specificity allows different image elements to generate meaning when composited together, their combined contribution to conceptual meaning suggests that image types should not be thought of in binary terms as being either objective and photographic or subjective and stylized. This book's introduction outlined how McCloud's discussion of the potential for images to be stylized in different ways provides a means of challenging binary separations of different image types. While McCloud demonstrates that drawn images can be realistic, symbolic, or abstract, subjective inflections are also evident in photographic images. Subjectivity intervenes before a photograph is taken, with the photographer deciding camera placement and framing. Prince notes ways that human agency can continue to shape the photographic image after it has been captured: "For example, flashing film prior to development or dodging and burning portions of the image during printing will produce lighting effects that did not exist in the scene that was photographed" (1996, 34). These subjective alterations have existed since the birth of photography, although they have been expanded as the medium has developed and entered the digital age. Traditionally, different production processes inhibit photographic images from taking on symbolic and abstract qualities as easily as drawn images. However, Burke's (2015, 203–14) discussion of film's ability to recreate the stylization of comics emphasizes the role digital filmmaking technologies have played in enabling filmmakers to freely manipulate the cinematic image, leading to many twenty-first-century comic book adaptations having highly stylized aesthetics that recall comics.

Cultural associations of drawn images with subjectivity generally and comics specifically with extravagant fantasy arguably permit heavy stylization in films that present themselves as comic book adaptations. These permissions exist in tension with the pervasive cultural tendency to equate the photographic image with realism, which potentially restricts the degree to which CGI can mold and stylize imagery in live-action films. The ontological properties of cinema are such that realism should not be thought of as solely dictated by an image's appearance. Cinema's capacity to present movement offers a kind of realism not apparent in still images, while the specific qualities of movement in live-action films present a new set of criteria that determine CGI's construction.

Tom Gunning (2007) proposes that a concept of cinematic realism based on movement rather than indexicality is more instructive when theorizing cinema in the age of digital imaging, as it is inclusive of forms of filmmaking that are not based on filming profilmic phenomena. Gunning builds on Christian Metz's (1974, 3–15) discussion of motion and temporality being central to cinema's "impression of reality." Metz argues that, while the photographic image connotes pastness, the moving image offers a sense of presence (5–6). Gunning adds that "motion always has a projective aspect, a progressive movement in a direction, and therefore invokes possibility and a future . . . we could say that through a moving image, the progress of motion is projected onto us" (2007, 42–43). Motion occurs in both space and time whether in a film or reality. We cannot contemplate moving images in the same way that we do still images, because to engage with moving images is to be involved in their progression into the future, which advances in tandem with the progression of reality. Gunning (39) asserts that our participation in motion is a visceral sensation, as we do not just see but also feel it. Since this participation occurs regardless of the kind of movement that is being presented, "Motion therefore need not be realistic to have a 'realistic' effect, that is, to invite the emphatic participation, both imaginative and physiological, of viewers" (46). Following Gunning, we participate in digitally rendered fantastical movements in the same way as profilmic movements. Kinetic phenomena that do not exist physically, such as Spider-Man's acrobatics, thus provide an impression of reality.

Gunning's inclusive conceptualization of cinematic movement in the abstract sense ignores specific qualities of movements. These qualities are of great importance when we consider the expense, time, and artistry devoted to ensuring digitally rendered forms in Hollywood films move in ways that adhere to laws of physics. This commitment suggests that, due to the cinematic image's kinesis aligning with the audience's experience of time and motion, there is also an imperative for the particularities of CGI's movements to match this experience. Prince's notion of "perceptual realism" provides a useful framework for the criteria informing special effects artists' attempts to create realistic CGI:

> A perceptually real image is one which structurally corresponds to the viewer's audiovisual experience of three-dimensional space. . . . Such images display a nested hierarchy of cues which organize the display of light, color, texture, movement, and sound in ways that correspond with the viewer's own understanding of these phenomena in daily life. (1996, 32)

Both profilmic and digitally rendered material in "realist" or "fantasy" films can exhibit these correspondences to the viewer's audiovisual experience of the real world (32). As such, even fantastic phenomena that audiences know have no physical referent can be presented as realistic by behaving as if subject to real physical forces. Movement plays a vital role in this process. No real human can swing from organic webbing emitted from their wrists. A central factor contributing to the perceptually realistic presentation of Spider-Man's actions in the *Spider-Man* trilogy, however, is that his digitally rendered body is designed to soar, dip, and dive as if subject to Earth's gravitational pull.

Due to still images in comics lacking actual movement and temporality, and therefore not automatically assimilating into a reader's experience of reality, comics present movement through unique suggestive means. These means, however, have abstract and specific qualities that draw comparisons to these qualities of movement in cinema. Andrei Molotiu's (2012) concepts of iconostasis and sequential dynamism reveal some significant strategies that comics can use to express movement abstractly. Molotiu defines "iconostasis" as "the perception of the layout of a comics page as a unified composition" (91) rather than a narrative sequence. Molotiu's concept of "sequential dynamism," in which energized relations between compositional and other elements propel the reader's eye along various trajectories that can align with or deviate from the sequential narrative flow, can complement iconostasis (89). Molotiu analyzes pages from early Spider-Man comics that deploy these strategies to create compositions imbued with a sense of kinesis. In regard to comics conveying specific qualities of movement, strategies include devices such as motion lines, multiple figures mapping different stages of a movement within a panel, and having a character start a movement in one panel that is completed in the next. In each case, the reader mentally completes these specific movements.

A double splash page from *The Amazing Spider-Man* vol. 2 #33 (September 2001), drawn by John Romita Jr., combines elements of these abstract and specific strategies for presenting movement to communicate meaning. An array of overlapping figures shows different moves in Spider-Man's battle against supervillain Morlun. While captions arranged in a steepening arc direct the reader's eyes from the top-left to the bottom-right, movement occurs chaotically in all directions, creating competing trajectories. Individual figures depict specific movements, such as punches and grapples. At points movements continue from one figure to the next, but most of the overlapping figures bear no explicit causal relation to one another. By refusing to present a clear temporal flow of events, the page functions as a unified

Spider-Man fights Morlun across a double splash page in *The Amazing Spider-Man* vol. 2 #33 (2001).

composition that conveys expressive kinesis rather than progression. The combination of specific moves, suspended from a clear temporal flow, with an abstract sense of motion showcases the ability and unrelenting stamina of both characters, while suggesting a potentially endless battle.

Although ontologically distinct from comics, the projective temporal flow and specific qualities of Spider-Man's digital body's movements in the film trilogy can create similar effects. In *Spider-Man 1*, as Spider-Man first swings from a skyscraper in pursuit of a criminal after Uncle Ben's (Cliff Robertson) murder, the virtual camera circulates tumultuously around his airborne body. The disorientating competing motion of camera and body involves the viewer in an energetic flurry while creating sensations such as giddiness and vertigo that are augmented by relations between body and space. Arcs formed as Spider-Man gains momentum on downward swings that propel him back upward recall those of a pendulum, thus simulating the effect of gravity on the movements of weighted objects. Spider-Man's initially clumsy, but increasingly assured, negotiation of obstacles—buildings, streetlamps, bridges—test his superpowers in a familiar environment to acclimatize both superhero and audience to his movements. The camera reflects Spider-Man's growing acquaintance with his abilities by gaining a greater sense of stability as the sequence develops: for instance, by following from behind as he progresses down the street. The street's linearity enables a clear mapping of Spider-Man's spatial trajectory and gauging of his speed. He overtakes cars moving in the same direction, the narrative of pursuit emphasizing temporal urgency. While comics can convey Spider-Man's energy and showcase his agility by holding him in stasis, cinema offers comparable sensations and displays by having him move through space and time in ways that are at once expressive, spectacular, and perceptually realistic.

The efforts to simulate gravity grant Spider-Man's digital body a sense of weight that is lacking in the ethereal gliding of Reeve's Superman's profilmic body. The special effects that present the two superheroes' powers thus further undermine the argument that digital images are removed from reality while photographic images are realistic. Digital bodies can be constructed to correspond with our understanding of physics, while profilmic bodies can be presented in ways that subvert gravity. Again, it is the specific stylization of an image, in this case by the nature of the special effects used in its creation, that constructs its relation to reality.

As the above analysis demonstrates, cinematic movement's affective sensations must be considered alongside the specific nature of the motion when analyzing the realistic qualities of CGI. Abstract and specific qualities of movements can be configured in both photographic and digitally rendered images to convey different levels of realism and thus different kinds of content.

The ontological qualities of CGI also contribute meaning to films in ways that are not accounted for in, but can be considered alongside, Gunning and Prince's conceptual frameworks. By focusing on the visceral experience and visual reception of moving images, respectively, neither Gunning nor Prince discuss intellectual processes in which audiences are engaged. Gunning's conceptualization of cinematic movement's impression of reality "depends on 'forgetting' (that is, on distracting the viewer's attention away from—not literally repressing the knowledge of) the technical process of filming in favor of an experience of the fictional world as present" (2007, 47). Meanwhile, Prince's use of the word "perceptual" echoes pervasive discourses that position images as perceptual—as opposed to conceptual—information, perceived by the eye rather than processed by the brain.

Other scholars argue that CGI can engage our mental faculties. Dan North (2008, 9) argues that special effects have a reflexive function, encouraging audiences to conceptually interrogate the image's form. Aylish Wood (2007, 6) uses the terms "seamless" and "inscribed" to describe how digitally created images can seek to be transparent in their construction or draw attention to their form. Both North and Wood propose that, through inviting audiences to marvel at special effects, films prompt an active awareness of the technology through which they were created. This conceptual processing can be encouraged by the perceptual qualities of the image; fantastic phenomena that exhibit a high degree of perceptual realism invite reflection on the technology that went into their creation.

Conceptual engagement with CGI can complement narrative comprehension. Sustained long takes that bounce and circle around the hero are a key way that the *Spider-Man* trilogy showcases digital filmmaking technologies. The longest of these occur in the first film's last, and second film's penultimate, shots, which last roughly thirty and forty seconds, respectively. Orit Fussfeld Cohen contends that the artifice of digital effects can be concealed through fast editing, which "prevents the spectator from perceiving the conjoined, digitally manipulated compound shot as a computer-generated product" (2014, 55). Following Fussfeld Cohen, it might be said that the prolonged takes of Spider-Man conversely foreground their digital composition. The free-flowing, unbroken movements of the virtual camera and Spider-Man's digital body emphasize their lack of physical restraints such as cranes and wires. These dynamic movements of camera and superhero also recall *Superman: The Movie*'s presentation of Superman's flight in long takes that showcase fluid movement. In developing this strategy by multiplying the camera and superhero's trajectories, the *Spider-Man* trilogy presents its spectacle as superior not just to previous Spider-Man texts but also previous superhero blockbusters. This narrative about the superior ability of the film's digital special effects technologies to navigate complex composite spaces entwines with the diegetic narrative concerning Spider-Man's mastery of space. As North (2008, 166–69) similarly outlines, the powers of the technology and of Spider-Man are in a reciprocal relationship as they draw attention to each other, engaging audiences in both simultaneously.

In the shots discussed above, the reciprocity of the digital filmmaking technology and Spider-Man is expressed through interlacing the abstract, perceptual, and conceptual qualities of digitally rendered movements. The giddy sensations of the swooping camera and Spider-Man's body combine with bounces that simulate the pull of gravity, while the elaborate qualities of each of these showcase the special effects' sophistication. The bodies of Spider-Man and his villains provide significant sites through which the discourse inscribed into the films on the relationship between CGI and reality is expanded. Examining the presentation of these bodies also elucidates how the films' deployment of CGI metamorphoses familiar traits of Spider-Man texts.

DIGITAL AND PROFILMIC BODIES

The superhero body is a source of spectacle, from costume and physique to performances of extraordinary movements. Prior to the *Spider-Man* trilogy, the profilmic bodies of actors or stuntmen presented this spectacle in live-action screen incarnations of Spider-Man. *Supaidāman* in particular utilizes the profilmic body to give its superhero a distinctive presence, Rayna Denison describing Supaidāman's pauses to strike poses before and during fights as "moments of character spectacle" (2015, 62) that assign a set of identifying stances to the hero. These pauses bookend and punctuate fluid fight sequences in which the superhero leaps and flips around, acrobatically dispatching his enemies. The fight sequences showcase not just the character as spectacle, but also the impressive physical agility of the actor or stuntman. The costumes and scale model work incorporated into fights between the bodies of enlarged villains and Supaidāman's robot Leopardon are additional forms of physical spectacle. These different kinds of spectacle foreground, and interweave, the diegetic skills of Supaidāman and the extradiegetic skills of performers and special effects artists. In *Superman: The Movie*, meanwhile, spectacular scenes of Reeve's profilmic body in flight also express characterization, such as the superhero's relationship with Metropolis and Lois. Even when the superhero body is solely profilmic, different kinds of complementary spectacle are employed to communicate meaning. The interactions between digital and profilmic bodies, or digital and profilmic elements of bodies, in the *Spider-Man* trilogy offer new ways to articulate characterization.

The increased threat posed by Spider-Man's villains as the trilogy progresses is marked on their bodies by increased use of digital imaging, thus developing the films' alignment of the power of digital filmmaking technologies with diegetic superpowers. In the first film, Norman Osborn/Green Goblin (Willem Dafoe) wears a physical costume that becomes a digital construct only in scenes where he is flying. In the sequel, Otto Octavius/Doctor Octopus's (Alfred Molina) mechanical appendages, the aspects of his form that possess superhuman strength and agility, in certain shots are profilmic models moved by puppeteers, but their more elaborate movements are animated through CGI. The arms' artificial intelligence comes to override Otto's mental functions, while they often completely replace his own limbs, his limp body dangling as the digitally rendered arms carry it around, the

Sandman becomes a giant digitally constructed ogre in *Spider-Man 3* (2007).

human body presented as a puppet for the digital. *Spider-Man 3*'s two villains' transformations are represented through digital manipulation of the body itself. Upon bonding with the alien symbiote and becoming Venom, Eddie Brock's (Topher Grace) profilmic body becomes inscribed with digital imaging, the structure of his face morphing to one with reptilian aspects. Flint Marko/Sandman's (Thomas Haden Church) powers are similarly realized through the human body morphing into a digital construct but completes this process through his whole body being replaced with a fully malleable digitally realized entity. In the climactic battle Sandman becomes a giant digitally constructed ogre, a state completely divorced from the profilmic human body while ensuring that he is literally, in terms of stature, the biggest threat in the trilogy.

The narrative of advances in digital imaging technology complements that of heightened threats posed to Spider-Man as the trilogy progresses. As Spider-Man's villains' bodies are increasingly replaced by CGI the diegetic threat intensifies. In attributing the nefarious qualities of these villains to their digital inscriptions, which are repeatedly placed in opposition to their humanity, the films themselves situate the physical and the digital as a binary. The films also complicate this dichotomy, however, through the interactions between Spider-Man's body's physical and digital qualities.

The superhero's body in the *Spider-Man* trilogy has provided a discussion point in discourses on the relation between the physical and the digital in Hollywood cinema. Two primary criteria that impact the reception of digital bodies emerge from Purse's (2013, 60–63) discussion of critical responses: the body must act and emote like a human or humanlike being, and the body must believably inhabit its surroundings. These criteria return us to discourses of perceptual realism. In each case, insufficient correspondences between digital bodies and real-world experience disrupt a film's verisimilitude. Many of the critics Purse surveys identify these failings in the *Spider-Man* trilogy. In the below analysis I examine ways in which Spider-Man's digital body is balanced against Tobey Maguire's presence to mitigate the digital body's lack of humanity. In the next section, I explore how Spider-Man's interactions with his surroundings develop as the trilogy progresses and resonate thematically. The strategies I identify metamorphose core themes of Spider-Man comics, thus circumventing restrictions that expectations of perceptual realism place on live-action films adapting comic book content.

Body language and facial expression are key features contributing to the humanity of a body in film (Purse, 62–63). Spider-Man's digital body puts little effort into conveying this humanity, instead committing itself to grand displays of agility. Besides the difficulty of constructing a digital body to express human emotions, Spider-Man's costume provides a further barrier, completely concealing the superhero's face. Aaron Taylor discusses ways in which the *Spider-Man* trilogy deploys Maguire's performance to surmount the expressive restriction of the digitized body and superhero's costume. Performances of physical humor in grounded scenes, when the actor wears a profilmic Spider-Man costume, and having Spider-Man remove his mask to exhibit Maguire's expressions both reveal not general human qualities but the idiosyncrasies of Maguire as performer, thus imbuing Spider-Man with the star's unique expressive qualities (Taylor 2017, 281–83).

Spider-Man's digital body does the acrobatic heroics while Maguire's body emotes.[7] This dichotomy reflects the division of superhero and civilian identities that Peter endeavors to uphold. His mask is of particular significance in this regard; by concealing his boyish features, Peter seeks to present as an adult—a Spider-*Man*—and escape his marginalization as a youth. A popular concern of Spider-Man texts, however, is the impossibility of separating the Peter and Spider-Man identities. While Peter/Spider-Man tries to construct a binary, the identities inevitably flow into each other on a spectrum.

As demonstrated in my analysis of *Amazing Fantasy* #15, in comic books juxtapositions of different forms and styles can evoke interactions between the identities. In the *Spider-Man* trilogy, the intermingling of Spider-Man's digital body and Peter/Maguire's physical presence provides a comparable means of presenting the inescapable interlacing of identities. Spider-Man's flawlessly agile digital body provides a potent representation of the infallible hero that Peter sees as an escape from his daily troubles. Scenes when Maguire's unmasked face is composited onto Spider-Man's digital body reveal that the superhero does not escape, but rather is infused with and driven by, Peter's humanity. This technique peaks in *Spider-Man 3* when a lengthy airborne battle is staged between two unmasked opponents: Peter in civilian clothes and Harry Osborn (James Franco) as Green Goblin. Both combatants' bodies oscillate between digital, profilmic, and hybrid digital/profilmic forms throughout the fight. Maguire's expressions amplify the intensity of specific moments. For example, after the disclosure of his adversary's identity, Peter's digital body clings to a tumbling chunk of wall before the camera moves inward to reveal a blend of bewilderment and terror across Maguire's face as Peter's world both figuratively and literally crumbles. Peter's and Harry's emotions resonate outside of the immediate moment, providing a culmination of all the feelings they have exchanged over the preceding films. Having both characters unmasked situates this battle as an emotional (and technological) climax of the trilogy. Furthermore, rendering Peter's civilian body through the CGI usually reserved for his idealized superhero self underscores how, just as Peter's problems torment Spider-Man, Spider-Man's actions impact Peter's life.

Throughout the *Spider-Man* trilogy, the superpowered body is a constant site of tension between the physical and the digital. This tension expresses fraught relationships, both between different characters and the doubled identities of individual characters. Another relationship through which identities are negotiated in superhero narratives is that of the superhero and the space they inhabit.

THE POLITICS OF SPACE IN SPIDER-MAN'S NEW YORK

By being set exclusively in New York, the *Spider-Man* trilogy explores an environment that is at once specific and a synecdoche of US urban culture. The ways in which different spaces are constructed and inhabited communicate the films' sociopolitical views.

EXTERNAL SPACE AND COMMUNITY

Despite typically being presented as synonymous with New York, Peter/Spider-Man belongs to a specific social group, the white working class. Although Peter's class and youth challenge conventions of representation in Golden Age superhero comics, his race and gender reaffirm broader exclusionary trends in the superhero genre. The figure of the superhero in general "remains grounded in forms of white heterosexual masculinity" (Hassler-Forest 2012, 196). This inhibits an inclusive exploration of identity. Examining how the *Spider-Man* trilogy presents and populates New York's external spaces allows one to evaluate the films' conceptualization of the city's cultural identity.

Although the network of iterations that comprise the Spider-Man franchise is dominated by texts centered on problems faced by white characters, characters of color have featured throughout its history. While 1960s Marvel comics did not directly engage with contemporary discourses on civil rights, Wright identifies a fostering of racial inclusivity in the way "Marvel was the first publisher to integrate African Americans into comic books" (2001, 219). Spider-Man comic books were the first to feature "random black bystanders. ... The first major African American supporting character in Marvel Comics was the *Daily Bugle*'s city editor Joe Robertson" (312), who debuted in *The Amazing Spider-Man* #51 (August 1967).

Writer J. Michael Straczynski's run on *The Amazing Spider-Man*, which was produced concurrently to the *Spider-Man* trilogy, provides a contemporary comic book point of comparison for the films' representations of race and New York's citizenry.[8] This run is pertinent due to being set in the franchise's longest ongoing comic book series set in Marvel's main comic book universe—officially designated as reality number 616 in Marvel's multiverse[9]—and at times directly engaging with discourses on race. By this stage in the 616 narrative continuity Peter has aged to an adult, although youth concerns are brought back into focus when Peter gets a job as a teacher at his old school.

The Amazing Spider-Man vol. 2 #36 (December 2001), produced early in Straczynski's run, depicts the aftermath of the 9/11 attacks and places particular emphasis on issues of race. In the comic, Spider-Man and other Marvel superheroes work alongside a multicultural New York citizenry to clean up debris and search for survivors. Spider-Man's narration expresses the need to challenge reactionary vilifications of the Other, for instance pondering "what do we tell the children? Do we tell them evil is a foreign face? No. Evil is the thought behind the face, and it can look just like yours." The final page encapsulates the comic's statement on the US being strengthened by embracing people of all races and ethnicities. This splash page portrays a multicultural ensemble of heroes stood before a US flag. New York's emergency services are first and foremost, backed up by serviceman and government agency staff, then key workers, and finally Marvel's heroes. Foregrounding ordinary people over superheroes suggests that whatever response is made needs to be taken in the interest of the wider community. However, the superhero genre's regressive tendencies are evident in this promotion of diversity. In the image, women are very much of a minority and eight of the eleven Marvel superheroes are white men.[10]

A multicultural ensemble of heroes stood before a US flag in *The Amazing Spider-Man* vol. 2 #36 (2001).

After the promotion of unity in *The Amazing Spider-Man* vol. 2 #36, which articulates ideas that counter racist voices, but similarly to 1960s Spider-Man comics integrates characters of color into crowds, many subsequent stories in Straczynski's run endeavor to explore experiences beyond those of the white male protagonist. For example, in *The Amazing Spider-Man* vol. 2 #37 (January 2002), Peter finds out that one of his students, Hispanic girl Jennifer, is homeless, and helps track down her brother, who has taken a drug overdose.[11] Elsewhere, in *The Amazing Spider-Man* vol. 2 #55–#56 (September 2003–October 2003), Peter is forced to question the sociopolitical system he upholds when he helps a Black girl, Melissa, find her brother, whom Spider-Man previously put in jail. In each of these stories Peter works to resolve individuals' problems, rather than reporting their transgressions to the authorities. While he does not take action to change the system under which these problems exist, the stories suggest that structural inequalities in contemporary New York inhibit the ideal of a unified society.

Despite being contemporaneous to Straczynski's run, the *Spider-Man* trilogy exhibits racial diversity to a similar degree as 1960s Spider-Man comic books, integrating characters of color into the general populace. The only Black character present throughout the trilogy is Joe "Robbie" Robertson (Bill Nunn). However, the ways that Spider-Man and other characters inhabit external spaces evoke more inclusive views on New York's community.

The films' spectacular realization of Spider-Man's movements articulates utopic ideas about social freedom and equality. Martin Flanagan argues that the opportunities Spider-Man's New York offers for physical mobility are linked to social mobility and proposes that this is evident in the superhero's movements: "The moral function of the superhero is also connected to mobility and freedom: to enforce a fair and equal distribution of space—essentially 'reclaiming' the streets from crime in the interests of ordinary citizens, while rescinding the right to move of villains" (2012, 45). The uninhibited dynamism of Spider-Man's movements express this egalitarian mobility. Furthermore, Spider-Man does not just exhibit Bukatman's conceptualization of utopia as movement, as discussed in the previous chapter, but pursues utopia through actions that protect New York's citizens.

While Spider-Man's movements symbolically express and narratively pursue an ideal of an equal and safe New York, the city itself plays a key role in evoking and enabling this utopia. Like Peter's body, the city is a site of transformation. As the trilogy progresses, a digitally manipulated New York takes on an increasing degree of elasticity to complement Spider-Man's fluid movements. In the first film, space gains its highest degree of malleability within

Spider-Man surfs on a digitally rendered door in *Spider-Man 3* (2007).

the diegesis when Green Goblin attacks the World Unity Festival. Digitally rendered segments of buildings fall toward the streets, presenting a direct threat to civilians' profilmic bodies. Space takes on greater elasticity upon being digitally dismantled in *Spider-Man 2*. When Otto's fusion machine is activated, metal is drawn toward it, causing structures to contort. The first time this happens, windowpanes bend inward until the glass shatters, digitally rendered shards propelled toward and killing Rosalie Octavius (Donna Murphy). In this case, as in the first film, digital environmental elements act antagonistically. *Spider-Man 2* also features instances of characters using dynamic environments to their advantage. For example, while fighting up the side of a clock tower, Spider-Man and Doctor Octopus both use a clock hand as a projectile. Spider-Man's digital body makes much more productive use of transformative space in *Spider-Man 3*. When Spider-Man saves Gwen Stacy (Bryce Dallas Howard) as she falls down the side of a skyscraper, he weaves through tumbling, digitally rendered rubble that turns from obstacle to aid as he catapults and springs off pieces to gain speed. Elsewhere, while chasing Sandman, Spider-Man surfs on a digitally rendered door that has been removed from an armored van. He attaches to the van and passing cars with strings of webbing to gain velocity from being towed. In both scenes, CGI transforms the city as crumbling walls and detached doors become mobile platforms.

The shared dynamism of superhero and city reconfigures the relationship between digital body and environment, which Purse outlines as one of the key criteria influencing the reception of digital bodies. Purse proposes that photorealism is not a fixed quality but can be seen as "a continuum between looser and more strident performances of photographicness" (2013, 60). Negative reception of Spider-Man's digital body stemmed from its "cartooniness" occupying the opposite side of the continuum than its urban surroundings (60). With each new film in the trilogy, however, space becomes more dynamic as it interacts in increasingly complex ways with Spider-Man's body, drawing the superhero and his surroundings into alignment on the photorealistic continuum.

While striving to make the films more perceptually consistent, bringing Spider-Man and New York into perceptual alignment by granting them a shared elasticity adapts key traits of Spider-Man comics and has narrative resonance. The symbiosis between Spider-Man and New York has been conveyed by imbuing New York with plasticity since Spider-Man's first comic book adventures. Bukatman observes that in Ditko's compositions "the physical space of the actual city became utterly unstable. Walls became floors and verticality was close to being entirely lost in his swirling circular forms" (2003, 207). The increasingly dynamic realization of city space in the film trilogy metamorphoses this quality of spatial fluidity. Spider-Man's positive harnessing of malleable city space as the trilogy progresses narrates the consolidation of his bond with New York as he masters his powers.[12] Meanwhile, by fostering spatiotemporal unity, tactile interactions between Spider-Man's body and environmental elements augment the films' representation of social unity. Spider-Man and New York's complementary elastic forms present the city as both a space of thrilling liberation and an ally in the fight against threats to the utopian ideal.

The fluid mobility that digital filmmaking technologies facilitate in the *Spider-Man* trilogy's cinematography further augments the city's quality of pliability and the expression of mobility for its citizens. The sequence in *Spider-Man 2* in which Spider-Man fights Doctor Octopus up a clock tower and on a speeding train exemplifies ways that the films use a free-roaming camera in digitally composited spaces to this effect. After an initial tussle Spider-Man's digital body falls down the clock tower, this fall presented in various shots in which the wall runs along the vertical or horizontal edges of the frame. Once Spider-Man and Doctor Octopus tumble onto the train the vertical setting is switched for a horizontal one, yet geometric properties remain unstable. Atop the train, as Spider-Man clings to the end of a carriage he is shown head-on, rushing wind caused by the train's velocity pushing him backward, likening his struggle to move along the train's rooftop to climbing up a building. When the fight shifts to the side of the train, the camera first frames the combatants from above in a composition that would usually be equated with a birds-eye-view but in this case is shot side-on with the train, the fact that the camera is upside-down providing a further directional skew. The shot's topsy-turviness is made explicit as the camera twists away, ending up peering down on the train from a high angle. Throughout this fight,

SPIDER-MAN AND THE MARVEL SUPERHERO IN THE TWENTY-FIRST CENTURY 101

Spider-Man clings to the roof of a train, framed as if he were climbing a wall, in *Spider-Man 2* (2004).

An upside-down shot shows Spider-Man and Doctor Octopus fighting on the side of a train in *Spider-Man 2* (2004).

The camera, having twisted away, peers down on Spider-Man and Doctor Octopus fighting in *Spider-Man 2* (2004).

surfaces oscillate between functioning as walls and floors, at times within single shots, verticality and horizontality becoming interchangeable.

New York's citizens are not just an abstract presence evoked by kinesis and staging. Spider-Man's encounters with a diverse citizenry affirm that he is fighting for and *with* a multicultural community, albeit while having privileged status. During the train-top battle Doctor Octopus sabotages the brakes. Spider-Man then saves the train by webbing to buildings to apply drag to the hurtling vehicle, causing him to be pulled taught over the train's nose as he clutches the webbing, arms stretched to the sides like Jesus Christ on the cross. The passengers reciprocate by carrying Spider-Man's unconscious body to safety; as they hold the hero's body above their heads, Spider-Man's arms spread to the side once again to evoke Christ. Spider-Man's mask is removed throughout this sequence, enabling not just his expressivity but also his pale complexion to be foregrounded. Dyer (1997, 15–18) outlines how Christian ideas of embodiment and transcendence structure notions of whiteness, with bodily suffering being the means though which the spirit transcends to attain a divinity constructed as constitutive of whiteness. From the Renaissance onward, Western art depicting the crucifixion rendered Christ as not just white but as the palest figure in the image (66–67). In *Spider-Man 2*'s train sequence, Spider-Man's pose and complexion root him in these traditions, the physical pain he endures draining his body of life till he passes out in testament of his spirit prevailing. Thus, while the group of passengers who surround and carry his limp body incorporates people of different genders, races, and classes—a microcosm of the film's conceptualization of New York's citizenry—Spider-Man is presented as a white savior figure.

When Doctor Octopus returns, the passengers stand together defiantly to block the supervillain's path to Spider-Man. Presenting this diverse community as an active ally to Spider-Man amplifies the film's contemporary resonance, Jeanne Holland asserting that "this scene enacts the post-9/11 theme of 'United We Stand'" (2012, 299). The *Spider-Man* trilogy seeks to offer a utopian vision of a multicultural citizenry collaboratively representing the identity and heroism of the US, yet this harmony is tainted by exalting the superhero through narrative and iconic tropes that privilege whiteness. Indeed, as Doctor Octopus shoves these citizens aside, a barely revived Spider-Man gestures to the few passengers holding him up to leave him to face the threat alone and, hunched and bleeding, stumbles forth to sacrifice his body once again.

Burke (2015, 34) argues that the *Spider-Man* trilogy's celebration of community aligns with post-9/11 sentiment at the expense of contradicting traditional elements of Spider-Man texts, namely the hero's individualism and the populace's distrust for him. What occurs, however, is a transformation of familiar traits from the Spider-Man franchise through placing them in dialogue with the contemporary sociopolitical climate. In Spider-Man texts

Spider-Man is pulled tight over a train's nose as he webs to buildings to stop the hurtling vehicle in *Spider-Man 2* (2004).

Spider-Man's limp body is carried by a group of New York's citizens in *Spider-Man 2* (2004).

it is most pervasively the adult establishment that denigrates Spider-Man, while other social groups, particularly Peter's peers, often provide support. The *Spider-Man* trilogy develops this trait by aligning Spider-Man with the wider community in external public spaces, rather than situating him alongside the establishment guardians of more exclusive internal spaces. Spider-Man's bond with New York's citizenry in these external spaces also extends the symbiotic relation Spider-Man has with the city to include the multicultural community as a key component of the Spider-Man/New York amalgam. It is through the combined efforts of community, Spider-Man, and city as a complete entity that New York's external public spaces are maintained as safe environments in which people can move freely. A harmonious multicultural community is thus inherent in the films' conceptualization of urban utopia, although the harmony is undermined through this community's dependence on a white savior.

NOSTALGIC CONSTRUCTION OF INTERNAL SPACE

In opposition to the *Spider-Man* trilogy's external spaces, internal spaces are governed by various kinds of white patriarchy. The focus on figures like Uncle Ben, Norman Osborn, and J. Jonah Jameson (J. K. Simmons) can be attributed to the films harking back to Silver Age comic books and bringing these into the center of the Spider-Man franchise, rather than adapting characters introduced in more recent texts. The *Spider-Man* trilogy's nostalgic inclinations are particularly evident in the design of key internal spaces. To assess whether the nostalgic presentation of these spaces functions in ways that are not simply regressive, it is necessary to first establish some instructive conceptualizations of nostalgia.

Svetlana Boym traces the history of nostalgia, outlining its etymological roots in two Greek words: "*nostos* meaning 'return home' and *algia* 'longing'" (2007, 7). Johannes Hofer created the word in 1688 to describe a medical condition suffered by people longing for a home from which they were displaced (Boym, 7–8). Notions of what nostalgia entails developed from a longing for a place to a longing for a time. As such, "nostalgia became less a *physical* than a *psychological* condition. . . . It also went from being a *curable* medical illness to an *incurable* (indeed unassuageable) condition of the spirit or psyche" (Hutcheon 1998, emphasis in original). Once nostalgia became about time rather than space the longed for object was made irretrievable since, while one can return to a place, one cannot go back in time. Theorizations of nostalgia often explore how this unfulfillable desire to return to the past impacts the present.

The suggestion made in my previous chapter that *Superman: The Movie*'s nostalgic stylization facilitates an evasion of contemporary concerns, and thus depoliticizes the film, aligns with Fredric Jameson's influential conceptualization of the nostalgia film. Superhero blockbusters have been discussed as examples of Jameson's nostalgia film: Hassler-Forest (2012, 48) applies the concept to *The Movie* while Wilson Koh (2009, 736–38) applies it to *Spider-Man 1*. In Jameson's postmodern theory, "the formal apparatus of nostalgia films has trained us to consume the past in the form of glossy images" (1991, 287). These glossy images replace the actual past, causing a loss of history that makes us unable to situate ourselves on a timeline. Jameson thus brands nostalgic stylization in films "an alarming and pathological symptom of a society that has become incapable of dealing with time and history . . . we seem condemned to seek the historical past through our own pop images and stereotypes about that past, which itself remains forever out of reach" (1988, 20). We are left in a perpetual present that cannot be located in relation to the past.

Other conceptualizations of nostalgia see the potential for a more successful negotiation of past and present. Boym recognizes that nostalgia can offer a conservative retreat into the past but also proposes an alternative function, arguing that "nostalgia, in my view, is not always retrospective; it can be prospective as well. The fantasies of the past, determined by the needs of the present, have a direct impact on the realities of the future." (2007, 8). Boym's formulation of two different types of nostalgia—restorative and reflective—distinguishes between retrospective nostalgia and nostalgia that can productively shape the future by negotiating past and present. Boym defines restorative and reflective nostalgia as follows.

> Restorative nostalgia stresses *nostos* (home) and attempts a transhistorical reconstruction of the lost home. Reflective nostalgia thrives on *algia* (the longing itself) and delays the homecoming—wistfully, ironically, desperately ... Restorative nostalgia does not think of itself as nostalgia, but rather as truth and tradition. Reflective nostalgia dwells on the ambivalences of human longing and belonging and does not shy away from the contradictions of modernity. Restorative nostalgia protects the absolute truth, while reflective nostalgia calls it into doubt. (13)

Restorative nostalgia mythologizes the past while reflective nostalgia acknowledges the imagined nature of myths and questions their foundations. In this sense, reflective nostalgia interrogates the conservative regression that Jameson identifies in nostalgia. Boym explores how, in the reflective model, different periods of time can be spatially juxtaposed, arguing that reflective nostalgia "cherishes shattered fragments of memory and temporalizes space" (15). While nostalgia developed from a longing for a place to a longing for a time, reflective nostalgia acknowledges the role space can play in the representation of time. Following Boym, coexisting spatial representations of different eras can examine the present by situating it in relation to knowingly imagined visions of the past.

While Boym notes that restorative and reflective nostalgia are not binaries, but can be mixed in different measures, Hutcheon (1998) provides a framework for understanding the function of contradictory tendencies in certain kinds of nostalgia. In outlining her conceptualizations of irony, nostalgia, and the postmodern, Hutcheon aligns nostalgia with a desire to retreat into the past but argues that when combined with irony it becomes reflective and critical about this retreat. Hutcheon opposes Jameson's assimilation of nostalgia and the postmodern, arguing instead that nostalgia in the conservative sense is modernist, but when it gains a reflexive edge through being tinged with irony it becomes postmodern. This ironized nostalgia exhibits the equivocal qualities inherent to Hutcheon's conceptualization of the postmodern, which always has "some mix of the complicitous and the critical at its ambivalent core" (1998). The nature of this complicitous critique is elucidated by Hutcheon's discussion of postmodern film, which "does not deny that it is implicated in capitalist modes of production, because it knows it cannot. Instead it exploits its 'insider' position in order to begin a subversion from within" (1989, 114). Postmodern texts cannot help but be complicit with the system in which they are produced but can use their "insider" status to undermine this system; they simultaneously inscribe and critique practices of the institutions in which they are made and the ideology that these institutions uphold. Hutcheon's conceptualization of the postmodern explicitly counters Jameson's. For Hutcheon the postmodern "is not synonymous with the loss of meaning and value but rather provokes discussion and analysis of how cultural meanings and values are constructed and negotiated" (Constable 2015, 81–82). Hutcheon's postmodern ironized nostalgia enacts this analysis of meaning through a critical negotiation of past and present. This negotiation has parallels with Boym's notion of reflective nostalgia. However, while Boym acknowledges that elements of restorative and reflective nostalgia can be present simultaneously, Hutcheon's conceptualization of the postmodern as intrinsically equivocal attributes complicitous qualities to all critical nostalgia. Ironized nostalgia contributes to cultural constructions of an idealized past while concurrently interrogating this process.

Spider-Man 1's complicity in dehistoricizing and depoliticizing culture is evident in an oft-recited anecdote in discussions of Hollywood and 9/11. An early trailer, in which Spider-Man uses a web spun between the Twin Towers to trap criminals in a helicopter, was pulled by distributer Sony following the attacks (see Leaver 2012, 155; Hassler-Forest 2012, 125–27; McSweeney 2014, 2). Koh argues that *Spider-Man 1*'s nostalgic mise-en-scène similarly erases history by constructing an idealized past:

> The set props in *Spider-Man* were chosen to make audiences experience an unreal, near non-specific era, one that spans half a century of real-world history, yet calculatedly compresses those decades to paradoxically co-exist with each other in every second of the film. In other words, the mode has more to do with current perceptions of a generalized past than with the authentic re-creation of a complex and specific reality. It simply reflects its producers' idealized interpretations of the past. (2009, 737).

The interior of Ben and May Parker's house in *Spider-Man* (2002).

While artifacts from different decades and contexts are overtly present in the film's mise-en-scène, however, it is important to acknowledge that individual spaces typically construct versions of relatively specific eras. Meaning emerges though the ways that these spaces are inhabited by characters and situated in relation to one another.

Ben and May Parker's (Rosemary Harris) house in *Spider-Man 1* is the primary site of nostalgia for an idealized 1960s US, when comic books were enjoying their Silver Age. The house is situated in a humble but cozy working-class suburbia. Pastel oranges, beiges, and floral patterns decorate the interior, while the most modern technology in the lounge is a wooden cased television. The first time we see the space, Ben is coded as working class by a literal blue collared shirt, worn casually under an unbuttoned waistcoat. The affectionate portrayal of Ben and May is accentuated by their loving relationship. While adhering to a breadwinner/housewife binary, they are in harmony as they pass each other objects and traverse the house. Mise-en-scène roots this space in the 1950s–60s, while its homely presentation and Ben and May's harmonious matrimonial union cast it as a working-class utopia.

This idealized vision of the past does not simply offer what Koh sees as "an appealing better-than-real illusion to escape into" (2009, 738). Boym argues that imagined pasts can avoid being regressive if they are recognized as imagined. Nostalgia can be for "the unrealized dreams of the past and visions of the future that have become obsolete" (2007, 10); for something that is recognized as never having existed, but that should have existed. The sense of Ben and May's house representing an ideal that cannot be maintained is established in the first scene set in this space. Ben discusses being made redundant after 35 years and mourns how his lack of knowledge about computers now leaves him unqualified for most jobs. The space is therefore not one of easy retreat from contemporary problems. Rather, contemporary developments are destabilizing its sanctity.

Capitalism is the force that threatens this working-class utopia, with Ben's corporation laying off employees for greater profits. The utopic presentation of Ben and May and concurrent vilification of corporate culture promotes their prosocial values as those that Peter needs to carry forward, encapsulated by the fact that it is Ben who imparts the wisdom inspiring Peter to help others: "With great power comes great responsibility." When first deployed in *Amazing Fantasy* #15, this now-famous worded identifier is presented in a caption, marking a solemn moment of personal reflection for Peter. In many subsequent Spider-Man texts the line is attributed to Ben. When Ben utters the worded identifier in *Spider-Man 1*, his gentle but assured tone gives the words a timeless quality. A slight smile cracks across his softly weathered face, in recognition of delivering a line that has resonated through popular culture and come to encapsulate Spider-Man's philosophy.[13]

The value of holding the needs of others over your own is in *Spider-Man 1* aligned with Ben and, through his nostalgic connotations, an idealized vision of the 1960s. The fact that the space that embodies this vision is always shown as impossible to retain, from its introduction when Ben's redundancy is announced to May being forced to sell the house in *Spider-Man 2*, makes it a site of reflective nostalgia, exuding longing for that which is pointedly presented as idealized. Rather than offering a nostalgic retreat into an imagined past, the ideals this space embodies are acknowledged as unfulfilled but upheld as worth aspiring to.

Through aligning these values with white patriarch Ben, the film also exhibits complicity with ingrained social structures. By presenting a parochial vision of working-class 1960s suburbia as the idealized utopia to which we should aspire, *Spider-Man 1* ignores significant political movements of that era, such as the women's liberation and civil rights movements. Hutcheon (1998) outlines the risk of Leftist nostalgic visions expressing conservative values, such visions often regressing to times when rights were denied to, for instance, women and minoritized ethnicities. This combination of subversion and regression exemplifies the complicitous critique that Hutcheon finds in postmodern nostalgia. In *Spider-Man 1*, the relay between Ben, Peter/Spider-Man, and New York somewhat counterbalances the film's location of idealized values of the 1960s solely in white masculinity. Ben is a benevolent patriarch whose values, when enacted by Spider-Man in New

J. Jonah Jameson's office in *Spider-Man* (2002).

York's external spaces, create a utopia that enables a multicultural populace freedom of movement, although the dependence of this utopia on a white savior adds another layer of complicity.

In contrast, *Spider-Man 1*'s capitalist patriarchs seek to maintain the establishment's exclusivity and restrict social mobility. The presentation of the spaces they inhabit adds to the film's commentary on sociopolitical values. One of these spaces, the *Daily Bugle* offices, harkens back to the same era as Ben and May's house. In comic books, Peter "began his freelance career during the newspaper's Golden Age in the mid-20th century, when newsrooms were smoke-filled and frantic in advance of tomorrow's edition" (McGowan and Short 2012, 115). The *Spider-Man* trilogy recreates this popular image of a newspaper office. There are modern elements, such as computers, but editor Jonah's office lacks a computer, instead featuring a row of television monitors and a phone, facilitating his patriarchal role of observing and commanding. The flow in and out of Jonah's office of people seeking orders further emphasizes his commanding role, while creating the hustle and bustle associated with Golden Age newsrooms.

The characterization of Jonah communicates *Spider-Man 1*'s perspective on this space. The film's Jonah recalls 1960s incarnations in both image and attitude. His square haircut, moustache, and suit recreate a look established in Silver Age comic books. Andrew A. Smith (2012) discusses Jonah's actions in comic books, demonstrating that, while for the most part villainous, at times Jonah has acted virtuously, for instance countering bigotry and exhibiting journalistic integrity. The *Spider-Man* trilogy's Jonah lacks these redeeming features. He also lacks more outwardly dangerous ones

Norman Osborn's apartment in *Spider-Man* (2002).

that the character has often displayed, such as hiring, or funding the creation of, supervillains to defeat Spider-Man. He aligns quite closely with the Jonah of the 1967–1970 animated series: a constant source of antagonism to Peter whose bluster is ultimately worse than his bite, generally ending each episode as a figure of comedic ridicule. Jonah bullies his employees and denigrates Spider-Man with sensationalist stories but is presented as a farcical figure.

Aaron Drucker (2012) argues that Jonah's Silver Age comic book characterization as a self-righteous, conservative figure facilitates critique of the establishment's attempts to dictate public thinking. An aspect of this establishment that Jonah specifically represents is the news media. The *Spider-Man* trilogy's caricatured presentation of Jonah as a bullish perpetuator of sensationalist falsehoods can be linked to the contemporary sociopolitical climate. Tama Leaver aligns Jonah's subversion of truth with the influence the news media had on the national response to 9/11, arguing that "the power and influence of media is both highlighted and, to an extent, critiqued in the *Spider-Man* films" (2012, 158). The farcical representation of Jonah parodies the reactionary response evident in the majority of US press coverage of 9/11 and the proceeding "war on terror," which, as explained by David L. Altheide, was "grounded in a discourse of fear" (2010, 11) that unquestioningly perpetuated the Bush administration's master narrative.

While the characterization of Jonah as an obnoxious, cigar-chomping, and penny-pinching mogul may seem to invite laughter over critical reflection, it portrays his mode of entrepreneurial capitalism as ridiculous and outdated. Rooting Jonah in past incarnations and historical stereotypes creates a

The Oscorp boardroom in *Spider-Man* (2002).

nostalgic vision of a capitalism that had a clear face with obvious faults. This nostalgia is reflective in that it does not cherish the values Jonah embodies, but rather appreciates our ability to easily recognize their flaws. Reflection prompts audiences to impress this awareness of the potential for the press to obscure facts onto their understanding of contemporary media.

The representation of Norman Osborn critiques entrepreneurial capitalism from a different perspective. Norman's apartment is filled with decadent Victorian décor. Carved wood furnishings, patterned rugs, and candlestick holders appear to have been passed down for generations. Large portraits in decorative frames adorning the walls also exhibit the imprint of Norman's ancestors, exuding the family's self-importance. This space's décor and emphasis on heritage convey that Norman's wealth is ingrained in his lineage.

In keeping with the décor's exhibition of ancestral privilege, the tribal masks displayed around this space are presented as treasures gained through Victorian imperialism. Jameson (1991, 35) identifies imperialism as the second stage of capitalism, preceding the current stage of multinational capitalism. Following this periodization, these masks align the Osborn family with an earlier form of capitalism than that which Norman's company Oscorp embodies, thus outlining the family's implication in the development of capitalism. The masks also provide an obvious reflection of the mask Norman wears as Green Goblin and suggest that sinister psychological traits are ingrained in his lineage. Consequently, while harking back to the past, this space is not one of nostalgic longing, but instead indicates the form of capitalism that Norman embodies and presents it as nefarious.

Harry Osborn and Peter's apartment in *Spider-Man* (2002).

While Jonah and Norman's entrepreneurial capitalism is associated with the past, and presented as ridiculous and villainous, respectively, Oscorp represents a more (post)modern form of globalized capitalism. By its faceless and decentered nature, postmodern multinational capitalism lacks specific spaces with which to be associated. Only one scene in *Spider-Man 1* presents a space exclusive to the guardians of this mode of capitalism. The scene is introduced by an exterior shot of Oscorp's skyscraper that tilts upward. Before the camera reveals much more than the first ten stories, the shot cross-fades to one of Norman sitting at the head of the boardroom table. Leaving a tilt to the top of the building incomplete somewhat abstracts this boardroom from the skyscraper, suggesting that the company's upper echelons are inaccessible. The boardroom's clinical design amplifies this sense of an untraceable and largely anonymous power. As the camera tracks back from Norman it reveals the formally attired board members sat around the table, five on each side and one at the other end, on identical leather chairs, a cup, saucer, and folder laid out before each of them. Symmetrical composition and hard lighting from above that ensures against shading imbalances enhance this regimentation. Eight out of the eleven board members are white men, exhibiting the perpetuation of patriarchal privilege within this mode of capitalism.

The power of this body over the individual is made evident when they force Norman to resign from his own company. Dafoe's uniquely creased visage is harnessed to mark out Norman's individuality as he cycles through heightened emotions. When Norman's proud smile falls upon hearing that the company is being sold his skin tightens over his cheekbones. His aghast frown shifts into a face scrunched in anger as he yells at the board members, then droops in defeat before his chin pushes forward, recalling Green Goblin's mask and pulling his skin taught in a look of menace. The board members meet Norman's impassioned outburst with cold rigidity and a hint of malicious delight. The film thus presents postmodern multinational capitalism as maintaining impenetrability through being governed by inaccessible, homogenous, and compassionless structures.

The spaces discussed above map different paths available to the *Spider-Man* trilogy's young protagonists. Peter can uphold Ben's prosocial values, pursue entrepreneurial privileges, or accept subservience within the corporate system. The Manhattan apartment that Peter and Harry share in *Spider-Man 1* expresses the teenagers' intermediary status, its décor and design situated at a crossroads between the different periods that the film uses to represent patriarchal figures and their values. Objects and styles from a range of times are collected together. Widescreen televisions and speakers are placed alongside wooden furnishings, a grandfather clock, and an abstract painting by contemporary modern artist Luc Leestemaker. The architecture itself also represents a clash of styles that evoke different periods, combining, for example, fluted columns reminiscent of classical design with industrial design elements such as steel stair railings. The apartment situates Peter and Harry apart from the specific temporal coding of the spaces aligned with different patriarchs, indicating the boys' opportunity to select which values to uphold.

Spider-Man 1 performs a reflective negotiation of different sets of values though the ways in which it presents, and positions its transitional young characters in relation to, key internal spaces. This negotiation is facilitated by the adaptive practices of superhero blockbusters. By reenvisioning icons of popular culture who have strong cultural associations with the eras in which comic books were in their Golden and Silver Ages, superhero blockbusters can reflect on culturally constructed visions of these eras. *Spider-Man 1* foregrounds these associations through affectionately gesturing to, and recreating elements from, Silver Age *Spider-Man* comics, which themselves now contribute to cultural perceptions of the mid-twentieth century as a simpler time when good and evil were clearly distinguishable. The film acknowledges the idealized nature of these perceptions of the past and, by situating them in relation to spaces representative of other times and values, explores a range of sociopolitical ideas. Yet the limitations of this range of ideas can be attributed to the limitations of the Silver Age comics that are the objects of reflective nostalgia. In its critique of entrepreneurial and postmodern capitalism, the prosocial values that *Spider-Man 1* offers as a positive alternative are rooted in, and thus rendered complicit with the representational

The presentation of Peter's apartment emphasizes his impoverishment in *Spider-Man 2* (2004).

limitations of, the idealized past associated with Silver Age comics. In terms of mentors—good or evil—for its central teenagers, the film only negotiates between different white men.

THE SERIALIZED STRUGGLES OF PETER AND MARY JANE

While Peter pursues Ben's prosocial values in the first film, the varied nature of a superhero's spectrum suggests that this role is not fixed for the sequels. The shifts that Peter undergoes in *Spider-Man 2* and *3* resituate him in relation to the potential roles presented to him in *Spider-Man 1*. Changes in Peter's characterization and circumstances also continue the trilogy's commentary on patriarchal structures, which is foregrounded in Mary Jane's narrative.

Peter's continued endeavors to place the needs of others over his own in the second film contribute to his worsened economic status. While Peter's poverty has long been explored in the Spider-Man franchise, Holland interlinks *Spider-Man 2*'s emphasis of this trait with contemporary circumstances. Holland argues that the film comments on the fact that "from 2001–04, the Bush Administration slashed domestic spending and redistributed wealth increasing the impoverishment of most Americans" (2012, 293), redirecting government funds to finance the "war on terror." The humbler residence that Peter now occupies expresses this sociopolitical commentary. The first time we see his new apartment its entirety is presented in one cramped shot that shows its dilapidated furnishings. A dull, grubby palette and dim lighting create dark corners that further close the space. The oldness of this

The presentation of Peter's apartment emphasizes Mary Jane Watson's loneliness in *Spider-Man 2* (2004).

apartment does not evoke longing for an idealized past, but instead suggests impoverishment in the present.

Spider-Man 2 also initiates a shift toward an exploration of Mary Jane's subjectivity. In the first two films, Mary Jane ascends a "rags to riches" arc, although she primarily functions as a love interest for Peter and Harry, and figure to be kidnapped by supervillains. Comics writer Gail Simone (1999) influentially illuminates the pervasiveness of this kind of role for female characters in superhero narratives on her "women in refrigerators" website, which lists examples of female characters being kidnapped, maimed, raped, and/or murdered to provide motivation for a male character. The name "women in refrigerators" refers to a storyline in *Green Lantern* vol. 3 #54 (August 1994), in which Green Lantern discovers that his girlfriend, Alex DeWitt, has been killed by a supervillain and her body left in a refrigerator. Miriam Kent (2021, 36–43) surveys the ways in which Mary Jane is reduced to both superhero girlfriend and woman in refrigerator in the *Spider-Man* trilogy, serving the development of male characters' narratives while frequently being sexually objectified. It is important to acknowledge, however, that *Spider-Man 3* takes significant steps to complicate this role. At the end of the second film, after imploring Peter to grant her the agency to make her own decision regarding whether she should date somebody who may place her life in danger, a celebratory shot exhibiting Spider-Man and the digital effects' powers is followed by a melancholic close-up of Mary Jane. This momentary contemplation of Mary Jane's feelings primes *Spider-Man 3* to explore her subjectivity and interrogate the patriarchal structures that subjugate her.

In *Spider-Man 3*, Mary Jane's treatment by patriarchal structures is illuminated through her treatment by Peter. This theme initiates the first time we see Peter's apartment, which remains the same as in the second film. Close-ups of Mary Jane sitting on Peter's bed are angled so that his police scanner, notable by its red LED display, is evident in the background, encroaching on their relationship and then forcing him away from her when it broadcasts information about a crime. Once Peter leaves, a wall-to-wall shot of the apartment recalls the one in which it was introduced in *Spider-Man 2*. However, brighter lighting makes the space less confining and outlines Mary Jane's isolation by positioning her alone in the width of the frame.[14] The space now emphasizes Mary Jane's neglect over Peter's socioeconomic status.

When Peter abandons Mary Jane in his apartment, he does so to help the wider community as Spider-Man. His actions later in the film serve a more selfish nature. The narrative conceit of Peter being bonded with the alien symbiote provides a means to push him to an extreme point on his spectrum of possible roles. Crucially, Peter's objectional traits are not simply motivated by an external force. Dr. Curt Conners (Dylan Baker) outlines how the symbiote "amplifies characteristics of its host, especially aggression," clarifying that the self-gratifying behavior Peter exhibits while bonded with the symbiote intensifies traits he already holds.

Spider-Man 3 makes clear that Peter harbors deplorable traits before falling under the symbiote's influence. For example, the particularities of Peter's attempted proposal to Mary Jane indicate his newfound affiliation with an entrepreneurial capitalist patriarchy that objectifies women. Peter's proposal equates wealth with romance. He selects an upmarket French restaurant as the venue and enlists a waiter to place the ring in Mary Jane's champagne glass. The fact that the waiter, played by cult icon Bruce Campbell, is so amicable with Peter subverts a running joke through the trilogy in which, as a wrestling announcer in *Spider-Man 1* then theatre usher in *Spider-Man 2*, Campbell disparages Peter. Campbell now embracing Peter signifies Peter being accepted by the gatekeeper who previously obstructed his access to wealth and high society. While succeeding in projecting himself as an affluent individual, however, Peter's self-absorption leads him to overlook Mary Jane's suffering, which is caused in part by him. The couple's growing segregation is conveyed by the scene's general progression from shot-reverse-shot cutting between long shots framed from behind each character, which include both in the frame, to narrower compositions. This progression culminates in a series of close-ups that isolate Peter and Mary Jane from each other, foregrounding Peter's bewilderment and Mary Jane's anguish. This division of man and woman exposes the form of patriarchy with which Peter is now complying.

The scenes in which these entrepreneurial traits intensify under the symbiote's influence oscillate between prompting audience distaste at Peter's callous actions and encouraging laughter at his pomposity. These perspectives are evident in other characters' responses to Peter. For example, Robbie and Betty Brant (Elizabeth Banks), the two *Bugle* employees most sympathetic to Peter, have expressions of shocked dismay when Peter aggressively confronts Eddie.[15] Elsewhere, female passers-by look on in bemusement as Peter swaggers down the street. This presentation combines the sinisterness of Norman and ridiculousness of Jonah, encompassing both sides of *Spider-Man 1*'s critique of entrepreneurial capitalism to ensure that Peter's actions are presented as utterly repugnant.

Peter's transformation culminates when he takes Gwen on a date to a jazz club. The scene pointedly jars with the rest of the trilogy through having Peter perform a musical number. This disruption establishes an unstable framework within which the film can push Peter to the furthest points of entrepreneurial repulsiveness and ridiculousness on his spectrum. As Peter performs for Gwen to incite jealousy in Mary Jane, his skilled piano playing and boastful dancing are incongruent with our knowledge and expectations of both Peter and Maguire ensuring that, even when Peter swings from a chandelier and recalls the fluid airborne movements of Spider-Man, his attempts at suaveness are laughably awkward. The horrific potential of Peter's entrepreneurial streak is laid bare after the musical number when he confronts and strikes Mary Jane.

While Mary Jane's subjugation in this scene denotes a lack of agency it is significant that, amidst all the disruptive elements, she emotionally grounds the scene and Peter. After Mary Jane is struck to the floor, a series of cuts between her and Peter show her physical pain and shock triggering a moment of self-realization in Peter. High angled shots accentuate Mary Jane's vulnerability, while in the reverse shots Peter's features quiver and shift into a horrified, wide-eyed expression. After Peter notices the black Spider-Man suit showing from under his shirt he flashes a look of shocked revelation at Mary Jane, indicating that she has sparked the realization that the symbiote has aggravated his recent shift in character. The prolonged duration of each take in this series of shots, particularly in contrast to the preceding rapidly edited musical number, outlines both characters' raw emotions. After Peter flees, a lingering medium shot of a desolate Mary Jane, still on the floor, directs audience empathy to her. Both Peter and the audience's identification with Mary Jane is vital to marking out just how far he has been pushed to a narcissistic extreme on his spectrum. Although, echoing women in refrigerators tropes, these events develop a male character's narrative arc, the equal attention given to both Mary Jane and Peter in this sequence emphasizes not just what she has revealed about him, but her emotional state.

Mary Jane and Peter gaze wistfully at each other at the end of *Spider-Man 3* (2007).

Mary Jane is primarily relegated to her role as kidnap victim in the third act, but the emphasis on her perspective poignantly resurfaces in the final scene, which opens on Mary Jane singing "I'm Through with Love" in the jazz club. As Peter enters, she stops, the melancholic score kicks in, and once again the two communicate in gazes. The film's pattern of conveying the couple's estrangement by dividing them into separate shots is broken in a medium shot that positions them on either side of the frame. This symmetrical composition suggests a rebalancing of the gender inequality that Peter has perpetuated throughout the film. Mary Jane and Peter's wistful expressions convey anguish over Harry's death and the destructive impact of Peter's actions on their relationship. Mary Jane then makes a gesture of forgiveness as she moves toward Peter and embraces him. The scene restages the climactic moment in *Some Like It Hot* (Billy Wilder 1959) when Sugar (Marilyn Monroe) sings "I'm through with Love" and Joe (Tony Curtis), dressed as Josephine, approaches and kisses her, causing her to see through his disguise. By alluding to this more affirmative and comedic moment in which doubled identities obstructing two people's relationship collapse, *Spider-Man 3* offers hope for Mary Jane and Peter's future. Although the mood of the two scenes is very different, the sense of Peter needing to be considerate to Mary Jane, and of her need for agency, is also suggested through the connotations of *Some Like It Hot*, which thematizes men seeing from feminine perspectives. While, in *Some Like It Hot*, upon dropping his disguises as Josephine and billionaire Junior, Joe removes the obstacles blocking his relationship with Sugar, Peter's obstacles come from within. Acknowledgement of this is writ large on Peter's sorrowful expression, which provides the film's final image, signaling that much work still needs to be done before Peter and Mary Jane can attain their happy ending.

Closing with this emulation of classical Hollywood cinema, rather than the exhibitions of CGI that end previous films in the series, offers melancholic reflection over celebration. This break in the series's conventions ensures that even audiences oblivious to the *Some Like It Hot* reference will comprehend the scene's significance. While the first film closes with a spectacular display of Spider-Man's abilities, as does the sequel—but follows this with a close-up on Mary Jane—the third film seeks to give Peter and Mary Jane equal weight. The sense of hope as Peter gazes regretfully into Mary Jane's sad but forgiving eyes suggests that, while unity and empathy with others are harder to pursue than self-gratification, they are necessary to fight for. *Spider-Man 3* ultimately reiterates the trilogy's appeal for prosocial values within a climate that favors capitalist enterprise, while additionally indicating the need for men to embrace feminine perspectives.

SPIDER-MAN'S EXPANDING CINEMATIC WEB

My analysis of the *Spider-Man* trilogy contributes to understanding of the role of CGI in superhero blockbusters and the nature of the superhero blockbuster's sociopolitical engagement in the twenty-first century. The strategies through which the trilogy creates meaning by interlacing CGI with profilmic phenomena reveal how digital filmmaking technologies provide superhero blockbusters with new ways to adapt the thematic tensions that superhero comics convey by juxtaposing different forms. A full appreciation of the complex meanings that CGI can create in superhero blockbusters requires attention to the interrelation of CGI's abstract, perceptually realistic, and conceptual qualities. Meanwhile, the construction of space, and the ways in which people of different races, ethnicities, genders, ages, and socioeconomic backgrounds inhabit these spaces provides a means through which the *Spider-Man* trilogy expresses sociopolitical meanings. Furthermore, certain internal spaces are designed to harken back to past eras and in doing so represent different values, with nostalgic constructions of key periods from Spider-Man's comic book history foregrounded. Interactions between past incarnations of a character and contemporary contexts are an inherent feature of a superhero franchise, which always offers a composite of competing elements rather than a unified vision. Consequently, superhero texts are primed to perform a reflective negotiation of past and present, yet by performing this negotiation within the franchise's parameters any critique that is expressed will inevitably exhibit forms of complicity with its target. Both the *Spider-Man* trilogy's adaptive and serial strategies provide means through which sociopolitical meaning is produced through (re)negotiating the meanings of previous Spider-Man texts.

Throughout my analysis I have also illuminated ways that the *Spider-Man* trilogy does not just metamorphose traits of other Spider-Man texts but also develops motifs and strategies established by *Superman: The Movie*. While the *Spider-Man* trilogy represents a significant moment in the development of the superhero blockbuster, Spider-Man's cinematic adventures did not end with Peter's wistful gaze into Mary Jane's eyes in the closing moments of *Spider-Man 3*. A planned fourth installment was cancelled, but to date Spider-Man has returned in two successive live-action film series. The two *Amazing Spider-Man* films reboot the superhero (recast as Andrew Garfield), seeking a different cinematic take on his origins. The next series of Spider-Man films—at the time of this writing comprising *Homecoming, Far from Home*, and *No Way Home*—introduces a new iteration of the superhero (portrayed by Tom Holland) into the MCU. Each series's approach provides a framework within which they continue, revise, and depart from the *Spider-Man* trilogy's strategies.

Both the *Amazing Spider-Man* and MCU *Spider-Man* series continue to use perceptually realistic while overtly spectacular CGI to realize Spider-Man's body and situate this idealized superhero self in opposition to Peter's civilian identity. These bodies' movements also have intertextual qualities, at times gesturing to the *Spider-Man* trilogy to conceptually elucidate the skillsets of their Spider-Men. The *Amazing Spider-Man* films emphasize improved special effects both in effort to assert superiority over the trilogy and convey Peter's rapid mastery of his powers. One prominent strategy sees Spider-Man freefalling from the top of a skyscraper, perceptual realism foregrounded as rushing wind appears to cause ripples in the fabric of his costume to enhance the idealized superhero body's sense of tactility. Peter's ultimate mastery of his powers and corresponding bond with Manhattan is affirmed in *The Amazing Spider-Man*'s final moments through restaging the celebratory swinging motif that closed the trilogy's first two films (although Spider-Man's acrobatic traversal of the city is now presented in multiple takes). Redeploying this motif creates continuities between series while asserting the achievements of Garfield's Spider-Man at the end of his first adventure.

The hero of the MCU *Spider-Man* films takes longer to master his powers and consolidate a bond with Manhattan. Stylistic allusions to the trilogy chart this process. Early on in *Homecoming*, Spider-Man pursues a van. Elements of the scene pointedly recall, while significantly departing from,

Spider-Man attempts to save a ferry that has been split in two in *Spider-Man: Homecoming* (2017).

the van chase in *Spider-Man 3*. Whereas in the trilogy-closer a highly experienced Spider-Man nimbly negotiates New York's streets by webbing to the back of the van and weaving through obstacles while surfing on a detached van door, in *Homecoming* the fledgling hero is dragged along clumsily on a string of webbing attached to the van, tumbling into bins and mailboxes. Later, when striving to save a passenger ferry that has been split in two, Spider-Man attempts to bind the halves with webbing and hangs suspended between them, arms stretched out like Christ on the cross as he strains to hold the ship together. The context and pose echo the sequence from *Spider-Man 2* in which the hero stops a speeding train. Again, comparisons between scenes highlight a significant contrast; while the earlier incarnation halts the train, Holland's Spider-Man fails to save the ferry. Visual allusions to the trilogy mark the early point at which the MCU's Spider-Man is situated in his heroic ascent.

Homecoming's van and ferry sequences occur outside of Manhattan—in the suburbs and Upper New York Bay, respectively—exemplifying a pattern whereby the first two MCU *Spider-Man* films situate the superhero outside of the towering metropolis that traditionally provides his comfort zone. *Homecoming* primarily stages its set-pieces in the surrounding New York area and features one at the Washington Monument. *Far from Home* takes Spider-Man out of America altogether, into European cities—Venice, Prague, and London—with much more horizontally orientated architecture than Manhattan. While the unfamiliar European settings exacerbate Peter's unease as he pains to navigate his identities as superhero and student, the skill with which he moves around them attests to his growing ability.

At the end of *Far from Home*, for the first time in the series we see Spider-Man ecstatically swinging through Manhattan, the film (re)deploying the celebratory swinging motif that carried through both previous film series.

The parallels that Spider-Man's dynamic movements through Manhattan draw with the preceding series proclaim that the superhero has now truly arrived home, both physically and in the sense of mastering his powers and embracing his superhero identity. The celebratory swinging motif's rooting in the *Spider-Man* trilogy is underscored in a mid-credits sequence when a familiar face from the trilogy shatters Spider-Man's elation. After Spider-Man lands in Midtown Manhattan, J. K. Simmons, reprising his role as Jonah, appears in a news bulletin broadcast on giant screens above Madison Square Garden to frame Spider-Man for attacks in London and expose his civilian identity. The nostalgic connotations of Simmons's Jonah are now doubled, harking back to both Silver Age comics and the *Spider-Man* trilogy. As such, his deceptive reporting is reflectively revealed as not simply a new phenomenon in the "post-truth" era of "fake news"—which as Christopher Holliday (2019) outlines are key thematic concerns of *Far from Home*—but as historically rooted, the character having been used to comment on such reporting since the 1960s. Spider-Man's triumphant return home is thus accompanied by the return of familiar problems, which accrue meaning through continuities with the *Spider-Man* trilogy.

The means through which Jonah's report frames Spider-Man—by playing reedited footage that misrepresents the superhero's actions—also contributes to *Far from Home*'s discourse on the untrustworthiness of digital technology. It therefore participates in the three Spider-Man film series' thematization of the threat of the digital. The *Amazing Spider-Man* films largely express this theme in the same terms as the trilogy, placing the digital in opposition to the human through CGI mutating supervillains' bodies to express their disconnect from humanity. The Lizard (Rhys Ifans) in the first film and Electro (Jamie Foxx) in the second are prime examples of human bodies superseded by CGI, which correspondingly psychologically corrupts the characters.

Whereas in the *Amazing Spider-Man* films the digital overwhelms the human, in the first two MCU *Spider-Man* films it is wielded by villainous humans. *Homecoming*'s supervillain Vulture (Michael Keaton), like Doctor Octopus in *Spider-Man 2*, creates mechanical appendages (in this case wings) which are mostly realized through CGI. Yet unlike Doctor Octopus, Vulture controls his extra appendages, and in doing so contributes to a discourse about human uses of modern technologies of war that threads through MCU films. *Far from Home* develops this exploration, the narrative concerning Peter deciding who should be responsible for the suite of weapons and surveillance technologies that deceased mentor Tony Stark (Robert Downey Jr.) has left to him. Creatures called Elementals initially appear much like Sandman's ogre form in *Spider-Man 3*. Yet the Elementals

Andrew Garfield's Spider-Man saves Michelle Jones in *Spider-Man: No Way Home* (2021).

are subsequently revealed to be sophisticated digital holograms used by supervillain Mysterio (Jake Gyllenhaal) to dupe Spider-Man into thinking Mysterio is a superhero and give him Tony's technologies. As such, CGI itself becomes a threat within the narrative, and "CGI's believability and power to convince . . . ultimately becomes its most threatening property" (Holliday 2019). In *Far from Home*, CGI's ability to attain perceptual realism renders it dangerously deceptive.

No Way Home draws together the three series' vilification of the digital. In effort to regain the secrecy of his civilian identity, Peter asks Doctor Strange (Benedict Cumberbatch) to cast a spell that will make everybody forget that he is Spider-Man. Disruptions to the spell cause rifts between universes, a premise that enables characters from other cinematic incarnations of Spider-Man to appear in Holland's Spider-Man's universe. In doing so, Holland's Spider-Man's intertextual dialogue with previous incarnations moves beyond stylistic gestures and into direct interactions. That Holland's Spider-Man's mastery of his abilities now equals his cinematic predecessors' is showcased in the film's finale when he teams up with Maguire's Spider-Man and Garfield's Spider-Man to take on a group of their villains. Staging this climactic battle at the Statue of Liberty, a monument emblematic of New York, further signifies Holland's Spider-Man's parallels with the other two incarnations through affirming his bond with the city. Yet the different points that these Spider-Men inhabit on the superhero's spectrum of possible roles are also evident. Having them all unmasked for the battle's latter half foregrounds the idiosyncrasies of each star's performance. The feelings that each Peter expresses also draw intertextually from their previous adventures. For example, Garfield's Peter's anguish and guilt over Gwen's death in *The Amazing Spider-Man 2* inflects his Spider-Man's chirpiness. When the tragic event is restaged upon Michelle Jones (Zendaya) falling down the side of the statue,

Garfield's Spider-Man performs the rescue that he failed to do for Gwen; as he clutches a relieved Michelle, he strains to simultaneously smile and hold back tears, conveying his pained redemption. The humanity ascribed to the Spider-Men through physical performance is in opposition to the villains' monstrosity that for most of them manifests as inscribed CGI. The Spider-Men's plan to "cure" the supervillains entails administering treatments that remove their overtly digital inscriptions.[16] The human thus triumphs over the digital while the three Spider-Men's humanity bonds them together, despite their divergent experiences and personalities.

While *No Way Home* returns Holland's Spider-Man to New York but explores his bond with other Spider-Men rather than New York's citizens, the *Amazing Spider-Man* films, following the *Spider-Man* trilogy, make efforts to extend Spider-Man's bond with New York into a bond with its citizenry. *The Amazing Spider-Man*'s biggest instance of Spider-Man, Manhattan, and its citizenry working in harmony occurs when a group of crane operators arrange the crane arms into a row of platforms for the web-slinger to swing from. The bond between Spider-Man, New York, and its citizenry is here conveyed through the very literal means of citizens moving physical structures to facilitate Spider-Man's mobility. As the crane operators mobilize, one shot prominently features a US flag behind the foreman, presenting their cooperation as an expression of US identity. Yet while these construction workers are racially diverse, they are all working class men. The sequence presents a multicultural citizenry working with Spider-Man and metamorphoses the franchise's celebration of working-class heroism, but its expression of diversity is limited in terms of gender.

The nature of the *Amazing Spider-Man* and MCU *Spider-Man* films' racial diversity and gendered dynamics is related to which previous Spider-Man texts they favor in their intertextual engagement. In refocusing on Gwen as Peter's romantic partner, the *Amazing Spider-Man* films adapt key events from an era of Spider-Man comics that built toward Gwen's death in *The Amazing Spider-Man* #121 (June 1973). This storyline "is often considered the end of the Silver Age of Comics" (Burke 2015, 276). Privileging this storyline thus underscores the *Amazing Spider-Man* films' departure from the trilogy's Silver Age nostalgia. Yet the *Amazing Spider-Man* films do not simply harken back to the period in which Gwen died in comics. As Taylor (2017, 276–77) argues, the films' representation of Peter is strongly modelled on the twenty-first-century reimagining of the character in *Ultimate Spider-Man* (December 2000–August 2011): hip and charismatic, with tousled hair and style informed by skater culture. Although Marvel's "Ultimate" line of comics in some ways reimagined characters with greater racial and ethnic diversity[17] the Spider-Man title primarily focused on a white American cast until it was relaunched as *Ultimate Comics: Spider-Man* (November 2011–December 2013), in which African American Puerto Rican boy Miles Morales took the Spider-Man mantle. The *Amazing Spider-Man* films' focus on a white central cast is linked to their rooting in the *Ultimate Spider-Man* comics; Miles subsequently got his cinematic debut in animated feature *Spider-Man: Into the Spider-Verse* (Bob Persichetti, Peter Ramsey, Rodeny Rothman 2018) which I argue elsewhere (Taylor 2022, 93–98) is industrially positioned as a subbrand to the live-action blockbusters situated centrally in the Spider-Man franchise, although uses this position to comment on racial, ethnic, and gender diversity in the franchise. In comparison to the *Amazing Spider-Man* films, the MCU *Spider-Man* films represent a notable increase in the racial and ethnic diversity of their central cast, despite still centering on a white Peter Parker and characters of color having "their existence constructed around their relationship to Peter" (Matthews and Tran 2023, 209). For example, Filipino American Jacob Batalon is cast as Peter's best friend Ned Leeds, with his characterization recalling Miles's best friend, Korean American Ganke Lee, from *Ultimate Comics: Spider-Man*. The MCU *Spider-Man* films also uproot themselves from franchise history by introducing new Black character Michelle Jones, known as MJ in reference to Mary Jane. Through intertextually engaging with more recent 2010s comics while further reworking the Spider-Man franchise, the MCU *Spider-Man* films avoid nostalgic visions that reproduce tendencies of representation from past comics.

While the *Amazing Spider-Man* and MCU *Spider-Man* films seek to grant female characters active roles, these representations are both developed and compromised through the films' negotiation of textual history. The *Amazing Spider-Man* films rework while also reproducing elements of Gwen's comic book narrative and infamous death that gave her a legacy as "perhaps the quintessential woman in the refrigerator" (Kent 2021, 31). Kent (58–63) argues that *The Amazing Spider-Man* knowingly subverts Gwen's textual history by repeatedly setting up then averting her death and giving her significant agency. Rather than being kidnapped by Spider-Man's enemies, Gwen uses her scientific knowledge to aid the superhero in fighting them. While Gwen continues to perform this role in *The Amazing Spider-Man 2*, her reversion back to the role of tragic victim with her death undermines the efforts to reframe the character.

Aunt May (Sally Field in the *Amazing Spider-Man* films, Marisa Tomei in the MCU) gains a more active role across the three film series. The MCU *Spider-Man* films in particular illuminate May's centrality to raising Peter and make her the embodiment of prosocial values: in *Far from Home* she organizes charity events while in *No Way Home* she works at a charity's community center and encourages Peter to help the displaced supervillains rather than simply return them to their universes to die. May's central contribution to Spider-Man's values is underscored in *No Way Home* when before dying she imparts one final teaching to Peter: "With great power there must also come great responsibility." Attributing this famous worded identifier to May reframes its wisdom as matriarchal.

This representation of May and her matriarchal values is, however, compromised by the MCU *Spider-Man* films' exploration of patriarchal figures. This exploration is shaped not just by juxtaposition of elements within the films, as seen in the trilogy, but also crucially by other MCU films outside of the Spider-Man series. Despite May's maternal role being foregrounded, Tony, a central figure in the MCU, provides a father figure for Peter. After his death in *Avengers: Endgame*, Tony's lasting impact on Peter is evoked even in May's death scene, the framing of May's failing body propped up in the screen's center-left, as Peter leans into the right, echoing the framing of Peter's last interaction with a dying Tony in *Endgame*. Although by this time in the series May has surpassed Tony as the bedrock of Peter's values, her importance to Peter and the tragic impact of her death is still situated in relation to Tony.

The complexities of the ways in which the MCU's serial structures affect its films' meanings are explored in the next chapter. This book's first two chapters have examined the adaptation of a network of texts into a single blockbuster film or film series. My comparisons between the three Spider-Man film series underscore how superhero blockbusters themselves become part of this network. I now examine how the adaptive practices of the superhero blockbuster are inflected in a model of serialization—itself adapted from superhero comic books—in which multiple interconnected series share a fictional universe.

CHAPTER 3

EARTH'S MIGHTIEST SUPERHERO BLOCKBUSTERS

Networked Seriality in the Marvel Cinematic Universe

The Superman story in *Action Comics* #1 ends with the eponymous hero seemingly falling in peril, a caption promising "to be continued." Seriality was thus established as a trait of the superhero genre upon its genesis. Seriality in superhero comic books developed from a linear chronology in a single series into a networked model, in which different characters owned by the same publisher could meet in one another's titles. Each individual superhero's series was situated in a shared universe. While *Superman: The Movie* inscribed strategies of serialization into the production and textuality of the New Hollywood blockbuster, the subsequent attempt to adapt the comic book model of a multiseries networked diegesis into cinema by introducing *Supergirl* (Jeannot Szwarc 1984) to the same universe was cut short by that film's commercial failure. Decades later, Marvel achieved great success in adapting this model to film. In 2012, Marvel Studios' *The Avengers*, in which characters from five previously released films in four different series come together as a superhero team, showcased the interconnectivity of what is officially dubbed the Marvel Cinematic Universe (MCU).[1] This chapter examines the stylistic and narrative strategies through which the MCU adapts a networked model of seriality. I focus on its ensemble films that most pointedly manifest this interconnectivity and provide sustained close textual analysis of *The Avengers*, but also survey the universe more broadly. By examining a key film from the MCU's network, I illuminate the ways in which an individual MCU film's intertextual strategies shape its meanings and inform viewers' understanding of the wider universe.

In adapting the shared universe model from comic books, the MCU builds on the modes of intertextuality practiced by preceding superhero blockbusters. Felix Brinker (2017, 208–9) identifies three key modes of textual interaction in the MCU: (multi-)linear serial storytelling, in which various film series unfold linearly while intersecting; transmedial serialization, in which series from other media also share the diegesis; and rebooting, remaking, and adapting, in which MCU texts maintain dialogue with texts set in other iterations of the universe. The first two modes create complex networks of textual connections within the MCU's diegesis, as texts from various series and media contribute events to a shared timeline. This textual configuration expands the serialization of narrative continuity found in film series like the *Spider-Man* trilogy. Audiences are encouraged to not just track characters and plots through past and present texts in a single series but to read across multiple series and media that exist in linear and parallel relations. Brinker's third mode indicates the vast array of texts set in other versions of the Marvel universe with which the MCU interacts in the networked model of adaptation explored in previous chapters. These other versions of the universe exist in tens of thousands of comics alongside iterations of Marvel franchises in other media. Each of these universes has its own timeline, and together they form a multiverse. The Marvel multiverse is a governing system, acknowledged and documented by both the publisher and fans, that encompasses all of Marvel's universes (see Proctor 2017). As with texts and incarnations within the textual network that comprises a superhero franchise, particular universes within the multiverse can gain prominence and wield great influence over the multiverse as a whole; Burke demonstrates that the MCU has gained such power in the Marvel multiverse, evident in how "the reorganization of the Marvel comic book universe since the emergence of the MCU has seen characters that appear in Marvel Studios productions emphasized over established comic heroes" (2018, 36).

In exploring the adaptive practices of the MCU, this chapter necessarily expands my focus from superhero franchises to universes in which superheroes from multiple franchises interact. This exploration requires attention to three interrelated kinds of adaptation in MCU texts: their ongoing dialogue with other Marvel texts, their adaptation of the shared universe model from comic books, and their metamorphosis of stylistic strategies that superhero comic books use to help manage fictional universes.

The chapter begins by identifying narrative and stylistic strategies developed in superhero comic books to manage vast networks of texts that share a fictional universe. I then map the organization of the MCU's textual network. This entails surveying MCU texts in media and formats other than the feature films, alongside merchandise and tie-ins, and considering the extent to which these contributions to the universe may impact interpretation of the films. The remainder of the chapter examines strategies through which MCU feature films manage the universe. I outline *The Avengers*' adaptation of comic book strategies of universe management and analyze how the resulting interactions with other texts shape the film's sociopolitical meanings. The audience does not need to be aware of the specific ways that comic book strategies are being adapted to comprehend the film's meanings, but knowledge of these practices grants understanding of how the meanings are formed and given force. I conclude by exploring the MCU's development after *The Avengers*, considering a range of texts but providing more detailed analysis of *Captain Marvel* and *Avengers: Endgame*. Finishing with this wider survey facilitates reflection on whether the sociopolitical values that underpin the universe have changed as it expands.

THE COMIC BOOK SHARED UNIVERSE

Understanding the strategies used to manage comic books' shared universes, some significant narrative formations in which these strategies occur, and key tropes through which they manifest provides a vital foundation for exploring the ways in which Marvel Studios adapts this shared universe model to cinema. In the 2017 edited collection *Make Ours Marvel*, essays by Mark Minett and Bradley Schauer, Brinker, and William Proctor represent distinct efforts to examine Marvel's narrative models. Each essay focuses on a different dimension of textual activity: Minett and Schauer's on the specific comic book narrative formation the "all-star team book" (i.e., ongoing series featuring teams comprised of superheroes who are already popular from solo adventures), Brinker's on the MCU's intertextual modes, and Proctor's on the Marvel multiverse. These essays elucidate significant strategies that are deployed to manage Marvel's textual networks. Minett and Schauer (56–62) analyze how all-star team books simplify and reiterate, rather than develop, characters' traits as part of their effort to manage multiple characters while not impacting the arcs they are undergoing in their solo titles. I will refer to such strategies as *compression*. A significant quality that Brinker illuminates is the "hierarchization of series and installments" (217). Organizing texts into *hierarchies* helps make the fictional universe accessible while complementing the process observed in previous chapters in which texts within individual superhero franchises jostle for centrality. Proctor (326–28) emphasizes the maintenance of causal, spatial, and temporal *continuity* across the textual network and how contradictions between different versions of a character are made sense of through the governing multiverse structure. Strategies of compression, hierarchization, and continuity maintenance manifest narratively and stylistically in superhero comic books and seek to make sprawling fictional worlds comprehensible. As nexuses for comic book universes, the narrative formations of the all-star team book and crossover event are prime sites where intersections between these strategies can be mapped.

The trope of the superhero versus superhero battle illustrates this point. Although DC established the narrative formation of the all-star team with the Justice Society of America, first appearing in *All-Star Comics* #3 (December 1940), Minett and Schauer (51–52) find that the superhero versus superhero battle, now commonplace in all-star team books and crossover events, originated in Marvel's 1960s comics. As outlined in the previous chapter, in this period Marvel debuted anxiety-ridden superheroes, whose personal torments were central narrative concerns. Martin Flanagan, Mike McKenny, and Andy Livingstone (2016, 119–20) explain that team comics provide new ways of aggravating the Marvel superhero's personal anxieties, while compounding a superhero's problems by forcing them into fraught interpersonal relationships with other insecurity-ridden superheroes. When Marvel characters meet one another, their internal conflicts are transmuted into interpersonal mistrust that often erupts in physical fights. The superhero versus superhero battle both offers fans the pleasure of seeing how different superheroes compare and forms an intersection between strategies of universe management. Richard Reynolds (1994, 40–41) discusses fans' inclination to map superheroes' relative strengths and weaknesses as "hierarchical continuity," in which fans collate their knowledge of various battles to position superheroes on a hierarchy based on power. This practice reveals that hierarchization in superhero universes takes forms beyond the organization of texts, such as the ordering of superheroes in relation to one another to help maintain continuity between characters. The transmutation of superheroes' personal anxiety to interpersonal tension also engenders compression of the former, as demonstrated in the formation of the all-star team in *The Avengers* #1 (September 1963). The story sees supervillain Loki tricking superheroes Thor, Iron Man, Wasp, and Ant-Man into fighting Hulk. While previous Hulk comic books explored Bruce Banner's struggles to repress his destructive alter-ego, Hulk, the struggle in *The Avengers* #1 becomes a physical battle between multiple combatants. Once Loki's ruse is exposed, the other superheroes work with Hulk to defeat Loki. By foregrounding the team's dynamic over Bruce/Hulk's psychological torment, this comic compresses ideas from solo titles.

The Avengers assemble to fight Loki on the cover of *The Avengers* #1 (1963).

All-star team books and crossover events also arrange a textual hierarchy. Morrison observes that DC's team the Justice League of America "had been assembled in 1960 to feature all of DC's best and most popular superheroes in epic battles against foes that no single superhero, not even Superman, could hope to face alone" (2011, 290). In promising more spectacular battles and fearsome adversaries, all-star team books situate themselves as superior to solo titles.

The covers of all-star team comics often announce this superiority. These do not possess the singular iconic pull of covers for superheroes debuting in solo titles, such as those for *Action Comics* #1 and *Amazing Fantasy* #15, which direct our attention to Superman and Spider-Man respectively by positioning the superheroes centrally. All-star team comics (and team comics more generally) frequently deploy more chaotic compositions, somewhat inevitably through the need, at least on a team's debut, to depict the whole team, while villains can gain central positions. On the cover of *The Brave and the Bold* #28 (March 1960), in which the Justice League of America debuted, each member of the team is engaged with a different arm of giant-starfish villain Starro, who dominates the page. The arms act as spokes of a wheel that whirl the reader's gaze around from one superhero to another. This dynamic composition expresses the intensity of battle against a colossal foe, foregrounding the promise of enhanced spectacle. The cover for *The Avengers* #1 shows the team, poised for battle, approaching Loki. Although in terms of stature Loki does not dwarf the superheroes, the image is presented from over his shoulder, placing him in the foreground and making him the largest figure, suggesting that the team face a threat bigger than their individual selves. As with *Amazing Fantasy* #15, the cover is also populated by speech balloons and captions that vie for reader attention. The competing pictorial and worded elements enhance the sense of adventure and peril that pushes the boundaries of what an individual comic can comfortably contain. A banner above the image affirms the comic's superior status by introducing the worded identifier "Earth's Mightiest Super-Heroes."

By contrast, the crossover event's strategies of textual hierarchy arrangement are more deeply ingrained into processes of universe management. Wright (2001, 278) identifies *Marvel Super Heroes Secret Wars* (May 1984–April 1985) as the first crossover event, the commercial success of which led to crossover events becoming regular features for both Marvel and DC. A crossover event concerns a story of such magnitude that it encompasses superheroes from across the universe or multiverse. Superheroes are either united against a common enemy, as in DC's *Crisis on Infinite Earths* (April 1985–March 1986), or divided into warring teams, as in Marvel's *Civil War* (July 2006–January 2007). The main storyline is told in a limited series. Supporting limited series and characters' ongoing series can tell other story threads. The main limited series is hierarchically positioned above the secondary limited series and ongoing series, which are supplementary but

A battle across the multiverse spans the front and back covers of *Crisis on Infinite Earths* # 1 (1985).

promise a richer experience. Crossover events' position of primacy in their textual network is harnessed to coordinate continuity. Crossover events trigger pivotal shifts in their universes or multiverses and often perform continuity maintenance. For example, the outcome of *Crisis on Infinite Earths* was the consolidation of DC's multiverse—a more tightly managed diegetic construct in contrast to Marvel's governing system—into a single universe.

As a prerequisite for such wide-reaching continuity maintenance, crossover events' main series compress the universe or multiverse into a single title while concurrently showcasing its breadth. The ontology of comic book imagery facilitates this dichotomous effort to contain and illuminate a broad fictional construct. Martyn Pedler (2009, 259) analyzes covers of crossover events' main series to demonstrate that comics' static artwork enables readers to scan detailed images. In being granted visual mastery over complex compositions, the comics reader gains mastery over the universes or multiverses that they represent. Yet rather than promising an omnipotent perspective, these covers tend to acknowledge limitation. For example, the "wraparound" cover of *Crisis on Infinite Earths* # 1 (April 1985) uses physical page space to represent narrative scope. A battle across the multiverse spans the front and back covers. Some characters and design elements from the front cover spread beyond its left edge. It is only when the comic is opened that the full composition is viewable. Even with the battle spread over the two covers, however, some image elements are cut off by the covers' edges. The unfolding covers represent the expansiveness of DC's multiverse, suggesting that the pages they encase explore this grand fictional construct and simultaneously indicating that a single comic cannot hope to contain the sprawling multiverse.

Team comics and crossover events employ a range of strategies that interlink compression, hierarchy formation, and continuity maintenance to make their expansive fictional universes and multiverses cohesive and manageable. These strategies can affect the meanings associated with characters, particularly when the characters are taken out of solo stories and placed in ensemble narratives. While the logics that govern these strategies could be applied to any media, some of the stylistic tropes though which they textually manifest harness comics form. As my subsequent analysis demonstrates, key principles underlying the hierarchical organization of comic book universes are reproduced in the MCU, while narrative and stylistic strategies that enact compression and map character hierarchies are adapted in MCU feature films.

THE MARVEL CINEMATIC UNIVERSE'S TEXTUAL HIERARCHY

Within the MCU's transmedial diegetic network, a media and textual hierarchy is maintained. While hierarchization is prominent in superhero comic books, it is also commonplace in other fictional universes and media franchises, manifesting in the interrelated practices of creators, industrial agents, and fans.[2] These hierarchies determine the degree to which particular texts can shape the diegesis and guide audience interpretation. Examining the discursive positioning, narrative scope, and stylistic strategies of MCU texts, merchandise, and licensed tie-ins enables one to map the extent to which these contributions to the universe can affect the universe's meanings.[3]

Despite the MCU being transmedial, the branding Marvel *Cinematic* Universe situates cinema as the universe's primary media. Feature films sit atop the MCU's textual hierarchy, functioning as "motherships," "an industrial buzzword to indicate the primary text that a transmedia story is built around" (Scott 2013, 46). Within this group of motherships, all-star ensemble films lead the whole fleet of texts, functioning comparably to comic book crossover events. The MCU is organized into phases, the first three of which are demarcated by all-star ensemble films that culminate, develop, or instigate story lines that ripple through the universe. In closing phase one of the MCU, *The Avengers* completes the opening phase's efforts to assemble the eponymous team and introduces supervillain Thanos (Damion Poitier; Josh

Brolin in subsequent films) in a brief mid-credit scene. Phase two's penultimate film *Avengers: Age of Ultron* (Joss Whedon 2015) fractures the team, a process phase three opener *Captain America: Civil War* (Anthony Russo and Joseph Russo 2016) intensifies by dividing most of the universe's superheroes across an ideological schism. Phase three has a two-pronged climax, *Avengers: Infinity War* (Anthony Russo and Joseph Russo 2018) and *Endgame*, which brings Thanos's plan to fruition. While the films released between these all-star ensemble films can develop central characters and build plotlines toward the universe-shaking events, other MCU texts are more restricted. For if feature films are the MCU's central texts, it is useful to think of the other entries to the network as their intertexts and paratexts. Jonathan Gray (2010) outlines how media intertexts and paratexts shape the meanings of the texts with which they interact. The range of forms that intertexts and paratexts take affects the nature of their textual interaction. Gray demonstrates that intertexts and paratexts can be "narrative extensions [that] render the story-world a more immersive environment" (2) or can provide frames and filters for the story world. The MCU feature films' intertexts in other media and formats are narrative extensions that can reframe understanding of the films while paratextual merchandise and tie-ins purely provide frames and filters.

The MCU's most prominent narrative extensions include comics, short films, and television shows. The television shows divide into two categories with distinct industrial frameworks that affect their placement in the MCU's textual hierarchy: shows produced by Marvel Television (a separate division from Marvel Studios) in collaboration with other companies and shows produced by Marvel Studios for streaming platform Disney+. The former stopped production as phase three ended and shortly before the latter started being released, consolidating Disney's efforts to make Disney+ the hub for MCU films and television.[4]

The characters and plots focused on in narrative extensions released prior to the launch of Disney+ can be separated into two groups: those that are secondary within the feature films and those that are not included in the films. Comics miniseries *The Avengers Prelude: Fury's Big Week* (April 2012–June 2012), network television series *Agents of S.H.I.E.L.D.* (ABC 2013–2020), short film *Marvel One-Shot: Agent Carter* (Louis D'Esposito 2013), and its follow-up network television series *Agent Carter* (ABC 2015–2016) are examples of the former. *Fury's Big Week* situates the narratives of certain films preceding *The Avengers* within the same week to enhance audience understanding of the universe's temporal continuity and fleshes out supporting characters from the films. Its main character is Nick Fury, a figure connecting the phase one films by orchestrating the Avengers' formation and played by star Samuel L. Jackson yet receiving little character development on screen. *Agents of S.H.I.E.L.D.* and *Agent Carter* take secondary characters that the films have largely finished with and develop them as protagonists. Thematically, these narrative extensions each continue to interrogate machinations of S.H.I.E.L.D.—the Strategic Homeland Intervention, Enforcement, and Logistics Division—that are central to *The Avengers*. The creative potential of these intertexts thus strongly parallels the role of secondary series in comic book crossover events, complementing hierarchically superior texts without affecting their central plots.

While narrative extensions that foreground secondary characters from the feature films build around the films' peripheries, those featuring unique characters claim their own spaces. *Runaways* (Hulu 2017–2019) is set in Los Angeles while *Cloak & Dagger* (Freeform 2018–2019) relocates its eponymous duo from their typical comic book territory of New York to New Orleans, these shows giving their superpowered teenagers cities unoccupied by other MCU superheroes. The Marvel Television series produced for Netflix—namely *Daredevil* (2015–2018), *Jessica Jones* (2015–2019), *Luke Cage* (2016–2018), *Iron Fist* (2017–2018), *The Defenders* (2017), and *The Punisher* (2017–2019)—are commonly concerned with personal threats and fights for control of specific areas within New York. This localized focus is distinct from the typically world-threatening events in feature films. These shows' opening title sequences demarcate their geographic or conceptual space, much like how comic book covers can signify scope. The opening titles of *Luke Cage* map the streets of Harlem onto the titular hero's body, enforcing the core bond between neighborhood and character. *The Punisher* opens with abstracted imagery of guns eventually forming the antihero's skull iconography, claiming guns and accompanying discourses as the show's unique conceptual space.

The physical and conceptual spaces that the Netflix shows claim intersect directly with one another but only indirectly with the feature films. Through this, they reframe interpretation of the MCU in distinct ways. In their series, the Netflix shows' characters never meet the films' characters but frequently interact with one another. Such interactions are rationalized by a shared geographical quality; while the Avengers fly through New York's skies, the Netflix superheroes operate at ground level. They are also grounded in a metaphorical sense, the shows offering franker presentations of superpowered violence than the family-friendly feature films. This "revisionary" take on the superhero genre offers an implicit critique of representations of violence elsewhere in the MCU. The forms of distance the Netflix shows cultivate from the feature films facilitate indirect critical commentary, although this distance risks the critical ideas being compartmentalized separately from the films' meanings.

In line with the production of MCU television shows joining that of the films at Marvel Studios and the corresponding industrial centralization of the MCU on Disney+, MCU television shows produced for Disney+ have much closer proximity to the feature films. This centralization exemplifies Schatz's argument that Hollywood studios' strategies of conglomeration entered a new era of stability in the twenty-first century and "key to the conglomerates' hegemony and their financial welfare in the early 2000s has been the strategic integration of their film and TV operations in the US" (2009, 21). Schatz was writing on the state of Hollywood in 2007, on the brink of streaming platforms coming to prominence (Netflix launched its streaming platform in 2007) and one year before the MCU began. Steaming platforms have intensified this integration of media conglomerates' film and television operations. After The Walt Disney Company acquired Marvel in 2009, the creation of Disney+ provided the conglomerate a hub for distributing and managing the Marvel characters' screen incarnations. Some very pronounced forms of managing the MCU's textual hierarchy have already manifested on Disney+. For example, in 2021 *Agents of S.H.I.E.L.D.* and *Agent Carter* started being listed in the category "Marvel Legacy Movies and Series" in certain territories (Barnhardt 2021), suggesting a downgrading of their status in the universe. Two years later, *Runaways* became the first MCU show to be removed from Disney+ (Gribbin 2023), thereby disconnecting it from the hub. These strategies that push shows produced by Marvel Television in collaboration with other companies down the MCU's textual hierarchy correspondingly affirm the higher status of the shows produced in the more integrated model by Marvel Studios for distribution on Disney+.

The closer proximity between the MCU shows produced for Disney+ and feature films manifests textually in more reciprocal relations. A newfound interplay between MCU television shows and films is evident in how, while the characters from the Netflix shows did not appear in the films, Marvel Studios' decision to grant Netflix's incarnation of Daredevil (Charlie Cox) a Disney+ show was signaled by the superhero's civilian identity Matt Murdock appearing briefly in blockbuster *Spider-Man: No Way Home*.[5] Meanwhile, characters in the films have acknowledged events from Disney+ shows, with *Doctor Strange and the Multiverse of Madness* (Sam Raimi 2022) referring to Wanda Maximoff/Scarlet Witch's (Elizabeth Olsen) actions in *WandaVision* (2021). The Disney+ shows also extend the narratives of much higher-tier film characters than the earlier network television shows, such as Avengers Scarlet Witch and Clint Barton/Hawkeye (Jeremy Renner) in *WandaVision* and *Hawkeye* (2021), respectively. Crucially, however, these are not the top-tier Avengers who have previously headlined solo films.[6] Yet other Disney+

shows introduce characters who then make the transition into films, such as *Ms. Marvel*'s (2022) eponymous hero (Iman Vellani) going on to team up with Carol Danvers/Captain Marvel (Brie Larson) in *The Marvels* (Nia DaCosta 2023) and *Loki* (2021–2023) introducing one timeline's version of supervillain Kang the Conqueror (Jonathan Majors), other versions of whom subsequently feature in *Ant-Man and the Wasp: Quantumania* (Peyton Reed 2023) and who was planned to be the villain of the next Avengers films.[7] The Disney+ shows are thus comparable to earlier MCU television shows in their focus on characters' personal development but unlike the earlier shows can contribute to the setup of seismic events that will occur in blockbuster films.

The Disney+ shows' negotiation of the televisual and cinematic in their longer form explorations of characters that respond to and feed into blockbuster films participates in broader contemporary discourse about the extent to which streaming platforms are breaking down traditional boundaries between television and cinema (see Comerford 2023). This negotiation is pointedly evident in *She-Hulk: Attorney at Law* (2022), which embraces the episodic televisual structure of the "case of the week" courtroom drama while bringing in characters from both MCU television shows and films, including A-List Avenger Hulk (Mark Ruffalo) for a few episodes. In its season one finale, *She-Hulk* uses its superhero lawyer's proclivity for breaking the fourth wall to reflect on the proximity of MCU television shows and films on Disney+. When Jennifer Walters/She-Hulk (Tatiana Maslany) begins to protest about the narrative descending into a superpowered punch up the on-screen action is suddenly replaced by the Marvel Studios menu on the Disney+ interface, as if the conglomerate is silencing her. She-Hulk proceeds to punch her way out of her show's block, clamber down the interface and enter the block for *Marvel Studios: Assembled* (2021), a documentary series about the production of MCU texts. In this "real" world, She-Hulk confronts K.E.V.I.N. (Knowledge Enhanced Visual Interconnectivity Nexus, voiced by Brian T. Delaney), an AI parody of President of Marvel Studios Kevin Feige. She petitions for an ending focused on character development rather than formulaic superhero spectacle. The closer proximity of *She-Hulk* to the MCU films thus facilitates more direct critique of their use of violent spectacle than the Netflix shows. Yet this self-reflexive critique is also complicit in its upholding of the MCU's governing structures. She-Hulk exiting and entering texts via the Disney+ interface enforces the platform's status as the MCU's hub. Furthermore, She-Hulk's mocking of the films' conventions ultimately maintains a distinction that aligns the televisual with character development and the cinematic with action spectacle. The shifting interplay between MCU television and film on Disney+ is reflected on only to uphold divisions.

She-Hulk punches her way out of her show's Disney+ block in *She-Hulk: Attorney at Law* (2022).

Elsewhere, MCU merchandise and licensed tie-ins forge direct links with the films through the construction of narrow filters. The vast majority of T-shirts and action figures representing Marvel superheroes feature the characters in their superhero, rather than civilian, identities. Hulk T-shirts present the green goliath in poses that accentuate his musculature. This filters out the character's psychological torment to define him by physical strength, thus compressing Hulk in more limiting ways than team narratives. Meanings are compressed along different lines in tie-in promotions that depict the whole team. Tie-in promotions accompanying *The Avengers'* theatrical release elided the film's interpersonal conflicts between superheroes. For example, in a cross-promotion appearing across Marvel comics in the months surrounding *The Avengers'* release, an image of the film's team marching forward accompanies an offer whereby members of Wyndham Hotels' rewards scheme can get free film tickets and a comic book.[8] This advertisement suggests that the camaraderie ascribed to the Avengers is enjoyed by Wyndham's loyal customers. This condensed understanding of the Avengers team must strain against central narrative texts that foreground discord between superheroes.

The above analysis outlines the varying ways in which the intertexts and paratexts that occupy the levels below the feature films on the MCU's textual hierarchy can or cannot shape audience interpretation of the films. Narrative extensions that explore the films' peripheries typically complement their meanings, while those that cultivate spatial and conceptual distance pose more challenges. Factors such as changes to the MCU's industrial management and distribution can contribute to shifts in the textual hierarchy while also enforcing established divisions. The filters provided by merchandise and tie-ins amplify certain ideas at the expense of others. Whatever meanings these intertexts and paratexts offer exist in relation to the films. The films manage the interpretative frameworks that their textual network offers by choosing which texts from this network to acknowledge. In this sense the films can actively encourage or discourage audiences from adopting the frameworks offered by intertexts and paratexts.

COMPRESSION IN *THE AVENGERS*

Compression in superhero universes is performed through various strategies, in both central texts and paratexts, that affect characters' meanings. To encompass the universe, the MCU's all-star ensemble films compress characters along similar lines to all-star team and crossover comics. True to the Marvel archetype, each MCU superhero contends with personal anxieties in their solo films. For example, in *Iron Man* (Jon Favreau 2008), Tony Stark/Iron Man struggles to reconcile his roles as weapons manufacturer and peace-seeking superhero, while in *Thor* (Kenneth Branagh 2011), the eponymous god (Chris Hemsworth) has his machismo tempered and learns to connect with nonsuperpowered humans on Earth when his divine powers are revoked. The often-conflicting positions each superhero negotiates on their spectrum of possible roles form the core of their collection of identifiable associations. This collection, which I refer to as a character's *associative framework*, comprises a range of elements that contribute to and express characterization. Solo films explore characters' associative frameworks in more depth, whereas all-star ensemble films select and compress elements. These approaches can reinforce or reconfigure the ideas a character represents.

By developing the above analysis of *Iron Man* and *Thor*, I will demonstrate how settings and genre conventions provide important interlocking elements in a character's associative framework. Situating its protagonist's ideological dilemma in the context of the "war on terror," *Iron Man* juxtaposes spaces of corporate America with deserts in Afghanistan and incorporates cinematography that emulates modern war films, such as handheld camerawork and fast zooms, into its action scenes. *Thor* introduces Asgard to the MCU, contextualizing this mythical realm by deploying fantasy tropes. To that end, the film opens on Thor's royal inauguration and showcases the gleaming grandeur of Asgard's decor. Gliding shots surveying vast crowds and triumphant music complement the thunder god's egotism. Once he is banished to

Earth, then, the humbler interiors of a small town in New Mexico facilitate fish-out-of-water comedy that teases out Thor's humility.

The settings and genre conventions present in a character's associative framework distinguish that character, but Marvel Studios' approach to genre is also a means through which characters intersect, thus maintaining both variety and continuity across the universe. Each MCU film blends distinct genre conventions with governing superhero formulas. Flanagan, McKenny, and Livingstone formulate the notion of a "genre fractal," defined as "a miniaturized replica, a repeat of the pattern in a scaled-down form" (2016, 88), to conceptualize the relation between these distinct qualities and encompassing conventions. In the MCU, fractal versions of other genres are placed within the superhero architecture of each film.[9] This strategy gives each film its own identity within a unifying structure. I would add, however, that characters and films can also be linked via the very elements that distinguish them. The *Iron Man* series bridges modern warfare and science fiction, its fictional technologies advancing contemporary military achievements in biomechanics and drone warfare. Meanwhile, *Thor* rationalizes its fantastical elements by suggesting Norse gods are aliens and thematizes the permeability of magic and science. The inter-series meeting point between modern warfare and fantasy, arranged by steering both toward science fiction, is underscored in *Thor* when a S.H.I.E.L.D. agent wonders if metallic Asgardian adversary the Destroyer is a suit of Iron Man armor. While, as observed in chapter one, *Superman: The Movie* exploits points of exchange between genres to illuminate the compatibility of Clark/Superman's different traits, the MCU harnesses points of intersection between characters' associative frameworks to draw together its universe.

Sociopolitical ideas are also woven into a character's associative framework. A Marvel superhero's personal struggle complements the negotiation of these ideas, which is performed in individual texts and dialogic interactions between texts. These negotiations can produce equivocal results, as illustrated by a brief survey of Captain America's and Iron Man's solo films. It is important to elucidate the values attributed to these characters since they are central to *The Avengers*' thematic development.

Set during World War II, Marvel Studios' *Captain America: The First Avenger* (Joe Johnston 2011) constructs a nostalgic vision of the war in which "an idealised America is set off against a sanitised Nazi party" (Vu 2016, 126). Terence McSweeney situates this representation firmly in line with that seen in many other Hollywood films, "which have dramatised World War II as it would like to be remembered by American culture at large rather than, in any meaningful sense, how it actually was" (2018, 100). Similarly to the *Spider-Man* trilogy, *The First Avenger*'s nostalgic sensibilities are complicit in perpetuating constructions of an idealized past. As demonstrated in my analysis the *Spider-Man* trilogy, however, the nostalgic tendencies of superhero texts can also perform reflective critical functions. This kind of critical reflection forms a key component of many Captain America texts. Johnson (2013, 153–96) explores how media franchises transform across space and time, as corporate owners pass them between different national sites of production and creative agents, while maintaining dialogue with their pasts. Superhero franchises generally rely on US cultural references, but their perspectives on national contexts shift. Initially created to stimulate the US war effort in World War II, Steve Rogers/Captain America later adopted a peculiar temporal relationship to this historical context. In *The Avengers* #4 (March 1964), the all-star team discovers that Captain America was frozen in ice at the end of World War II and thaws him out. Captain America's subsequent status as emblem of the US military past transposed to the present has frequently been used in Captain America texts to critique the nation's historical and contemporary wartime politics.[10]

The First Avenger's naïve patriotism is somewhat counteracted in scenes that parodically reflect on Captain America's earlier use as propaganda. In one vibrant sequence, Captain America (Chris Evans), sporting a costume modeled on his 1940s comic book incarnation, promotes war bonds on the home front and performs for troops in United Service Organizations shows. His media history is further mapped in shots of children and soldiers reading *Captain America Comics*; Captain America starring in a film; and a stage show recreating the iconic cover of *Captain America Comics* #1 (March 1941), on which he punches Adolf Hitler. On the actual comic book cover, Captain America strikes a diegetic incarnation of Hitler, but in the film his adversary is a stage actor playing Hitler and positioned before a backdrop of gasping chorus girls dressed in US flag-themed outfits. The gaudy artifice, which exemplifies the sequence's tone, ascribes these qualities to the comic book cover to critique the use of superheroes to promote jingoism. However, this sequence can also be interpreted as affectionately tracing Captain America's media history and—as Flanagan, McKenny, and Livingstone (2016, 104) argue—mocking a bureaucratic military system that prioritizes public perception of the war over letting soldiers fight. The compatibility of Boym's concept of reflective nostalgia and Hutcheon's discussion of postmodern nostalgia as a form of complicitous critique, discussed in the previous chapter, highlights this sequence's critical function. The film parodies coarse US propaganda that simplifies World War II, on the one hand, while its strategies of misrepresentation and sanitization, comparable to those found in the original propaganda, celebrate the nobility of US soldiers, on the other.

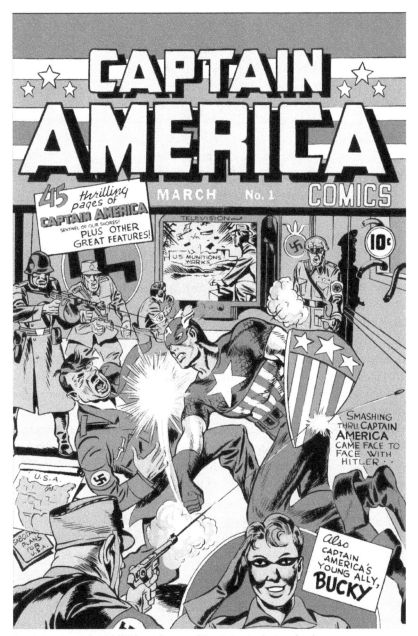

Captain America punches Adolf Hitler on the cover of *Captain America Comics* #1 (1941).

Captain America punches a stage actor playing Hitler in *Captain America: The First Avenger* (2011).

This process of reflectively problematizing past texts through parody, while simultaneously yearning for the past those texts represent, testifies to Hutcheon's (1989, 93–117) identification of postmodern parody as a key vehicle for complicitous critique. In her discussion of parody in postmodern film, Hutcheon identifies an "insider-outsider doubled position" (109) in which the films both continue and critique practices of the institutions in which they are made. We can think of Marvel and DC superhero blockbusters' insider position as twofold, as they are produced both inside the dominant US ideology and, within this system, inside their franchises and multiverses. Consequently, Marvel Studios texts can critically reflect on other texts from their franchises and the MCU but will always be corporately motivated to promote, and expected to exhibit forms of continuity with, these texts that are themselves rooted inside dominant US ideology. Instances of complicitous critique in Hollywood's superhero blockbusters are thus inflamed by their adaptive practices and modes of intertextuality.

While *The First Avenger* presents 1940s US military attitudes as at least transparent, even if the film is ambivalent about whether they need scrutinizing or commending, the *Iron Man* films explore the obfuscating entanglement of military and commercial interests in the twenty-first century. Tony's relation to the military-industrial complex, the nature of his capitalist enterprise, and the ways in which nationality factors into these issues shift across the series. The first two films feature Middle Eastern and Eastern European terrorists involved with US weapons manufacturers who pursue lucrative contracts with the US military. *Iron Man 3* (Shane Black 2013) reconfigures this relationship when its purportedly Asian terrorist, the Mandarin (Ben Kingsley), turns out to be a fictional figure constructed by an American businessman, implicitly suggesting that the stereotyped terrorists in the previous two films are themselves constructs of the US imaginary. The villainous businessmen provide counterpoints to Tony, refracting different elements of the entrepreneur who began the first film as the leading weapons supplier to the US military. Despite maintaining this dimension of corporate corruption, the films largely present Tony's personal brand of capitalism as righteous. The *Iron Man* films' serialized interrogation of the military-industrial complex thus treads a precarious path between critiquing and championing US power structures. In a different way than *The First Avenger*, the MCU's intertextual exchanges again elicit equivocal sociopolitical ideas.

Superhero team narratives endeavor to preserve characters' distinct qualities while consolidating links between characters. In *The Avengers* #1 each superhero is introduced in an environment familiar from the series in which they originated. They are then brought together in spaces with which none of them are associated. In subsequent issues, the Avengers adopt Tony's New York mansion as their headquarters. Marvel Studios' *The Avengers* follows a comparable trajectory, introducing each superhero in their own space before drawing them together in neutral environments and finally in New York. Interestingly, the characters' home environments are not locations that they inhabited in previous films. Rather, they are spaces that economically communicate a range of their respective superheroes' associations. Bruce is introduced in a Calcutta slum, a space that, like others to which he retreated in *The Incredible Hulk* (Louis Leterrier 2008), provides refuge from US authorities. Steve is first seen in a dilapidated boxing gym, evoking his background of combat in a bygone era. Tony's corporate and technological frameworks dovetail as—while wearing his Iron Man armor—he connects the energy source for his new Manhattan skyscraper, Stark Tower. Later in the film, Thor emerges from a thunderstorm that connotes his elemental powers.

When selected elements of characters' associative frameworks are foregrounded and compressed in *The Avengers*' character introductions, the accompanying sociopolitical ideas are also filtered. Steve's and Tony's introductions delineate distinct values for each man. Flashbacks to Captain America's noble wartime deeds associate him with camaraderie, bravery, and duty while the gym's obsolescence suggests that these values are now outmoded. As Steve pounds a punching bag, these values are transposed into the isolated former champion's body. While Steve is secreted in the gym, Tony's enterprise suffuses the heart of commercial America. Tony's values of socially conscious if egocentric capitalism pursued through technological ingenuity are celebrated in Stark Tower, which is illuminated by renewable energy and adorned with his surname in huge glowing letters. Even after Tony removes his Iron Man armor, the capitalist aspirations of Manhattan's glittering cityscape and Tony's technologies remain inscribed on his body via the glowing energy source built into his chest. These introductions select primarily positive values to compress into the men's bodies. The parodic elements of *The First Avenger* and concerns over Iron Man's implication with the military-industrial complex are omitted.

To further elucidate how the compression of associative frameworks contributes to the film's sociopolitical meanings, it is useful to examine characters who are more marginalized in the MCU. For the team's cinematic debut, Natasha Romanoff/Black Widow (Scarlett Johansson) is the only female Avenger and, alongside Hawkeye, one of only two team members to have not previously headlined a solo film. Her introduction in *The Avengers* negotiates this low status. Natasha is assigned a discrete space, a warehouse in her native Russia, and appropriate spy genre codification, as the secret agent is being held captive by a man in military uniform and two henchmen. Wearing a short black dress and tights, she is tied to a chair, arms bound behind her so that her back is slightly arched and chest thrust forward. This presentation recalls the frequent objectification of female characters in comic book art (see Cocca 2014). Natasha is thus situated as sexualized object. A cutaway shot to a mirror, partly concealed by haphazardly piled paintings and weapons, connotes duality, reminding the viewer of the strength Natasha is hiding. While the theme of deception is inherent to the spy genre, the use of an ornate framed mirror, an object associated with the maintenance of female beauty, to reflect Natasha's sexualized physique ascribes feminine exhibitions of surface beauty to her specific mode of deception. In the interaction between space, genre, and body, themes of espionage compound the cultural association of femininity with duplicity.

Natasha's facade shatters when she unleashes her concealed power. By her skillful use of the chair, the object of her performed immobilization, as a weapon, Black Widow's own objecthood is reconfigured as she nimbly dispatches her captors. Brown (2016, 54) applies Mary Ann Doane's discussion of femininity as masquerade when arguing that "by employing an exaggerated masquerade of femininity," Black Widow encourages men to underestimate her ability and sexualize her body, lowering their guard before she overpowers them. Brown is quick to note, however, that in doing so, she remains an object of the male gaze, defined by her sexuality to the extent that sexual manipulation becomes Black Widow's primary power. While the male superheroes' bodies are inscribed with their selfhood, Black Widow's body expresses her ongoing struggle between subjecthood and objecthood. The film is reflexive about her marginalized status, but her power, her contribution to the team, renders her complicit in her own marginalization. The general devaluing of female characters in the MCU and superhero genre is exacerbated in exclusory merchandising trends, including the "almost complete absence of superheroine toys" (55). Indeed, Joanna Robinson, Dave Gonzales, and Gavin Edwards outline how, for the toys produced based on Marvel Studios' *The Avengers*, "there were multiple sizes and types of action figures for each member of the team, except for Black Widow, who had a single four-inch figure" (2023, 181).[11] The filtering out of female characters in MCU merchandise reflects and reinforces their marginalization in the films.

Flanagan, McKenny, and Livingstone do not consider whether their notion of genre fractals can be applied to all-star ensemble films. The above analysis demonstrates that the opening act of *The Avengers* streamlines the practice of placing fractal versions of cinematic codes into an encompassing system. Characters' associative frameworks are compressed into single spaces and ultimately their bodies. The compression removes more ambiguous elements from certain characters' solo characterizations. As in Marvel comics, this process facilitates a shift of emphasis from personal torment to interpersonal tensions. Being attuned to how each character's simplified set of values is formed primes us to observe the ways in which these values are challenged and complicated as superheroes who embody different ideas interact with one another.

ASSEMBLING THE CHARACTER HIERARCHY

The all-star ensemble films that drive the MCU's overarching causal continuity feature altercations and fights between superheroes, borrowing this trait from superhero comic books to manage hierarchical continuity. As I have shown, the character introductions in *The Avengers* assign each superhero a unique identity loaded with sociopolitical ideas. The ways in which these are presented establish degrees of power and status. These ideas are subsequently infused into the hierarchy that develops out of characters' interactions and through which certain characters and traits are championed. Examining the character hierarchy provides a means to outline which values the film privileges and to interrogate its sociopolitical allegiances. The following analysis examines a selection of significant encounters between characters in *The Avengers*, ranging from physical clashes to battles of wit, to chart the emerging hierarchy.

The first physical battle negotiates the upper echelons of the character hierarchy. Iron Man, the exemplar of humanity's technological accomplishments, faces Norse god Thor, who possesses magical strength and commands storms with his hammer, Mjölnir. A forest provides the arena. In comic books,

Symmetrical image composition and panel layout present an evenly matched fight between Iron Man and Magneto in *AVX: Vs* #1 (2012).

balanced compositions and page layouts are common strategies for presenting superhero versus superhero battles. For example, a two-page spread from *AVX: Vs* #1 (June 2012), part of a limited series that showcased superhero versus superhero battles during the *Avengers vs. X-Men* (May 2012–December 2012) crossover event, features evenly laid out rows along the top and bottom thirds of the pages, while the fighting superheroes, Iron Man and Magneto, are granted equal space in the center. Symmetrical image composition and panel layout suggest the combatants' equivalence. The Iron Man versus Thor fight in *The Avengers* adapts this strategy. As the superheroes exchange blows, a back-and-forth editing rhythm enforces a sense of balance. Each superhero demonstrates advantages in certain areas while at other times using unique powers to the same effect. For example, Thor's hurled Mjölnir and Iron Man's repulsor-propelled kick each drive the other superhero through trees, exhibiting the weapons' distinct qualities but equal force. The balance created in comics through still images is metamorphosed into cinema through rhythmic editing and movements that reflect each other in their impact.

The presentation of Iron Man's and Thor's weapons underscores the characters' differences while mapping the intersection of their associative frameworks.

Thor's lighting charges Iron Man's Armor in *The Avengers* (2012).

The double page spread from *AVX: Vs* #1 and the Thor vs Iron Man scene from *The Avengers* connote the characters' associative frameworks through a visual device that originated in comics, which Burke identifies as "krackle": "The abstract colored shapes that convey a superpowered character's abilities" (2015, 219). Krackle can be used to represent powers that do not have tangible properties, such as Magneto's telekinetic manipulation of metal, which *AVX: Vs* #1 presents as purple irregular orbs. Thor and Iron Man's digitally rendered lightning bolts and repulsor beams are understood to have tangible forms within *The Avengers*' diegesis, yet their glowing colors and obtrusive presence function in a highly stylized, rather than perceptually realistic, mode. This trait supports Burke's claim that the deployment of krackle in film pointedly recreates the stylized modes of representation associated with comics. In *The Avengers*, Thor's white lightning bolts emanate luminous blue light and fire in jagged lines. These colors connote the cold Nordic environments in which Thor's mythology originated. They are contrasted by the warmth of Iron Man's streamlined orange beams. Products of his engineering, the beams projected from Iron Man's repulsors connote his extravagant wealth through recalling the color of the hot rod on which he based his exoskeleton's paintwork in Marvel Studios' *Iron Man*. The distinct appearances and conceptual connotations of these different kinds of krackle encapsulate aspects of the characters' associative frameworks. Concurrently, the color and shape of Thor's lightning indicates its electrical properties, creating an obvious link to Iron Man's technology. This link is made explicit when Thor fires a bolt at Iron Man that connects in a shower of sparks and supercharges the armor, enforcing the bridge between Thor's magical and Iron Man's technological frameworks that had its

Loki's reflection is positioned as Black Widow's in *The Avengers* (2012).

foundations laid in previous films. The striking colors and shapes of digital krackle in *The Avengers* forego strict perceptual realism to convey conceptual qualities of the powers they represent, which illuminate relations between characters.

The battle ends as a tie, effectively elevating Iron Man to the status of a god. The technologies that the entrepreneur has developed enable him to engage in evenly matched physical combat with Thor. This encounter grants both characters high hierarchical status while asserting Iron Man's superiority over other humans, continuing the valorization of his brand of capitalism.

When mapping the hierarchy's lower levels, it can be instructive to seek out parallels that are drawn between superheroes and supervillains. Thor's adopted brother, Loki (Tom Hiddleston), *The Avengers*' main antagonist, can transform and teleport his body, complementing his inclination for trickery. In this respect, his counterpart is master-of-deception Black Widow. In one scene, when Black Widow interrogates Loki, the two engage in a contest of psychological manipulation. Black Widow succeeds in getting Loki to unwittingly reveal his ploy, and Loki succeeds in igniting Black Widow's guilt over past misdeeds. As with Iron Man and Thor's fight, mirroring strategies connote an equal match. At one point Black Widow's and Loki's postures mimic each other: both perform composure by sitting with their hands in their laps, leaning forward slightly. The image that most encapsulates Black Widow and Loki's comparability, however, occurs as Loki approaches the glass door of his prison cell. Black Widow is shot to the right of the frame while the camera is situated inside the cell so that Loki's enraged reflection shows on the left. The earlier shot of a mirror in Black Widow's introduction

Hulk's hunched posture and long arms recall those of a gorilla in *The Avengers* (2012).

suggested that she was concealing her true nature; this reflection provides a clear representation of her psyche. While denoting that Loki has got into Black Widow's head, the shot also and more provocatively suggests that he was already there in the sense that he is positioned as *her* reflection.

Through this interaction and its contrast to Iron Man and Thor's battle, *The Avengers* refines the ways in which gender, physical ability, and nationality factor into the character hierarchy. Their equivalence places Black Widow and Loki, two non-American characters, at a comparable point on the hierarchy. (Loki is from the realm of Jotunheim but associated with Europe due to his heritage in Norse mythology and Hiddleston's British accent.) The malicious potential of Black Widow's abilities is underscored through association with Loki. If Black Widow's powers of deception are interlocked with her femininity, moreover, Loki's duplicity makes him a feminized man, the antithesis of Thor's muscular masculinity.[12] Ascribing feminized masculinity to the film's villain situates this quality even lower on the character hierarchy than Black Widow's femininity, in marked opposition to the spectacular heroics of Iron Man and Thor. Tellingly, when Iron Man and Thor battle, Loki spectates and schemes.

Encounters that pit opposed body types against each other also underscore the character hierarchy's governing principles. Bukatman discusses Hulk as exemplary of a type of superhero that bodily manifests "an aggressive hypermasculinity, a compensation for psycho-sexual anxiety that depends upon a ruthless suppression or . . . an obliteration of the feminine" (2003, 61). In *The Avengers*, digital imaging enables Hulk's hypermasculine musculature to be realized to inhuman proportions. Upon Bruce's first transformation into Hulk, he hunts his antithesis: Black Widow's feminine body. Hulk's roars, hunched posture, and long arms recall those of a gorilla. The juxtaposition of gorilla and slender feminine body recalls the horror-fantasy tradition of the King Kong franchise, beginning with Merian C. Cooper and Ernest B. Schoedsack's 1933 film. In Marvel Studios' *The Incredible Hulk* and *Age of Ultron*, female characters calm Hulk by arousing his affection, much like King Kong's female companions. As Hulk charges after Black Widow in *The Avengers*, however, the sexual connotations only signify the vulnerability of the feminine to the masculine. Once Hulk catches up with her, he swats Black Widow with one arm, propelling her into a wall. This casual swipe grants Hulk an effortless victory. Later in the film, Hulk gains a comparably easy victory over Loki, smashing the god repeatedly against the floor. Hulk's defeats of Black Widow and Loki assert the superiority of hypermasculine brawn over feminine duplicity.

The film's negotiation of Iron Man's and Captain America's values is given center stage. Robert Downey Jr.'s star persona augments the challenge that Tony poses to Steve and advances the film's celebration of the entrepreneur. Downey's star persona is underpinned by his widely publicized struggles with drug addiction and transitions from prosperous celebrity lifestyle to periods in rehabilitation and jail. These traits resemble Iron Man's comic book characterization, particularly the character's bouts with alcoholism and numerous losses of fortune. Downey's star persona and the Iron Man comics thus act as complementary intertextual forces informing the MCU's Iron Man. Dominic Lennard (2012, 25–31) explains that, even after years of sobriety, both the press and Downey's film roles perpetuate the troubled aspects of his persona. The cover of August 2008's *Rolling Stone*, released the same summer as Marvel Studios' *Iron Man*, exemplifies this tendency, presenting Downey as a troubled figure, stubble-ridden in a prison-orange hood under a headline reading "To Hell and Back with Robert Downey Jr." A fictional cover for *Rolling Stone* in Iron Man provides an interesting counterpart, showcasing Tony, confident and sharply dressed, with the headline "Tony Stark Wants to Save the World." These two covers trace a shared trajectory as they jointly proclaim that Iron Man primes both the fallen actor and "B-list Marvel star" (Morrison 2011, 378) to ascend to A-list status. In *The Avengers*, Tony boasts about his self-made success while branding Steve a "laboratory experiment," thus asserting superiority over a superhero whose powers were bestowed on him by an external force. Evans's celebrity status underscores the contrast of Tony and Steve. At the time of *The First Avenger*'s release, Evans was best known for his role as Johnny Storm/Human Torch in *Fantastic Four* (Tim Story 2005) and *Fantastic Four: Rise of the Silver Surfer*

Tony Stark exerts superiority as he stands opposite Steve Rogers in *The Avengers* (2012).

(Tim Story 2007). Downey is a star, known for his idiosyncratic persona; Evans is an actor, known for performing roles.

Steve's and Tony's values are directly pitted against each other in an altercation in a laboratory owned by S.H.I.E.L.D. Within the film, S.H.I.E.L.D. represents the US military-industrial complex. Steve's patriotism engenders unwavering trust in S.H.I.E.L.D., whereas Tony's individualism and previous experiences with corrupt military bodies stoke his suspicion of the agency. After revealing that he is running a decryption program on S.H.I.E.L.D.'s systems, a condescending Tony confronts Steve, maneuvering his invasion of S.H.I.E.L.D. into a direct affront to the soldier. Tony's Black Sabbath T-shirt denotes his love of heavy metal, an element of his associative framework that *Iron Man* director Favreau interlocks with Downey's persona, stating in a 2008 interview with *Superherohype* that the star "captures that bad boy attitude ... That's why we open with 'Back in Black' [by AC/DC]" (quoted in Lennard 2012, 28). Tony's attire pointedly contrasts with what he dubs Steve's "spangly outfit," a uniform that symbolizes Steve's devotion to the US military. Tony's suspicions of S.H.I.E.L.D. are later validated when it is revealed that they have been developing weapons of mass destruction for intergalactic war. Tony's brand of capitalism is thus presented as liberated and able to pose necessary challenges to the military-industrial complex, while Steve's staunch patriotism allows the military-industrial complex to operate unchecked.

The reconfiguration of elements from characters' associative frameworks that began in their introductions continues in their hostile interactions. This process outlines distinctions and links between characters while a hierarchy emerges that favors certain qualities. Strong masculinity is championed, but the two physically strongest characters, Thor and Hulk, are removed from the film's central thematic discourse because they do not represent the United States. (Bruce is pursued by US authorities and finds refuge in foreign territories.) The central clash between Captain America's and Iron Man's values positions nationality as a determining factor in the hierarchy. *The First Avenger*'s equivocal perspective on Steve's World War II mentality was initially repressed in *The Avengers*, but it returns in the presentation of him as naïve. Meanwhile, the celebration of Tony's entrepreneurialism is augmented. By granting the film's American characters privileged status, *The Avengers*' efforts to interweave the thematic concerns of the series that it draws together perform a critique of US military structures that remains complicit with US hegemony.

CONSOLIDATING THE UNIVERSE

The organization of the character hierarchy is finalized during *The Avengers*' climactic battle in Manhattan: a space central to the superhero genre that in this film, significantly, is Iron Man's home environment. By this point in the film, the characters' values have undergone processes of compression, unpacking, and reframing via intertextual strategies that draw on understandings of the characters from previous Marvel texts alongside understandings of stars and genre conventions. Examining the ways in which these values are arranged and interlaced in the finale's pivotal moments reveals the qualities and sociopolitical ideas that the hierarchy ultimately endorses.

The hierarchy's finalization occurs not despite but through the film's efforts to resolve tensions and unify the team. The moment when Bruce enters the final battle and demonstrates a substantial degree of agency over Hulk heralds the team's harmonization, entwining his personal development with the team's gelling. An invading alien race, the Chitauri, descend on humanity, and a colossal armored creature called a leviathan swims through the sky. Upon arriving at the battleground, Bruce morphs into Hulk and punches the leviathan, causing the creature's armor to scatter as its body crumples. Iron Man fires a missile at the leviathan's exposed flesh, blasting the monstrosity into pieces. The team's musical theme then rises triumphantly as the Avengers form a circle around which the camera rotates. Any sense of equality in this evocation of togetherness, however, is undermined by the preceding action. Hulk's brawn and Iron Man's technology defeated the leviathan. The hierarchy again favors physical strength and the American entrepreneur.

Marvel superheroes advance on alien invaders in *Secret Invasion* #6 (2008).

Another continuous take that weaves the superheroes together further illuminates how efforts to unite the team concurrently solidify the character hierarchy. The shot begins with Black Widow, having hijacked an alien aircraft, being overtaken by Iron Man. The camera follows the armored entrepreneur as he momentarily lands on the streets and fires a repulsor beam for Captain America to deflect toward Chitauri with his shield. This joint attack symbolizes the two superheroes' reconciliation. Iron Man then flies toward Hawkeye, who is perched on a roof. The camera is led by an arrow fired by Hawkeye to Hulk, who is joined by Thor on the back of another leviathan. This long take adapts a strategy that developed in team comics and crossover events in which splash pages depict the scale and participants of epic battles in detailed images. For example, a double splash page from *Secret Invasion* #6 (November 2008) features a mass of Marvel's superheroes advancing from the right of the page on alien invaders. The superheroes significantly encroach on their opponents' side of the page, forming an overwhelming force. Yet imbalance is also evident among the superheroes, as some of Marvel's most famous superheroes—including Captain America and Iron Man—occupy the center of the image. *The Avengers*' long take performs comparable functions to this splash page: emphasizing the battle's scope,

Captain America grows despondent and his super-strong skin gets wounded in *The Avengers* (2012).

presenting the team as a united force, and maintaining a character hierarchy. The means through which certain superheroes are privileged are, however, metamorphosed. In a comics panel, lead characters can be placed centrally and in the foreground. Cinema's capacity for camera and character movement allows characters to be favored through different spatial means, not to mention temporal ones. In the long take under analysis, each superhero occupies a certain kind of space—the street, a rooftop, or airborne—on the environment's vertical axis, except for Iron Man, who traverses ground and sky. Iron Man also features in the shot for longer than any other character, linking the first four Avengers in the relay. The roaming shot favors Iron Man, making him the needle that sews the team together.

This long take also develops the superhero blockbuster trope of following superheroes' aerial movements in long takes. Rather than following lone heroes and emphasizing their bond with their cities through complementary kinesis, as seen in *Superman: The Movie* and the *Spider-Man* trilogy, *The Avengers*' long take transitions between teammates, underscoring their relations with one another. Fluid kinesis creates the abstract feeling of utopia that Dyer identifies in musicals, while the team's navigation of streets and skies enacts Bukatman's conceptualization of movement as utopia, both outlined in chapter one. Within these expressions of utopia, Iron Man—the film's embodiment of corporate New York—becomes the force that unifies the team and integrates them into the city. Furthermore, Stark Tower's semi-destruction in this final battle initiates its transformation into Avengers Tower for future films. Tony's enterprise sustains a team of superheroes who can protect humanity and uphold urban utopia.

Captain America exhibits camaraderie throughout the battle but also strains in a post-9/11 world where terror can reign from Manhattan's sky. The soldier grows despondent, and his super-strong skin gets wounded. Yet his values triumphantly resurface in the battle's decisive moment. Earlier, Steve accused Tony of only fighting for himself and of not being "the guy to make the sacrifice play." At the battle's culmination, Iron Man performs exactly this kind of selfless act when carrying a nuclear missile, which S.H.I.E.L.D. launched to defeat the Chitauri at the expense of destroying Manhattan, into a portal leading to the Chitauri mothership. For McSweeney, this moment shows "a new generation of hero embodying the spirit of the 'Greatest Generation'" (2014, 131–32). By embodying Captain America's spirit, Iron Man assimilates it into his own values. This move ascribes camaraderie, courage, and self-sacrifice to Iron Man's entrepreneurial capitalism. Furthermore, these endangered values are revitalized by Iron Man's technology. The protective exoskeleton ensures that although Iron Man makes "the sacrifice play," he does survive, underscoring his transcendence to godlike status.

Combining the two sets of American values in Iron Man thwarts S.H.I.E.L.D.'s callous plan. However, this final critique of the military-industrial complex renders S.H.I.E.L.D.'s nuclear missile vital to the Avengers' victory, the missile resolutely defeating the Chitauri by destroying their mothership. Foregrounding Captain America's values causes the missile to raise an aspect of the US strategy in World War II that Captain America's associative framework represses: the atomic bombings of Hiroshima and Nagasaki. The combination of Captain America's and Iron Man's values correspondingly maps mentalities ingrained into the US World War II effort onto the post-9/11 United States. If Iron Man's technology revitalizes Captain America's values, the nuclear missile, another technology of war that has historically been deployed to protect these values, is implicated in this celebration. Extreme force is presented as a deplorable but necessary way to retain noble US values. The film's interrogation of the military-industrial complex enmeshes S.H.I.E.L.D.'s reprehensible tactics with the values championed by Captain America and Iron Man. *The Avengers'* endeavors to compress characters' associative frameworks and then unify them in a single gesture thus renders the gesture profoundly equivocal.

Although the strategies through which the MCU is managed in *The Avengers* engender meanings laced with contradiction, the character hierarchy that the film forms is remarkably secure. As I have shown, various criteria coalesce to situate Iron Man firmly at the top. He embodies Western progress; his technological accomplishments place him alongside gods and allow him to become Earth's savior; he reconciles past and present US values; and he is played by the film's biggest star. The only quality that the film favors for which Iron Man does not exhibit superiority is physical strength. His unarmored body is less muscular than Hulk's, Thor's, or Captain America's. Interestingly, Iron Man elevates himself over these characters through his posturing in a manner similar to Loki. Tony acknowledges this at one moment, when he realizes that Loki covets Stark Tower due to its ostentatious assertion of an individual's superiority. Identifying Iron Man's arrogance in Loki's villainy is the film's primary critique of Iron Man's entrepreneurialism. However, the scene in which Tony and Loki meet in Stark Tower just before the final battle, effectively as leaders of opposed forces, presents Tony's attitude as the more stable. The trickster god loses his composure upon being taunted by Tony and hurls the entrepreneur out of a window. Tony prepared for this, however, and is caught mid-fall by an upgraded Iron Man exoskeleton. In this moment, Loki's resort to physical violence is shown as a failing, whereas Tony's boastful provocations, technologies, and forward thinking enable his victory. Iron Man's godlike status is asserted not just through his possessing powers comparable to Thor's but also through his outwitting of Loki.

THE UNIVERSE'S CONTINUED EXPANSION IN THE "INFINITY SAGA"

The process observed in *The Avengers* through which meanings of previous texts are harnessed, reaffirmed, and reworked continues in subsequent MCU films. Each new film forges intertextual relations with other nodes in the textual network. Through strategies of compression and hierarchization adapted from comic books, the all-star ensemble films manage the universe's continuity, while other films and narrative extensions in other media expand and enrich the universe. These modes of narrative and stylistic intertextuality shape the meanings of individual films and the values that circulate the universe. Intertexts and paratexts that are not explicitly called upon in a film can still affect understanding of it, particularly in cases where they complement rather than challenge its meanings. The character hierarchy can be rearranged, and its governing criteria revised, as new characters are introduced, encounters between characters are staged, and events transpire. I now explore this process in phases two and three of the MCU, which together with the first phase form the "Infinity Saga," throughout which magical gems called infinity stones emerge and are ultimately wielded by Thanos in the infinity gauntlet. I survey a range of texts but provide more sustained analysis of *Captain Marvel*, the first MCU blockbuster to be headlined solely by a woman, and *Endgame*, which provides the saga's climax. Focusing on these two films enables me to examine whether a key tenet of the MCU's character hierarchy affirmed in *The Avengers*—its devaluing of the feminine—alters as the universe expands and consider the extent to which the hierarchy shifts by the saga's end.

In the solo films that immediately followed *The Avengers*, the central superheroes are decompressed. In *Iron Man 3*, Tony's self-assured demeanor is deconstructed through the deployment of conventions of buddy films. The various buddies Tony pairs up with outline deficiencies in his character. *Captain America: The Winter Soldier* (Anthony Russo and Joseph Russo 2014) poses new challenges to Captain America's patriotism when corruption is revealed at the core of S.H.I.E.L.D., effectively pitting the star-spangled hero against America's military-industrial complex. It emerges that S.H.I.E.L.D. has been infiltrated by HYDRA, a fascist organization with links to Nazism. The film casts a critical eye on the military-industrial complex, although HYDRA's involvement ultimately pins the blame on a foreign body. The layers of allegory that typify MCU feature films' critique of the military-industrial complex are stripped away in *The Punisher*, which undertakes a more direct examination of illicit tactics undertaken by the US government in the "war on terror." Although this approach implicitly critiques *The Winter Soldier*'s more cautious methods of interrogation, the show continues the film's championing of masculine brawn as vital to rebellion.

Phases two and three introduce the first female-led screen texts to the MCU. *Agent Carter* offers a feminist perspective on S.H.I.E.L.D.'s corruption. Set in the postwar 1940s, the show probes the historical roots of S.H.I.E.L.D.'s corruption alongside sexism within S.H.I.E.L.D., suggesting links between these issues. The show premiered in 2015, the same year as *Jessica Jones*, which offers a complementary discourse on rape culture in the present day. These Marvel Television shows provide potent critiques of the MCU's marginalization of the feminine. However, the shows' positioning as hierarchically inferior to the largely male-centric films applies a suppressive force to their meanings when read in relation to the wider MCU.

As a blockbuster film, *Captain Marvel* has the potential to intervene more directly in the MCU's underpinning structures. Since her 2012 comic book relaunch, Captain Marvel ascended the 616 comics universe's character hierarchy, as evident in crossover event *Civil War II* (July 2016–February 2017) centering on a disagreement between her and Iron Man. Captain Marvel was thus primed to climb the cinematic universe's ranks. Marvel Studios' *Captain Marvel* concerns its protagonist struggling against the oppression of patriarchal structures. At the start, unbeknownst to Carol, her memories of her past on Earth have been repressed by alien Yon-Rogg (Jude Law), commander of a military task force serving the Kree Empire. Upon being captured by Skrulls—another alien species—Talos (Ben Mendelsohn) sifts through Carol's lost memories. This sequence provides a powerful articulation of the different layers of patriarchy that have contained and controlled Carol: the memories show her experiencing sexism as a child and during her miliary training; it later becomes apparent that Yon-Rogg concealed these memories to manipulate her; and another man, Talos, is controlling the presentation of these memories, searching through them for his own needs. Through the course of the film, Carol fights through these layers of oppression to regain her memories and consequently her agency, in doing so becoming superhero Captain Marvel. Yet certain strategies limit her capacity to also dismantle the MCU's masculinized structures.

The film's 1995 temporal setting restricts its ability to directly critique other MCU texts. Jessica Taylor and Laura Glitsos situate *Captain Marvel* in "an emergent trend of solo, female-led superhero films" in which the films' "location in aesthetically distinct pasts . . . is a reflection of contemporary ambivalence towards feminism, wherein female empowerment is both championed and contained" (2023, 656). Situating the film's feminist themes in the past suggests that women's structural oppression does not exist in the present. This postfeminist move involves critiquing 1980s and 1990s popular culture, rather than MCU texts. Most pointedly, Carol arrives on Earth by crashlanding into a Blockbuster video rental store, upon which she mistakes a cardboard cutout promoting *True Lies* (James Cameron 1994) for an adversary and shoots a photon blast at it which decapitates Arnold Schwarzenegger, thereby symbolically retaliating against the film's sexism. Subsequently, she picks up a VHS of *The Right Stuff* (Philip Kaufman 1983), while elsewhere the film features numerous allusions to *Top Gun* (Tony Scott 1986). *Captain Marvel* responds to these 1980s films' depictions of space and the air force, respectively, as the domain of men in its depiction of a female pilot turned astronaut. Taylor and Glitsos argue that the humorous tone with which *Captain Marvel* stages these critiques of 1980s and 1990s pop culture makes them akin to its jokes about phenomena like dial up internet speeds, locating them in a past that "we as a society are beyond" (660). The sexism of 1980s and 1990s Hollywood cinema is presented as a relic that twenty-first-century blockbusters like the MCU films have shed.

Continuity with other MCU films is maintained through having Carol team up with Fury, who at this point in the universe's timeline is a S.H.I.E.L.D. agent. To play this younger Fury, Jackson is de-aged using digital processes. Holliday discusses the increasing application of such technologies in twenty-first-century franchise blockbusters, where "Hollywood's current tendency

Nick Fury lovingly fusses over Goose the Flerken in *Captain Marvel* (2019).

toward prequels, sequels, and spinoffs, as well as its 'reboot' production culture ... has become highly conducive to digital de-aging processes" (2021–2022, 226–27). The MCU exemplifies these practices, using digital de-aging processes to locate characters on its increasingly complex timeline(s) (228–29), the technology thus helping maintain temporal continuity. As the central connector of *Captain Marvel*'s past to the MCU's present, the presentation of Fury provides a means for the film to reframe understanding of the wider universe. This is also the first MCU film to decompress Fury. As the future-director of S.H.I.E.L.D. lovingly fusses over Goose the Flerken—an alien species that distinctly resemble cats—or cheerily sings the Marvelettes' "Please Mr. Postman" into a washing up brush, *Captain Marvel* reveals the warmth in a figure that had previously only been the Avengers' stern orchestrator. Whereas many other superhero blockbusters place the digital in tension with the human, digital de-aging processes are here used to showcase Fury's, and by extension S.H.I.E.L.D.'s, humanity. Although during the narrative Fury goes rogue, he does so both due to awareness that S.H.I.E.L.D. has been infiltrated by Skrulls and intuiting that Carol's cause is just. The fact that he has apparently faced no disciplinary action when we see him comfortably back in his S.H.I.E.L.D. office—which he now shares with Goose—at the film's end indicates that his honorable actions were congruent with the agency's values. Far from participating in other MCU texts' critique of S.H.I.E.L.D., in having the agency embodied by a star who carries great weight yet in this digitally aided performance shows levity, *Captain Marvel* presents the universe's representation of the US military-industrial complex as caring and just.[13]

While contributing to the MCU's ongoing discourse about the military-industrial complex and US values, *Captain Marvel* seeks to intervene by modifying these values' celebrated qualities. This intervention plays out in gestures to the universe's hierarchical continuity. The presentation of

Captain Marvel radiates orange and blue krackle as she soars through the sky in *Captain Marvel* (2019).

Captain Marvel's powers intertextually situates her alongside the MCU's championed male Avengers, even if the 1995 setting prevents her from directly interacting with them. When breaking free from the Skrulls, Captain Marvel exhibits great physical strength and combat skills like Captain America, then upon shattering the restrainers that imprison her hands shoots photon blasts akin to Iron Man's repulsor rays. Later in the film, after her full powers are unlocked, Captain Marvel soars through the sky like Iron Man and radiates orange and blue krackle—combining Iron Man and Thor's colors—in a way reminiscent of how Thor sizzles with lightning in *Thor: Ragnarok* and *Infinity War*. Unlocking these powers is the result of Carol regaining her memories and identity through the help of Maria and her daughter Monica (Akira Akbar). When reprogramming her costume's colors to disassociate from the Kree, Carol bases her costume's color scheme on Monica's US Air Force T-Shirt "since we're on the same team," asserting her bond with Monica and their wider affinity to US values. Furthermore, Neal Curtis (2020, 940–41) notes the significance of *Captain Marvel* amending the character's 1969 comic book origin by changing the Kree warrior who gives Captain Marvel her superpowers from male to female. The superpowers that situate Captain Marvel alongside the men atop the MCU's character hierarchy are thus rooted in sisterhood and femininity, which the film interlocks with US values. The film reframes the universe's hierarchical continuity's governing principles by infusing them with femininity but does not upturn them: physical force and US values are still the most favored traits. Kent (2021, 133) and Dove-Viebahn (2023) also demonstrate that, although Captain Marvel is aided by Black women, the film ultimately centers her white femininity. In its moves to elevate femininity in the MCU's governing structures, *Captain Marvel* enshrines the centrality of whiteness.

While solo films can attempt to intervene in the MCU's underpinning structures, all-star ensemble films continue to manage an ever-expanding universe through means that reinforce or reconfigure the character hierarchy. One significant approach that emerges is to divide the universe's growing number of superheroes into smaller groups. Hierarchy formation is enacted within these groups and through their interactions. The two teams in *Civil War* congregate around Tony and Steve. These physically powerful white male embodiments of differing US values lead teams that include women, Black men, and characters coded as foreign. Key tenets of this organization are denoted spatially when the teams battle at an airport. Iron Man and Captain America lead their respective forces as they march toward each other. The matter-manipulating Vision (Paul Bettany) and Scarlet Witch are relegated to hovering behind their teammates. This pair's foreign-coding and Scarlet Witch's femininity, alongside the immaterial qualities of their powers, are in marked opposition to the championed qualities of their team leaders, thus continuing to order the character hierarchy along criteria set in *The Avengers*.[14]

In other ways, the renegotiation of character roles in *Civil War* challenges the universe's underpinning values. The film begins with an Avengers operation in Nigeria that ends tragically. This initiates a discourse on America's role in international conflict. Tony's support of and Steve's opposition to the government's proposed monitoring of superheroes seemingly invert their respective commitment to individualism and national loyalty in *The Avengers*, but these altered positions develop their continuing arcs. Tony's revised position follows him being made to question his ego in *Iron Man 3* and *Age of Ultron*, in which Tony's technologies and self-possession breed the titular megalomaniacal artificial intelligence. Steve's increasing distance from and suspicion of US institutions can be traced from *The Avengers* and *The Winter Soldier*. *Civil War*'s reluctance to endorse either position makes its sociopolitical stance ambiguous, but the emerging discourse contributes to an increasing engagement with issues of globalization in the MCU. Significantly, *Civil War* also introduces T'Challa/Black Panther (Chadwick Boseman) to the MCU, priming one of Marvel's most prominent Black superheroes to upset the universe's centering of whiteness. Black Panther's opposition to US superheroes operating without regulation emblematizes the racial dimension of *Civil War*'s thematization of US imperialism. These challenges to the MCU's racial structures are developed in *Luke Cage*'s and *Black Panther*'s (Ryan Coogler 2018) more sustained explorations of Black identities. The technological superiority of Black Panther's nation Wakanda also upsets Tony's and America's positioning atop the world's power structure. The political meanings of individual texts thus remain equivocal, their ambiguities aggravated by intertextual dialogue, but shifts in the values underpinning the MCU's character hierarchy become evident not just in solo films but also all-star ensemble films.

The dynamics within and between the groups into which *Infinity War* organizes the MCU's superheroes continue certain shifts in the identities and values that the universe's character hierarchy favors. Characters initially team up with others with comparable associative frameworks. The group including Iron Man, Doctor Strange, and Spider-Man are linked by their geographical home of New York. The Guardians of the Galaxy and Thor are linked by genre conventions of science fiction and comedy. Scarlet Witch, Vision, Black Widow, Captain America, and Sam Wilson/Falcon (Anthony Mackie) are grouped as "foreign" outsiders, the latter two having disassociated from the United States following *Civil War*. When seeking technological aid outside of the US, Captain America directs his group to Wakanda, reinforcing the African nation's position of power in the MCU. The Wakandans provide not so much a group as an army, led by their king Black Panther when Wakanda provides the stage for the film's climactic battle. Iron Man, Thor, Captain America, and Black Panther ultimately fulfill leadership roles in their groups or armies, affirming the dominance of strong masculinity but also somewhat opening out the character hierarchy in terms of nationality and race by indicating that the top level is no longer exclusive to white American characters. Steps toward a less restrictive hierarchy are also expressed in the representation of powers. Iron Man's new nanotechnology and the Wakandans' holographic technology appear to manifest and manipulate matter in comparable ways to Doctor Strange's and Scarlet Witch's magic. This harmonious new stage in the MCU's meeting of science and magic situates the magical powers held by characters lower down the hierarchy alongside the powers of some of the groups' leaders.

These shifts in the character hierarchy do not, however, continue unimpeded. In its efforts to provide a grand conclusion to the storyline set in motion upon Thanos's reveal in *The Avengers*, *Endgame* prominently gestures back to *The Avengers* and, in doing so, reentrenches values championed in the MCU's first all-star ensemble film. Thanos's success in harnessing the infinity stones to eliminate half of all life in the universe provides *Endgame* a compression strategy through which many characters are temporarily erased, allowing the film to focus on a more limited selection of characters. Following a jump of five years in diegetic time, the superheroes from *The Avengers* are foregrounded over other surviving characters through each having developed in ways that strikingly reframe key elements of their associative

Captain America wields both Mjölnir and his shield in *Avengers: Endgame* (2019).

frameworks. Among these, Tony and Steve have retired from superheroics, the former's pursuit of responsibility now satisfied through fatherhood, the latter refocusing his camaraderie into leading support groups for survivors of Thanos's massacre. Thor is once again prompted to question his worthiness, resulting in him becoming overweight and drinking heavily in a characterization that fuses the riotous excesses of Vikings with representations of frat boys in teen movies. Black Widow has advanced from soldier to commander of an intergalactic superhero taskforce, this new role continuing *Captain Marvel*'s manoeuvring of women up the character hierarchy's ranks.

As with *The Avengers*, the character hierarchy's organization is, however, secured in *Endgame*'s climactic battle. The battle's opening bout pits *The Avengers*' three most powerful men—Captain America, Iron Man, and Thor—against Thanos. Thor's flabby physique provides the only modification to what these three previously represented, his capability in taking on Thanos while wielding both Mjölnir—which can only be held by one who is "worthy"—and axe-hammer Stormbreaker suggesting that a hypermuscular male physique is not essential to his worthiness.[15] The three superheroes' interactions, meanwhile, combine and underscore familiar values. Early in *Endgame*, Tony produces a new shield for Steve, complete with Captain America's patriotic iconography, thereby resuming the exchange of American values between Iron Man and Captain America. When facing Thanos, these values are elevated via Thor's divine powers. The thunder god's ability to turbocharge Iron Man's armor is repeated, this time intentionally, as Thor channels lightning into the armor, enabling the entrepreneur to fire a multibeam repulsor attack that knocks Thanos back. Captain America subsequently harnesses the god's power upon lifting Mjölnir. As Captain America fights one-on-one with Thanos, shield emblematizing his noble

The Marvel Cinematic Universe's female superheroes assemble in *Avengers: Endgame* (2019).

US values in one hand and hammer of the gods in the other, those national values are presented as worthy of divinity.

The championing of US identity continues even after Thanos smashes Captain America's shield. After struggling back to his feet, with a trembling hand, Steve tightens the buckle that fastens the remaining half of the shield to his arm before standing alone but steadfast before hordes of alien invaders. This action (re)binds Captain America's unyielding bravery to his nationality. Steve's resolve is rewarded moments later when he is joined by his own army, almost all of the universe's superheroes—those previously eliminated by Thanos now resurrected—arriving on the battlefield then launching into war upon the Captain's command.

After the embodiment of US values, now rendered divine, leads the charge, the universe's numerous superheroes are showcased to varying degrees. Each hero's contribution negotiates their place on the character hierarchy. Black Panther and Captain Marvel, the two introduced since *The Avengers* who most disrupt the universe's underpinning structures, participate in a relay wherein key characters take turns carrying the infinity gauntlet. Captain Marvel is granted her own grand entry to the battle, blasting down from space and attracting Thanos's ship's fire before destroying it in a striking demonstration of her incredible power. Upon collecting the gauntlet from Spider-Man, Captain Marvel is joined by the MCU's other female superheroes, who assemble in a single shot. Yet as Sabrina Mittermeier argues, "this brief moment hardly does much for empowerment and rather serves as a reminder of missed opportunities" (2021, 425). The instance of Marvel's leading women working together strikes like a synthetic gesture rather than a genuine expression of sisterhood since in most cases it does not stem from existing relationships: many of these women have not even met, let alone interacted, in previous MCU texts.

Captain Marvel's thematization of sisterhood is compressed in a way that renders it hollow.

Captain Marvel brings the gauntlet to a place on the battlefield where three men who do have a well-established history together—Iron Man, Thor, and Captain America—stage a final showdown with Thanos. Upon engaging in physical combat with Thanos and therefore joining Scarlet Witch as the only women to directly fight the alien despot in the battle, Captain Marvel provides a final contribution that affirms her growing importance in the universe's character hierarchy. Yet Thanos punches her away and all seems lost as he moves to activate the infinity gauntlet. It is subsequently revealed, however, that Iron Man has discreetly removed the infinity stones. Iron Man then exhibits Captain America's willingness to put his life on the line in restaging his own "sacrifice play" from *The Avengers*. As Tony configures his exoskeleton—the technological triumph of his personal enterprise—to harness the infinity stones' magic and finally eradicate Thanos at the cost of his own life, he declares, "I am Iron Man." This worded identifier first uttered in the MCU at the end of *Iron Man*, when combined with Steve's values, reaffirms the attribution of individual responsibility for the greater good to Tony's brand of capitalism. Iron Man's death opens space atop the MCU's character hierarchy for others to fill, and the shifts enacted by characters such as Black Widow, Black Panther, and Captain Marvel indicate that changes in its racial and gendered dynamics are occurring. Yet Tony's sacrifice—which supersedes Black Widow's earlier sacrifice to provide the film's emotional climax—also leaves the universe indebted to the white male American entrepreneur who proved its savior. The positions of primacy that the superhero Iron Man and the film *The Avengers* hold in the MCU's character and textual hierarchies exert a strong influence on *Endgame*, which as an all-star ensemble film sets a course for the universe going forward.

THE MCU BEYOND INFINITY

The ongoing intertextual exchanges in the MCU interlace individual films with an array of associations, which through their interaction engender equivocal sociopolitical meanings. The organization of the character hierarchy and the values that it champions, however, are clearly delineated within individual all-star ensemble films. These values can grow to underpin the MCU as they are reaffirmed in other texts. They can conversely be eroded by texts that directly subvert or implicitly critique them. The capacity for any MCU text to critique values that hold prominence within the universe is always inhibited by its situation within, and thus complicity with, the Marvel multiverse and cinematic universe. New characters, texts, and ideas have to contend with the weight of characters, texts, and ideas that hold positions of dominance in the character and textual hierarchies. Like the process in which texts and incarnations vie for centrality within a superhero franchise, texts and superheroes that share a universe are engaged in an ongoing process of negotiating their places on hierarchies.

My analysis has illuminated two main ways in which Marvel Studios films adapt comic book strategies of universe management. First, the films use cinematic form to articulate relations between characters and other universe elements, often metamorphosing tropes developed in comic books that express such relations in drawn images. Second, modes of intertextuality traditionally practiced in Hollywood are modified and combined with Marvel's modes of intertextuality. Stars' personas imbue characters with meanings, which are interwoven with meanings that characters already hold from other texts. Genre is similarly harnessed in strategies of universe management. Fractals of different genres are deployed in MCU films to differentiate and interlace the universe's characters and spaces. Thus, the MCU adapts strategies honed in decades of comic books for managing an ever-expanding textual network and combines these with revised forms of Hollywood modes of intertextuality. Each intertextual gesture draws on and reworks associations from their sources. These reconfigured associations produce further meanings through their interactions, which play out in narrative and stylistic strategies. Understanding the ways in which MCU films elicit and guide intertextual modes of reading allows one to analyze how meanings form in MCU texts and assess the cohesiveness of these meanings. The framework I have established for analyzing MCU texts' adaptive practices thus proves vital to interpreting the MCU as it continues to expand, while being primed to examine other superhero blockbusters that adapt comic books' shared universe model of seriality.

MCU texts released after *Endgame* continue the ongoing negotiation of values that underpin the character hierarchy. Moves to diversify its upper levels in terms of nationality are evident in *Shang-Chi and the Legend of the Ten Rings* (Destin Daniel Cretton 2021), the first MCU blockbuster headlined by a Chinese superhero, and *Eternals* (Chloé Zhao 2021), which concerns superpowered synthetic beings from space who represent a range of national and ethnic identities, along with the MCU's first openly gay superhero, Phastos (Brian Tyree Henry). Racial dynamics are examined in Disney+ show *The Falcon and the Winter Soldier* (2021) which, following Steve passing the Captain America mantle to Sam, explores the implications of a Black man carrying the shield. *The Falcon and the Winter Soldier* primes Sam to enter the MCU character hierarchy's upper echelons when he subsequently headlines a film, this trajectory from television to film also evidencing the reshaping of the MCU's media hierarchy following the launch of Disney+. *Black Widow* (Cate Shortland 2021), meanwhile, finally gives the first female Avenger a solo film, yet having this set in the past after her present-day death mitigates against it impacting the MCU's overarching structures (Taylor and Glitsos 2023, 667). *Black Panther: Wakanda Forever* (Ryan Coogler 2022), as Marvel Studios' first blockbuster with a Black female lead, offers a much more significant intervention, maneuvering T'Challa's sister Shuri (Letitia Wright) into adopting the Black Panther mantle and, in doing so, placing Shuri in a position of great power in the MCU.

The more disparate structure of the MCU's fourth and fifth phases is evident in how, at the time of this writing, there have not been any all-star ensemble films to consolidate or inhibit emerging shifts in the universe's hierarchies. The current overarching MCU storyline, "The Multiverse Saga," explores Marvel's multiverse. In doing so, it can harness the opposing potentials that alternate timeline narratives in superhero texts offer for reimagining or reentrenching a superhero universe's underpinning structures, which I explore in the next chapter.

CHAPTER 4

THE STRANGEST CONTINUITY OF ALL

Alternate Timelines in Fox's X-Men Films

After its opening title sequence, *X-Men: The Last Stand* (Brett Ratner 2006) cuts to a warzone where the superhero team fend off attacks from robots in the flaming wreckage of a city. This apocalyptic scenario is ultimately revealed to be a simulation in the X-Men's training facility, the "Danger Room." This simulation is reflective of how the X-Men franchise, since comic book storyline "Days of Future Past," published in *The Uncanny X-Men* #141–42 (January 1981–February 1981), has recurringly imagined alternate timelines. Alternate timelines are a far more widespread narrative strategy in the superhero genre, yet the X-Men franchise is significant not just in its frequent use of alternate timelines but the fact that it produced the first superhero blockbuster to deploy the strategy: 2014's *Days of Future Past*. This chapter analyzes the use of alternate timeline tropes in *Days of Future Past* and *Logan* to explore some of the divergent ways that the narrative strategy has been adapted into cinema and the ways in which it can shape a film's, and the wider franchise's, meanings.

The X-Men franchise is well suited for imagining alternate scenarios. Launched shortly after Spider-Man, in *The X-Men* #1 (September 1963), the X-Men develop the Marvel model of the superhero as social outsider, being branded on the cover of this debut issue as "the strangest super-heroes of all." As a preconstituted team, the X-Men lack the isolation of characters like Spider-Man or the tensions that arise from solo superheroes being brought together in an all-star team like the Avengers. Although drama still develops between teammates, a primary source of anxiety comes from the premise of the X-Men's superpowers as genetic mutations rendering them superheroes who, as the worded identifier goes, are "sworn to protect a world that hates and fears them." Despite the plasticity of the mutant metaphor enabling mutants to represent a range of minoritized social groups, the original X-Men team's lineup of primarily heterosexual American white men inhibited their embodiment of Othered communities (Fawaz 2016, 145; Darowski 2014, 41). The team were reformed for their relaunch as the "All New All Different" X-Men in *Giant-Size X-Men* #1 (May 1975), which introduced a more international and racially diverse team. In this all new era, *The Uncanny X-Men* "quickly became Marvel's most popular title—both in terms of sales and critical appreciation" (Reynolds 1992, 85). The era's run of X-Men comics written by Chris Claremont with art primarily by Dave Cockrum, John Byrne, and John Romita Jr. continues to prove central to the network of texts in various media and iterations that comprise the franchise. While all superhero franchises are fluid, the X-Men's interchangeable team and narrative device of mutation offer great scope for enacting shifts in the franchise's underpinning identity formations. Established X-Men can gain central positions in the franchise and become hard to dethrone, but new mutants can be added at a creator's whim. The premise facilitates reimagining the team and alternate timelines provide a means to rethink the franchise more radically in ways that can harness the mutant metaphor and reformulate its sociopolitical meanings.

This chapter begins by mapping the history and some key functions of alternate timelines in superhero comic books. I then analyze ways in which different styles and tropes have been critical to shaping alternate timelines in X-Men comics, focusing on comic book stories that directly inform the plots of *Days of Future Past* and *Logan*. I proceed to analyze the films. As with previous case studies, spaces and bodies are central to the films' construction of meaning. Examining these aspects unveils *Days of Future Past*'s and *Logan*'s divergent uses of alternate timeline tropes. The X-Men franchise is distinct from my previous case studies, however, in being rooted outside of the US metropolis. The presentation of spaces outside of US cities in *Days of Future Past* and *Logan* is crucial to the meanings that the alternate timelines generate, while interlinked with the presentation of bodies. Despite X-Men texts frequently foregrounding of issues of social prejudice, tendencies of superhero blockbusters whereby muscular white masculinity is privileged are also prevalent in X-Men films. Alternate timelines have the potential to reimagine such structures, and the two films' differing presentations of Logan/Wolverine's (Hugh Jackman) body, of itself and in relation to female characters and people of color, provide a locus for the extent to which they envision such shifts. Finally, the impact of these strategies on the film series's central timeline and broader X-Men franchise is gauged by examining the endings that *Days of Future Past* and *Logan* provide for their alternate timelines.

EXPLORING ALTERNATE TIMELINES

Alternate timelines in superhero comic books take various forms, such as being presented as a potential future or parallel universe within a story that occurs in the main universe, a new reality that has temporarily replaced the central timeline, or "imaginary" stories that take place in their own bounded texts. For my understanding of alternate timelines, which encapsulates all of these approaches, the key word is *alternate*. Designating a timeline as alternate requires the existence of a "prime" timeline.[1] An alternate timeline is set apart from the prime timeline. Its difference is communicated through explicit and implicit means that can be textual and discursive. This difference is underpinned by a balancing of familiar continuity with the strangeness of the alternate timeline. As such, another meaning of the word alternate, that of continuously oscillating between two points, is instructive, as the alternate timeline alternates between familiarity and strangeness. While negotiation of familiarity and variation is inherent to superhero texts, being a central feature of genre, media franchises, and adaptation, alternate timeline narratives push variation into the realm of the strange, their status facilitating more extreme changes to familiar characters and worlds. In their oscillation between familiarity and strangeness, alternate timelines can perform different functions.

Superhero comics begun to explore alternate timelines in the 1960s. DC used an alternate timeline in a significant act of continuity maintenance in 1961's *Flash* #123, in which story "Flash of Two Worlds!" establishes a multiverse that positions DC's Golden Age continuity on a secondary timeline parallel to the Silver Age one. In this case, the alternate timeline designation is used to rationalize inconsistencies that had accumulated over two decades of storytelling by bracketing off the Golden Age incarnations of DC's superheroes (Ndalianis 2009a, 278–79). In the same period that DC established its multiverse, the publisher started using the name "imaginary stories" for stories situated outside of narrative continuity that radically revise core elements of a character. Brian Cronin (2010) identifies "Mr. and Mrs. Clark (Superman) Kent!" in *Superman's Girlfriend Lois Lane* #19 (August 1960), which features Clark revealing his identity as Superman to Lois and marry her, as the first story that DC officially dubbed imaginary. In 1977, Marvel started series *What If?* that served a similar purpose to DC's imaginary stories, each issue exploring what could have happened if a defining event in the prime universe's fictional history had occurred differently. *What If?* stories are explicitly positioned as occurring in alternate universes within Marvel's multiverse. Labeling a story as imaginary or a "what if?" scenario permits free rein to alter familiar character and world elements since these are preserved in the prime timeline.

The possibility and pleasure of these alternate timelines depends on the prior establishment of narrative history. Hence why, for both DC and Marvel superhero comics, at least a decade worth of stories was published before alternate timelines were first deployed. The same can also be seen with the MCU which, after developing for over a decade since 2008's *Iron Man*, started its own animated *What If...?* series (Disney+ 2021–) and began exploring the multiverse in other texts. The fact that alternate timelines depend and indeed thrive on narrative history provides one explanation for why, as superheroes' narrative continuity has accumulated and adaptations in other media have proliferated over the years, alternate timelines have become more prevalent.

The potential for alternate timeline narratives to perform continuity maintenance provides a key reason for their increasing use as fictional history accumulates. As both DC and Marvel's comic book continuity has become incredibly complex and often contradictory, the publishers frequently adopt the strategy pioneered in "Flash of Two Worlds!" distributing unruly narrative elements across a multiverse to streamline the prime timeline. Ever since DC's *Crisis on Infinite Earths*, this strategy has typically been enacted in multiverse spanning crossover events such as DC's *Flashpoint* (July 2011–October 2011) or Marvel's *Secret Wars* (July 2015–March 2016). In discussing DC crossover events that use alternate universes to enact continuity maintenance, Brown argues "these series repeatedly explain to readers how superhero multiplicity is acceptable and containable because the comic book universe is imagined to displace multiplicities across either space or time" (2019, 31). Despite negotiating an array of alternate timelines that revel in the multiplicities of fictional history, these events ultimately "confirm the primacy of the dominant canonical universe. Other realms and timelines may exist, but they are the variations" (31). The multiversal conceit provides a means for publishers to clean up, and reinforce the central status of, their prime timeline.

In their reimagining of familiar franchise elements, alternate timelines can have significant sociopolitical implications. Ramzi Fawaz argues that

> *What If?* stories have the potential to experiment with creative possibilities that remain beyond the political scope of contemporary comic

book imaginaries . . . The value of *What If?* stories, then, lies in their imaginative premise, namely the possibility of asking the superhero, and its most compelling fantasies, to *do* and to *be* something else. (281, emphasis in original).

By virtue of existing outside of the prime timeline, alternate timelines are relatively free from strictures imposed by owning companies, fans, narrative conventions, and other forces that seek to police superhero franchises. As such, they can rework and interrogate ideas that underpin a franchise. For example, *Superman: Red Son* (June 2003–August 2003) rewrites the American icon's origin by asking what would have happened if Superman's rocket had landed in the USSR rather than the USA. The resulting story reflects on how nationality shapes Superman's identity while remapping international power dynamics and thus enacting the kind of seismic geopolitical ruptures denied to stories set in the prime timeline.

Having alternate timelines set apart from the prime timeline enables them to fundamentally revise traits that are central to the franchise yet potentially leaves the ideas they generate on the franchise's periphery. Eco (1972, 19) argues that the iterative structure of superhero comic book serialization, in which the world is reset back to equilibrium at the end of the story, works ideologically to enforce the status quo. Correspondingly, in each of their adventures, superheroes exhibit civil consciousness rather than political consciousness, protecting the established order and not interrogating its politics. Eco argues that imaginary stories help to preserve this "kind of oneiric climate" (17) in which the worlds that superheroes inhabit do not change, as these stories provide a space for superheroes to undergo radical developments that is discursively bracketed off from the main storyworld (17–18). Narrative experimentation is facilitated in imaginary stories through means that maintain the stasis, both temporal and political, of the superhero's core adventures.

Eco was writing specifically about Superman comics in the era of superhero comics that Henry Jenkins (2009) identifies as defined by self-contained stories. Yet Marc Singer (2018, 40–42) argues that even as superhero comics came to foreground serialized continuity, the iterative structure remains, it just takes longer for the storyworld to reset (multiple issues, years, or even decades). While maintaining the continued relevance of Eco's arguments about superhero comics' iterative structure, however, Singer challenges Eco's claim that superheroes never exhibit political consciousness, citing Superman's early role as a champion of the oppressed (38) and the antiestablishment currents of Marvel's 1960s superheroes (40). As demonstrated in previous chapters, the politics of a superhero franchise are by no means fixed.

Even if the basic premise of a character's story is constantly reiterated, the politics can shift as new texts engage in dialogue with sociopolitical contexts, trends in popular culture, and other texts in the franchise.

Eco's understanding of imaginary stories is accurate in that their discursive positioning as imaginary places them as subordinate to and apart from the prime timeline, which via the naming logic is positioned as "real." However, Eco does not account for the dialogic exchanges that can occur between incarnations of a superhero. Different forms of textual hierarchization that police, but cannot completely control, the dialogic exchanges between texts have throughout this book emerged as a key feature of superhero franchises. Certain texts are always given greater weight in the franchise and other texts strain against this weight. The discursive differentiation between real and imaginary stories is another mechanism that privileges certain texts but again one which, while exerting significant force, cannot completely quash the potential for subordinate texts to infiltrate the franchise's core.

Crucially, stories set in alternate universes are still part of their franchise. As such, ideas explored in imaginary stories can inform other texts in the franchise and even become central features, as evident in how the 1960 imaginary situation of Clark/Superman marrying Lois would in 1996 occur in the prime timeline. Imaginary stories can thus provide spaces in which the alteration of key aspects of a superhero act as initial inroads into more wide-reaching efforts to revise a franchise's underpinning politics. This potential is demonstrated by *What If?* #10 (August 1978), which asks what would have happened if Jane Foster—rather than Donald Blake—had found the hammer of Thor and gained the god's superpowers. Jane proceeds to become superhero Thordis before her power is transferred to her male counterpart. Despite granting a woman the superpowers held by a male character, by ultimately returning the power to the familiar man the story reinforces the centrality of events in the prime timeline. Correspondingly, the championing of white masculinity is reinstated. Yet the story's experimental spirit was decades later reframed and achieved much greater impact on the franchise. In the 616 comics universe, from 2014 to 2018 Jane held the mantle of Thor, her storylines often interrogating and dismantling Asgard's patriarchal structures (see Flegel and Leggatt 2021, 99–109). Jane's Thor also enacted further moves toward the center of the franchise through featuring in MCU blockbuster *Thor: Love and Thunder* (Taika Waititi 2022). Ideas initially explored as "what if" speculation can plant seeds that grow over time.

Alternate timelines may be deployed to affirm core elements of the prime timeline, but they can also inform shifts in that timeline. The discursive positioning of a timeline—as "real," "imaginary," a possible future, etc.—helps determine the weight given to particular stories within a franchise, yet ultimately superhero multiverses and franchises are fluid. Both the discursive and textual qualities of a story need to be considered when evaluating the relationship an alternate timeline establishes with the prime timeline and extent to which it may reshape the franchise.

STYLE AND NARRATIVE STRATEGIES IN THE X-MEN'S COMIC BOOK ALTERNATE TIMELINES

The alternate timelines featured in the two comic book storylines that I primarily discuss in this section have different relationships to the prime timeline. "Days of Future Past's" alternate timeline is presented as a possible dystopian future that is juxtaposed against the present-day prime timeline. In this future, the remaining mutants are hunted by robots called Sentinels and held in camps. A band of surviving X-Men execute a plan to send Kitty Pryde's consciousness back in time to her younger body in effort to prevent this future from transpiring. In contrast, the alternate timeline in "Old Man Logan," which ran in *Wolverine* vol. 3 #66–72 (August 2008–June 2009) and *Wolverine: Old Man Logan Giant-Size* (November 2009), is not directly juxtaposed against the prime timeline. "Old Man Logan" has the feeling of an extended "what if?" narrative, asking "what if Marvel's supervillain's won?" The story is set fifty years after Marvel's supervillains teamed up and killed most of Marvel's superheroes. Logan has renounced both violence and the superhero mantle Wolverine but is recruited by Hawkeye to drive across a transformed US. Style and narrative strategies are used in these storylines to negotiate familiarity and strangeness in narrative history, spaces, and characters.

Every creator working on an established superhero reworks familiar yet pliable characters and worlds. As outlined in this book's introduction, Lefèvre (2007, 8) locates the individuality of a comics artist's imagery in the ontology of drawn images. A long-running superhero franchise's prime timeline, then, is far from stylistically stable: in being passed between tens or hundreds of creators over decades of stories it comprises an array of interpretations. Alternate timeline stories differ in degree rather than kind, giving creators more freedom to radically revise elements.

The relation that an alternate timeline's artist(s) have to the prime continuity informs their stylistic approach. "Days of Future Past" is drawn by John Byrne, inked by Terry Austin, and colored by Glynis Wein. At the time, this was *The Uncanny X-Men*'s regular art team. Byrne, Austin, and Wein were therefore distinguishing the alternate timeline from their own

The "Days of Future Past" alternate timeline's Kitty Pryde and New York are introduced in *The Uncanny X-Men* #141 (1981).

established look for the series. The story's opening splash page immediately announces the distinction through starkly reworking a familiar space and character. The opening caption in the page's top left identifies the setting as New York, as confirmed by the Empire State Building behind this caption. Yet the city's iconic specificity is left behind as the reader's eyes roam across and down the page to dilapidated buildings and debris-strewn streets. This

The present-day Kitty Pryde attempts to navigate the Danger Room in *The Uncanny X-Men* #141 (1981).

world is literally askew, presented at an angle so that buildings slant to the left while a dislodged lamppost leans to the right, causing a "one way" sign to point downward, indicating this space's descent from what it once was. The arrow also points to an aged Kitty in green overalls that indicate her

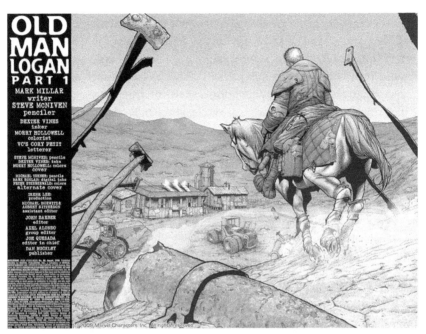

The Western genre's iconography is foregrounded when we are first shown the alternate timeline of "Old Man Logan" in *Wolverine* vol. 3 #66 (2008).

incarceration. While the design of spaces and characters is central to this alternate timeline's strangeness, narrative shifts between timelines underscore the distinct color palettes of future and present. Upon the first shift to the present, the future's dark greys, blues, and greens are suddenly replaced by the vivid tones culturally associated with comic book fantasy. Bright yellows and reds dominate a splash page that provides a sharp contrast to the preceding sequence, depicting a younger and less assured Kitty attempting to navigate the Danger Room. These stylistic differences between the drab future and hopeful present are maintained throughout the story.

The creative team's relationship to the series is different for "Old Man Logan." Of the storyline's core creative team, writer Mark Miller had written *Wolverine* vol. 3 #20–32 (December 2004–November 2005) but artist Steve McNiven had not previously worked on the series. While Miller and McNiven's reenvisioning of Wolverine was not directly situated in relation to one particular interpretation of the character, it negotiated the familiar and strange through reframing elements of his associative framework, particularly Wolverine's links to the Western genre, the character having long been associated with the gruff yet honorable figure of the Westerner (see Shyminsky 2006, 397).

The centrality of the Western genre's iconography to the alternate timeline of "Old Man Logan" is showcased in our first glimpse of this bleak future in *Wolverine* vol. 3 #66. A double splash page depicts Logan on horseback returning to his farm in a dusty desert. Other elements, such as a modern tractor and combine harvester sitting in states of disrepair, make clear that this timeline is not set in the past. While, at the time of publication, in the X-Men's prime timeline the team had relocated to San Francisco, Logan's farm is in Sacramento, California, marking his estrangement from his (now mostly deceased) team. The desolate landscape, which shows no trace of the city's former urban center, is indicative of the fates of many other cities Logan travels through in "Old Man Logan." If, as explored in previous chapters, superheroes are intrinsically linked to the modern city, the fall of most major US cities in "Old Man Logan" reflects the fall of superheroes.

While "Days of Future Past" and "Old Man Logan" are each realized by a core creative team who craft the alternate timelines in a distinct style, alternate timelines can also be constructed by a range of creative teams. For example, one of the X-Men franchise's most extensive explorations of an alternate timeline, the crossover storyline "Age of Apocalypse" (February 1995–June 1995), had various creative teams working on its multiple titles. In this case, the designs of the reenvisioned characters and world become a central factor in unifying the event, even when inflected with an artist's individual style. Whether it be Adam Kubert's distinctly feral rendition of Wolverine, hunched over with veins bulging down his arms and hair spread out as wide as his torso, or Joe Madureira's more cartoony Wolverine, with smoothly rounded arm muscles, angular face, and shorter hair, both share the same snarl baring jagged teeth, costume with red triangles on the forehead akin to warpaint, and metal stump in place of a left hand. This last detail signifies the character's altered history. In this timeline, Wolverine and former teammate Cyclops's familiar animosity intensified to the extent that a battle between the two marked itself on both bodies, with Wolverine losing a hand and Cyclops an eye. Character designs do not just unify different artistic styles but also manifest the timeline's history.

Pushing familiar character traits to extremes or reframing them in surprising ways are key narrative strategies in alternate timeline stories. These strategies take different trajectories in the treatment of Magneto by "Days of Future Past" and of Wolverine by "Old Man Logan." The reframing of Magneto in "Days of Future Past" had a lasting impact on the prime continuity, initiating a shift across the master of magnetism's spectrum of possible roles from evil supervillain to sympathetic superhero. Magneto's new role in "Days of Future Past" is first indicated through visual allusion to the X-Men's leader Charles

Age of Apocalypse's Wolverine as drawn by Adam Kubert on the cover of *Weapon X* #1 (1995).

Age of Apocalypse's Wolverine as drawn by Joe Madureira on the cover of *X-Men: Alpha* #1 (1995).

Xavier. As Kitty returns to her surviving comrades in the opening sequence, a wheelchair-user, whose torso and face are off-panel, approaches the group. Such an image in an X-Men comic would typically herald Xavier's arrival but this assumption is immediately proven mistaken when Kitty addresses the character as Magneto. The next few panels show Magneto convincing the team of their plan's importance. Over the course of these panels, through coming to adopt both Xavier's means of mobility and role of rallying the team, Magneto's reframing as team leader becomes apparent.

Placing the persecution of Jewish people in the Holocaust within Magneto's associative framework is a key means through which "Days of Future Past" initiates Magneto's transformation in the prime timeline. Focusing the storyline on Jewish teenager Kitty centers Jewish identity. Furthermore, the internment centers in which mutants are held are pointedly reminiscent of Nazi concentration camps, thus foregrounding this historical genocide of Jews. For instance, the "M" for "mutant" displayed on all interred mutants' overalls recalls the badges on Nazi concentration camp prisoners' clothes (Smith 2014, 70). This alternate timeline's mutants are situated metaphorically—and Kitty directly—as persecuted Jews. Magneto's association with persecuted Jews subsequently becomes direct in the prime timeline when it is revealed, in *The Uncanny X-Men* #150 (October 1981) and *The Uncanny X-Men* #161 (September 1982), that he is a Jew whose parents died in the Holocaust. This revelation provides a rationale for his radical methods for countering mutant oppression as a supervillain and context in which he considers if these actions changed him from persecuted to persecutor and made him akin to the Nazis. After handing himself in to stand trial, *The Uncanny X-Men* #200 (December 1985) ends with a morally redeemed Magneto accepting Xavier's offer to replace him in overseeing the X-Men, completing the shift to a role first glimpsed in the alternate timeline of "Days of Future Past."[2]

While Magneto changes, via frameworks introduced in "Days of Future Past," into a new role in the prime timeline, over the course of "Old Man Logan" the titular mutant transforms from his strange role as pacifist to his more familiar violent self. Logan's renouncing of violence, revealed to have occurred after he was duped by Mysterio's illusions into murdering the X-Men, is rooted in his love for his teammates, an aspect of his characterization that X-Men texts frequently place in tension with his role as loner. Logan's pacifism thus intensifies a familiar quality of his character. The storyline's penultimate chapter ends with Logan completing a shift along his character spectrum by fully resuming the violent role of Wolverine. The transformation is announced with a double splash page simply comprising the worded identifier "SNIKT!" in huge and blocky blood red letters,

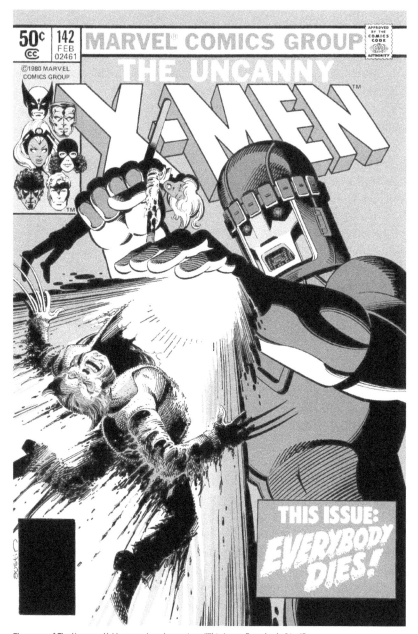

The cover of *The Uncanny X-Men* #142 (1981) promises, "This Issue: Everybody Dies!"

denoting Wolverine popping out the adamantium (a fictional metal) claws that protrude from his knuckles for the first time in fifty years. After exacting revenge for the murder of his family, Wolverine ends the storyline riding off into the sunset—now embodying both the look and violent mentality of the Westerner—to go topple the villains who have overrun the country, thus affirming his position at a familiar violent and heroic point on his spectrum.

One particularly extreme change that characters commonly undergo in alternate timelines is death. In recent decades, comic book superheroes die with increasing frequency in their prime timelines. Yet Singer (2018, 42) points out that this does not offer the kind of significant narrative change that Eco sees as prohibited in superhero comics; it is only a matter of time till a deceased superhero is alive again. Superhero conventions facilitate restoration in a range of ways, from characters being resurrected through sorcery to an incarnation from an alternate timeline joining the prime timeline. Character deaths in the prime timeline are often publicized months in advance and pitched as real-world media events; for instance, the "Death of Superman" storyline was particularly successful at attracting mainstream media coverage. Superhero deaths in alternate timelines are treated differently. For characters whose deaths occurred prior to the narrative, significant changes to the world that their deaths cause are explored in detail; for example, "Age of Apocalypse" explores of a world transformed following Xavier's death. In terms of quantity, alternate timeline narratives delight in killing swathes of superheroes in single strokes. Qualitatively, deaths can be sudden and without ceremony. The sadistic pleasure that alternative timeline stories take in wholesale and abrupt deaths is evidenced by the cover of *The Uncanny X-Men* #142, which contains the conclusion of "Days of Future Past." A caption excitedly promises, "This Issue: Everybody Dies!" while the image shows a Sentinel clutching Storm's limp body in one hand and incinerating Wolverine with a blast emanating from the other. While a bloodthirsty means of harnessing the narrative freedom that alternative timelines offer, the trope of wholesale and unceremonious superhero deaths enhances the bleakness of the worlds depicted, enriching their dystopian visions' meanings.

In alternate-timeline comic book stories, distinct art styles, altered spaces, redesigned characters, and tropes such as wholesale character deaths emphasize changes in the fictional world. Over the course of the storyline, elements can gravitate back to the familiar or push further away from it. This reenvisioning of franchise elements facilitates the stories' exploration of the values associated with famous characters; what happens to these values when they are transformed or lost, and how does this impact the universe? Films *Days of Future Past* and *Logan* adapt these strategies for envisioning alternate timelines to rework familiar elements from both the wider X-Men franchise and 20th Century Fox's X-Men films' prime timeline.

FOX'S X-MEN FILMS' FRACTURED CONTINUITY

The continuity of Fox's X-Men films splinters in various ways. The first three films—2000's *X-Men*, *X2* (Bryan Singer 2003), and *The Last Stand*—follow a linear chronology set, as the first one declares, in "the not too distant future." *X-Men Origins: Wolverine* (Gavin Hood 2009) then turned the clock back, being a prequel focusing on Wolverine. Subsequently, four team films relaunched the main series, recasting many major characters and revising narrative continuity. *X-Men: First Class* (Matthew Vaughn 2011) explores the formation of the X-Men in the 1960s, followed by three films that each jump forward a decade: *Days of Future Past* is primarily set in the 1970s, *X-Men: Apocalypse* (Bryan Singer 2016) in the 1980s, and *Dark Phoenix* (Simon Kinberg 2019) in the 1990s. Concurrently, other films exhibit varying textual relations to the main series, resulting in a fractured body of films that construct strands of continuity while often embracing multiplicity. *The Wolverine* (James Mangold 2013) picks up its titular hero's story after *The Last Stand* while *Logan* largely disregards narrative and stylistic connections to the main series films; *Deadpool* (Tim Miller 2016) sees Ryan Reynolds reprise his role from *Origins: Wolverine* but in a markedly different interpretation of the character, while *Deadpool 2* features its own alternate timeline in the form of a postapocalyptic future that Cable (Josh Brolin) seeks to avert; and *The New Mutants* (Josh Boone 2020) features a group of young mutants whose adventure has no overt relationship to events in the main series.

Paratextual materials provide a more definite, but by no means conclusive, designation of timelines for Fox's X-Men films. The Online Marvel Database, maintained by fans, collates universe designations from officially published materials. At the time of this writing, the database separates the films into three separate timelines: the "original" timeline; the "revised" timeline following the events of *Days of Future Past*, which includes the *Deadpool* films and *The New Mutants*; and *Logan*'s alternate timeline. Conversely, the X-Men Movies Wiki considers *Logan* as part of the revised timeline, due to statements from director James Mangold. I consider *Logan* as an alternate timeline narrative due to it foregrounding alternate timeline tropes, including stylistic and tonal distinction from the prime timeline, a vision of a bleak future, and deaths of core characters.

Days of Future Past and *Logan* metamorphose narrative and stylistic elements from the "Days of Future Past" and "Old Man Logan" comic book storylines, respectively, while also dialogically engaging with the wider network of X-Men texts. Discursively, the films' alternate timelines are positioned comparably to those of the comic book storylines. *Days of Future Past* places its dystopian future in direct juxtaposition to the film series's prime timeline. In attempt to avert the dystopian timeline, the future Wolverine's consciousness is transported back to 1973 to prevent Mystique (Jennifer Lawrence) from assassinating Dr. Bolivar Trask (Peter Dinklage): an event that leads to the creation of unstoppable Sentinels. *Logan*, meanwhile, effectively explores a "what if" scenario, presenting a world in which there are no more superheroes, the X-Men having been killed by Charles Xavier (Patrick Stewart) losing control of his psychic powers. Now a chauffeur who looks after Charles, Logan is reluctantly recruited to escort young mutant Laura (Dafne Keen), who is revealed to have been artificially created using Logan's DNA and thus has strikingly similar mutant powers, across America.

Style is a crucial means through which *Days of Future Past* and *Logan* stake their alternate timelines' relationships to the film series's prime timeline. Familiarity and strangeness are negotiated in both films via a central tension between mutability and stability that manifests in the presentation of spaces and bodies.

RELOCATING SUPERHEROES' SPATIAL PARAMETERS

The X-Men franchise is emblematic of a broadening of spatial locales beyond the urban metropolis in 1950s and 1960s US superhero narratives. This shift can be linked to the postwar movement of middle-class Americans out of city centers and into suburbs.[3] Superhero comic book stories from this period that explore small town life include those of Superman spin-offs Superboy and Supergirl. Superboy, first appearing in *More Fun Comics* #101 (January 1945), was the superhero identity Clark adopted when growing up in Smallville, while Supergirl—Clark's cousin Linda Lee—initially lives in Midvale, which she describes upon her debut in *Action Comics* #252 (May 1959) as "a pretty little town." Upon their comic book debut, the X-Men were located in New York State near many of their fellow Marvel superheroes but boarded at Xavier's school in suburban Westchester. The first X-Men film introduces the school in Westchester although progresses toward a finale on the Statue of Liberty, thus establishing the series and twenty-first-century superhero blockbuster in the Manhattan iconography central to the superhero genre. Subsequent X-Men

The mountainside temple in China in *X-Men: Days of Future Past* (2014).

films, however, explore a wider array of locales outside of cities and the US. *Days of Future Past* and *Logan* use such settings in their alternate timelines.

MALLEABLE SPACE AND TIME IN *DAYS OF FUTURE PAST*

Days of Future Past opens on a shot of Manhattan's deteriorated skyline, its once-triumphant skyscrapers diminished. The camera glides forward to reveal a gaping hole in the Empire State Building which it proceeds to drift through. Whereas forward penetration through urban space is in *Superman: The Movie* deployed to celebrate city space, the motif is redeployed here to reveal its destruction. *Days of Future Past* subsequently depicts Sentinels attacking a group of X-Men in the ruins of Moscow before the heroes regroup in China. These international story settings are representative of the global composition of contemporary Hollywood production. In this era, "many films are made in several locations with finance, actors and crew drawn from a number of countries" (Goldsmith, Ward, and O'Regan 2010, 1).

While international settings can help increase appeal to global audiences and allow Hollywood studios to take advantage of international filming locations where local governments offer appealing economic incentives (Goldsmith, Ward, and O'Regan 2010, 12–13), it is important to note that story setting and shooting location do not always align. A blockbuster's representation of a story setting can affect the film's sociopolitical meanings. Regarding *Days of Future Past*'s scenes set in Moscow and China, neither Russia nor China are credited as filming locations. Furthermore, the lack of specification of a place within China indicates a generalized understanding of the nation. The presentation of both settings supports this accusation of a generalized depiction. Central Moscow's crumbling landmarks are surveyed before the action moves to a generic industrial space devoid of national specificity beyond some Russian text on walls and objects. The mountainside temple that comprises the film's China foregrounds traditional architecture replete with elaborately carved—albeit deteriorating with age—décor that includes iconography of Chinese dragons. This depiction constructs an orientalist view of China as defined by mysticism and pastness. While identifying these settings by their most familiar landmarks and iconography is comparable to the film's presentation of Manhattan, it is crucial to also consider their narrative use. The sequence in New York is accompanied by Xavier's narration ending on the rumination "is the future truly set?" This introduces the theme of time being malleable that is central to alternate timeline narratives in which the alternate is directly juxtaposed against the prime timeline. Yet Russia and China provide only places of refuge for the X-Men. It is through travelling to the past that the future dystopia can be averted.

The primary story settings in 1973 are New York (mainly Westchester), Paris, and Washington, DC, thus locating the fight to avert dystopia in the US and Western Europe. A short sequence in Saigon, showing US troops evacuating the Vietnam War, provides the only exception. Forlorn US mutant soldiers unknowingly await transferal to Trask Industries. This exploitation of mutants is added to the real-life atrocities the US enacted in the Vietnam War. Trask's vilification of mutants is thus discursively linked to the US's actions in the Vietnam War. The film indicts the US as perpetuators of hatred. Yet Saigon only features as a place to escape, which is achieved when Mystique liberates the mutants. The remaining 1973 scenes occur in Western settings that provide spaces where positive change can be enacted.

In *Days of Future Past*, the malleability of time is interlocked with malleable space as the cinematic image's spatiotemporal properties are manipulated. The presentation of mutant powers is a key way in which spatiotemporal malleability is expressed. In the X-Men franchise, many mutants have abilities that disrupt laws of space and time, such as teleportation and superspeed. Comics, with its construction of time through spatial forms, offers powerful means of presenting such spatiotemporally disruptive superpowers. In an article that explores the ways in which comics can use static images to represent complex spatiotemporal configurations, Ndalianis concludes by linking such localized spatiotemporal disruptions to "the multiple and parallel timelines that have haunted the comic book throughout its history" (2009b, 247). The spatiotemporal plasticity of comics form reflects, and provides ideal means for exploring, the branching timelines of superhero narratives.

Magik opens a stepping disk to escape Warlock in *The New Mutants* #21 (1984).

X-Men comics often manipulate the medium's conventions of spatial design to represent powers that subvert laws of space and time. For example, when drawn by Bill Sienkiewicz, the "stepping disks" that Magik opens to travel through dimensions and time appear as ovals or gashes within narrative space. In opening portals that share the whiteness of the page on which the comic is printed, it is as if Magik is tearing through the panel itself, creating her own areas of gutter that lead to new spatiotemporal settings. In a panel from *The New Mutants* #21 (November 1984), Magik opens a disk to escape alien Warlock. The disk's unstable squiggly edges express its rupture to both the comics page and the diegetic world's spatiotemporal coordinates. Although the portal stabilizes into an oval in the next panel, the volatility of Magik's power at this early stage of her development subsequently takes her into an alternate future timeline in *The New Mutants* #32 (October 1985). With Magik's teleportation power, ruptures to the comics page, diegetic spatiotemporal coordinates, and the narrative timeline are interlinked.

Fox's X-Men films metamorphose strategies that manipulate comics conventions of spatial design in techniques that disrupt traditional spatiotemporal conventions of the cinematic image. As discussed in chapter two, the digital image lacks the celluloid image's indexical relationship to profilmic material, while digital imaging can further dislocate the cinematic image from physical space. Much digital imaging strives to be perceptually realistic but it can alternatively present fantastic phenomena that breach laws of physical space. For example, when mutants teleport in X-Men films, highly stylized CGI manifestations mark their spatial ruptures. When Magik (Anya Taylor-Joy) first casts a portal in *The New Mutants*, jagged blue lines fizzle and

Quicksilver runs along the circular wall in *X-Men: Days of Future Past* (2014).

pulsate as the space around her warps; Nightcrawler (Alan Cumming) leaves tangles of navy vapor each time he disappears and appears in *X2*; shades of glowing purple sprawl out from the portals that Blink (Fan Bingbing) opens in *Days of Future Past*. These forms of digital krackle operate in a highly stylized mode, emphasizing the spatiotemporal disruption of the mutants' powers that are visualized in defiance of perceptual realism.

3D versions of *Days of Future Past* offer additional avenues for spatial manipulation. As Owen Weetch (2016, 2) outlines, in 3D films aspects of the image can either appear to protrude out of the screen, into what is called negative parallax, or recede into the depth of screen space, which is called positive parallax. When Blink opens multiple portals in individual shots, these are positioned at different levels of positive parallax, thus accentuating the space's depth and showcasing her mastery of manipulating its spatial coordinates.

Yet Blink's portals not breaching the screen into negative parallax limits her disruption to the cinematic image. As Weetch outlines, use of negative parallax is commonly perceived as particularly disruptive, a popular criticism of 3D cinema being that "negative parallax distracts from diegetic absorption" (17). Weetch challenges such reductive discourses by exploring 3D's expressive capacities. In fact, *Days of Future Past* harnesses the disruptiveness of negative parallax to convey Quicksilver's (Evan Peters) disruption to time and space, thereby breaching the screen to enhance narrative meaning. When Quicksilver assists Wolverine and Xavier (James McAvoy; Patrick Stewart in the alternate timeline) in breaking Magneto (Michael Fassbender; Ian McKellen in the alternate timeline) out of imprisonment at the Pentagon, his superspeed proves crucial to escaping a blockade of guards in a kitchen. Upon facing the guards, Magneto urges Xavier to "freeze them" but the telepath currently lacks the power to issue such psychic commands. Quicksilver steps in by effectively freezing time via his own means: moving so fast that everything around him slows to a near halt, pots and pans (having been levitated by Magneto) suspended mid-air. To the tune of Jim Croce's "Time in a Bottle," Quicksilver jaunts around the room of bottled time, clearing a path by repositioning the guards to strike themselves or one-another and prodding bullets to alter their trajectories. The sequence initiates with Quicksilver running along the circular wall, the camera that faces him while tracking backward angled as if turned ninety degrees so that he appears upright. This redeploys the motif of superheroes penetrating the depth of cinematic space while defying gravity but elongates this space through having drops of water in negative parallax seemingly glide toward Quicksilver as he runs through them. The jarring protrusion of these droplets, which should be falling horizontally across the image toward the floor but are halted by Quicksilver's trajectory, underscores how his superspeed subverts both space and time. As Quicksilver's casual manipulation of events continues in subsequent shots his interactions with objects and people span negative and positive parallax, for instance plucking a plate from negative parallax then frisbeeing it into positive parallax, and knocking a newspaper into negative parallax. This nimble navigation of space protruding from and receding into the 3D image reinforces Quicksilver's transcendence of spatiotemporal laws.

Quicksilver's disruptive movement through stilled space also plays with spatiotemporal tensions inherent to the cinematic image. Whereas in comics motion is suggested through still images, in cinema still images are played in rapid succession (traditionally twenty-four a second) to give the impression of actual movement. Laura Mulvey (2006) argues that stillness is therefore inherent to the cinematic image yet is concealed by traditional practices of film exhibition. For Mulvey, digital technologies like DVDs that allow us to freeze the cinematic image reveal this hidden stillness. In echoing Metz (1974)—discussed in chapter two—Mulvey observes that "while movement tends to assert the presence of a continuous 'now,' stillness brings a resonance of 'then' to the surface" (13); cinema's movement brings the "then" of the still photograph into the "now." In revealing the cinematic image's stillness, digital technology brings back its pastness—its evocation of then—while providing a means to interlace this with the presence—the now—of moving images. *Days of Future Past* harnesses this potential. As Quicksilver moves through near-frozen space, cinema's stillness exists simultaneously with its movement, and their corresponding temporalities are blended. Digital image manipulation and compositing are thus employed to create interplay

The US flag waves behind Mystique in *X-Men: Days of Future Past* (2014).

between movement and stillness that expresses the film's theme of time being malleable. Digital filmmaking technologies provide the means to aestheticize the mutability of time.

The different levels of disruption to the cinematic image enacted by Blink and Quicksilver reflect their degrees of agency in averting the dystopian timeline. Blink is played by Chinese star Fan Bingbing and therefore provides a more authentic representative of China than the temple setting yet is still situated in this space where characters cannot directly affect their timeline's fate. The limitation imposed on this setting is reflected in the presentation of Blink's mutant abilities; she teleports around this space in positive parallax. Quicksilver, meanwhile, exercises his powers in US locations where his superspeed flaunts negative parallax and interlaces the cinematic image's temporalities. Quicksilver's is presented as the more spatiotemporally disruptive power, reflective of how the film grants the Western mutants in 1970s Western settings the capacity to enact change.

This distribution of agency over altering the timeline, and its sociopolitical implications, are affirmed in the film's climax. In Washington DC, Magneto issues a threat to humanity, addressing government officials and Trask, along with a global audience of television viewers. The film cross-cuts between Magneto's speech and the X-Men of the dystopian future futilely defending themselves from a Sentinel attack. Whereas cross-cutting is typically used to present simultaneous events, here it asserts the interrelation of past and future, expressing via montage that hate begets hate. The violent effects of Magneto's words are laid bare in shots of the future mutants being massacred as he speaks. When the speech culminates in him mobilizing mutants for war, Blink's body is fatally pierced by three Sentinels, affirming how for all her power of spatial manipulation, her fate is dependent on past actions.

The turning point comes when Mystique confronts Magneto. After immobilizing Magneto by shooting him, she points the gun at Trask. Xavier intervenes, telepathically communicating with Mystique by freezing the world around her and manifesting a psychic image of himself. As with Quicksilver's powers, this recurring way of presenting Xavier's powers in the X-Men films utilizes digital compositing to blend stillness and motion, allowing characters to converse in a space dislocated from the flow of the world. It is via this feat of spatiotemporal manipulation that Charles convinces Mystique to spare Trask's life. Upon Mystique dropping the gun, the remaining mutants of the future disappear along with their robotic adversaries, signaling that Mystique's act of mercy averted that timeline. As she walks away, the camera moves into a close-up in which the US flag waves behind Mystique, her vivid blue skin and red hair matching the flag's primary colors. In harmonizing Mystique and the flag, this composition aligns the virtue that Mystique has just shown with US values, underscoring the film's location of the capacity for positive change in the US

Days of Future Past's aesthetic of spatiotemporal malleability and narrative provide a response to Xavier's opening question, optimistically asserting that the future is not set. Its use of international story settings and presentation of mutants' movements through these spaces are key to shaping the stylistic identity of its alternate timeline and corresponding meanings.

THE IRREVERSIBLE DECLINE OF URBAN SPACE IN *LOGAN*

Whereas *Days of Future Past* draws on science fiction tropes in its presentation of a malleable alternate timeline, *Logan* foregrounds the Western genre in its construction of a bleak future where corruption is embedded. The strategies for presenting *Logan*'s timeline in many respects act as a response to and rejection of those in *Days of Future Past*. This response reflects a contemporary set of discourses promoted by certain prominent figures in Hollywood such as *Dark Knight* trilogy director Christopher Nolan, who vocally oppose an overreliance on digital imaging along with 3D presentation (see Ressner 2012). Meanwhile, following the commercial downturn of 3D presentation in many major territories, Hollywood studios were less inclined to 3D presentation by the time of *Logan*'s production.[4] Although not featuring time travel, *Logan* reaches back to genres and styles associated with cinema's past to present an unforgiving future that comments on contemporary US politics.

In returning to tropes of the Hollywood Western, *Logan* eschews the trend of blockbusters showcasing story settings from around the world.

Laura gazes out of the limousine window, transfixed by Oklahoma City's garish neon lights, in *Logan* (2017).

Comic book storyline "Old Man Logan" concerns a journey across a transformed US; *Logan*, in dialogue with contemporary discourses on immigration, transforms the journey into one of border crossing. The mutants begin in Mexico and must navigate through the United States to North Dakota, where Laura can cross into Canada. Kent underscores the contemporaneous resonance of this narrative: "The rhetoric of Trump's election campaign and subsequent presidency amplified the urgency, and inequality, of a situation in which the legal protections of undocumented immigrant children in the US were becoming increasingly diminished" (2021, 128). *Logan*'s production broadly corresponded with the election campaign of Donald Trump, who became president of the United States in 2017 and made the construction of a wall between the US and Mexico a central campaign pledge. If, following Bukatman (2003), a superhero's unrestricted movements express utopianism, borders that inhibit movement mark *Logan*'s timeline as dystopian. *Logan*'s dialogue with contemporary US politics thus locates Trump's policies as dystopian. While in *Days of Future Past* mutants' fantastic movements break laws of time and space to avert dystopia, in *Logan* the mutants struggle to cross national borders as Logan and Charles's mutant powers deteriorate. *Days of Future Past* expresses hope for forging a better future; *Logan* is pessimistic about contemporary society's trajectory.

Despite their differences, both films' dystopic visions align urban decline with the end of superheroes. In *Days of Future Past*'s alternate timeline cities have been destroyed; in *Logan* they have ideologically decayed. *Logan*'s spatial dynamics negotiate the dialectic between "civilization" and "the wilderness" that Jim Kitses (1969, 11) identifies as central to the Western genre. Although Kitses outlines how this dialectic can be framed differently in individual texts to give either side positive or negative connotations, *Logan* presents a purely bleak view of the civilization associated with its cities while the wilderness offers a route to liberation. From Kitses's (11) list of concepts that Westerns can associate with civilization, "restriction" and "corruption" are the most apt for describing *Logan*'s cities. El Paso and Oklahoma City are the main cities featured as story settings. These are primarily seen from Logan's limousine in scenes that convey their corruption. In El Paso, a scene in which Logan chauffeurs a group of raucous frat boys pointedly comments on the culture of the city. As the limo passes a border between Mexico and the US, the boys obnoxiously chant "USA" at the queue seeking to cross. The imagery of border crossing and xenophobic nationalism resonates with Trump's rhetoric. Later in the film, as Logan, Charles, and Laura arrive in Oklahoma City, Laura gazes out of the limousine window transfixed by the garish neon lights promoting venues and products. The city is coded as a place of capitalism run rampant, the crass apotheosis of the civilization that encroached on the freedom of the old west and a far cry from the superhero city of shimmering achievements.

While contemporaneous discourses of border crossing are inherently bound to capitalism, with Trump scapegoating immigrants for economic hardship in the United States, *Logan* develops these links via its narrative of a US company commodifying Mexican girls and mutants. The film's corporate villains, the Alkali-Transigen research company, are responsible for almost ending mutantkind through lacing food products with drugs that suppress mutation. Similarly to *Days of Future Past*, where Trask experiments on mutants to aid the production of weapons, in *Logan* Alkali-Transigen's genetic experiments breed mutants in the wombs of Mexican girls to craft into weapons to sell, thus envisioning what Kent (2021, 125) discusses as biocapitalism. The mutants' representation of marginalized social groups goes beyond metaphor, with the film directly representing the Mexican girls' children being commodified.[5]

Sanctuary from the capitalist forces of persecution is located outside of cities. The Munson family farmhouse provides the most wholesome refuge when Will (Eriq La Salle), Kathryn (Elise Neal), and their son Nate (Quincy Fouse) welcome Logan, Charles, and Laura for a home cooked meal and night's sleep. Trees with full foliage and a carefully maintained lawn surround the house, representing a tamed wilderness where life is nurtured. The Munson's farmhouse provides a counterpart to the Starrett family homestead in *Shane* (George Stevens 1953), a classic Western referenced multiple times in *Logan*. The Starrett homestead promises a place where *Shane*'s titular gunslinger (Alan Ladd) can pursue an honest life working the land; the

Munson house similarly offers respite from violence and persecution. Yet the intertextual gesture underscores how such sanctity is under threat from corrupt forces. As with *Shane*'s ruthless cattle baron, in *Logan* land baron Jackson (Lennie Loftin) seeks to oust the Munsons. Significantly, whereas *Shane*'s Starretts are white, the Munsons are Black. Making the persecuted family who represent an ideal of American freedom Black, while Jackson and his thugs are white, gives the discourse on freedom and corrupt civilization a racial dimension rarely framed in such a way in classical Westerns.[6] Jackson ultimately proves nothing but fodder when Alkali-Transigen's forces arrive with X-24: a bestial clone of Wolverine. X-24 also ruthlessly kills Kathryn and Nate, thus furthering the film's portrayal of corporate capitalism's violence against people of color. Corporate capitalism, in not simply quashing the individual but commodifying them, renders the classical Western villain quaint, instilling the sense of this dystopian timeline being one in which the battle between freedom and corrupt civilization was lost long ago.

Logan's presentation of its dystopian future as unalterable is expressed stylistically through foregrounding the profilmic in both its story settings and realization of mutant powers. Most uses of digital imaging in *Logan* are constructed to be "seamless" (Wood 2007, 6), their presence concealed. As explored in chapter two, tension between the digital and profilmic can be used expressively within superhero films. The means through which *Logan* sets itself against the heavily digital aesthetics of other X-Men films recasts this strategy by using an opposition between the digital and profilmic to distinguish between timelines across films. If the malleability of digitally manipulated images in *Days of Future Past* affirms the film's philosophy of the future being changeable, the profilmic imagery of *Logan* takes on a rigidity that suggests the timeline cannot be altered.

The presentation of Charles Xavier's powers in *Days of Future Past* and *Logan* is indicative of their timelines' differences. In *Logan*, Charles's uncontrollable bursts of psychic energy prompt the image to vibrate. As director James Mangold explains on the DVD commentary, this effect was achieved by the comparatively rudimentary technique of vigorously shaking the camera, then running the footage through consumer-grade software that stabilizes camera shaking, resulting in "warbling, warping imagery." This technique gives Charles's power a unique quality. When he uses this power at a hotel in Oklahoma City, Alkali-Transigen's elite task squad the Reavers are frozen in their tracks, recalling the blending of movement and stillness achieved through digital compositing in previous X-Men films. Yet the image's vibrations instill everything with motion, undermining this stillness. Rather than the precise control over time, space, and psychic communication

Logan brandishes X-Men comics next to a television playing *Shane* (1953) in *Logan* (2017).

that Xavier exercises in previous films, here the pulsating image conveys his power's instability. The low-tech means of visualizing Charles's power, achieved in the first part through the distinctly physical technique of shaking the camera, conveys the degeneration of his mutant abilities and corresponding deterioration of the world.

Logan's emphasis on the profilmic is central to strategies through which the film positions itself as "realistic" and contributes to a discourse on realism vs. fantasy. These strategies echo those of previous superhero blockbusters that assert realism. Brooker outlines the discourses of realism through which *Batman Begins* was framed, which interlock its "insistence on physical stunt work and old-school effects rather than CGI" (2012, 94) with its use of crime thriller conventions. *Logan*'s foregrounding of the profilmic combined with its use of Western conventions and intertexts (rather than crime thrillers) works comparably, proclaiming a realism that resists associations with superhero fantasy. Elisavet Ioannidou gets to the crux of the cultural stakes of such strategies, arguing that the *Dark Knight* trilogy films construct themselves as realistic in effort to be positioned as mature and thus "defy the popular belief that superheroes are for children" (2013, 236). In such a formulation, realism is aligned with the adult, fantasy with the childish.

Logan reveals how this formulation situates the childish as naive. The film itself is discursively positioned as "adult" due to its graphic violence gaining it an "R" rating for domestic theatrical release, indicating that it is not intended for the wide audiences typically sought by superhero blockbusters. *Logan*'s rejection of many of the main series X-Men films' stylistic and narrative strategies manifests in Logan explicitly decrying superhero fantasy. In the Oklahoma City hotel room, he confronts Laura about her X-Men comics, lecturing, "You do know they're all bullshit, right? Maybe a quarter of it happened, and not like this. In the real world people die, and no self-promoting asshole in a fucking leotard can stop it. This is ice cream for bed-wetters." Logan's swearing asserts his and the film's perspective as an adult one, as he accuses superhero comics of providing a retreat from reality. Yet the film does not sustain a purely demeaning perspective on superhero fantasy. Crucially, Logan delivers this speech while standing next to a television on which *Shane* plays. Framing the superhero comic books he brandishes and Western film together draws a clear link between the superhero and Western genres, thus undermining a binary in which the former is childish and naïve while the latter is adult and realistic.

After Logan leaves, Laura watches the final moments of *Shane*, captivated by Shane's mournful monologue about a life of violence being inescapable once a man is set on that path. Laura absorbs Shane's moral teachings, the same way that we understand her to have pored over her X-Men comics. The Western genre is thus, like the superhero genre, presented as one that enthralls children, yet its fantasies are shown to have the potential to teach moral lessons. Earlier, Charles told Laura that he watched *Shane* at her age, this information suggesting that *Shane* informed his lifelong pursuit of peace between mutants and humans. The superhero genre is given similar positive qualities later when we see one of Laura's young mutant friends clutching a Wolverine action figure, this toy providing reassurance while embodying the fight against persecution. Western and superhero texts are shown to be capable of teaching productive moral messages.

Superhero fantasy is also redeemed through more direct narrative means when "Eden," the destination in North Dakota where Laura plans to join the other young mutants, proves to be real. Earlier in the film, Logan had discovered that the coordinates for Eden are provided in one of Laura's comics, causing him to consider it fiction. Eden's existence renders superhero comics not misleading "bullshit" but a compass to the young mutants' salvation. Eden is a desert outpost that leads to the woodland route to Canada. These woods are the site where the mutants face a final onslaught from Alkali-Transigen. The Reavers' cybernetic appendages, four-wheel drives, and assault rifles are a destructive technological intrusion in this Edenic space. Furthermore, they unleash their ultimate biotechnology: X-24. The children counter these technologies with their mutant abilities. While many of these powers are realized through CGI, indicative of how the film has by this point redeemed and become more comfortable with portraying superhero fantasy, they have elemental qualities that link them to the natural surroundings. As a group of young mutants kill the Reavers' leader Donald Pierce (Boyd Holbrook), they bind him to the ground with grass that tightens into a suffocating cocoon while pummeling him with frost, electricity, and air pressure. Nature wins over technology, albeit nature manifested through fantastic abilities realized by digital imaging. Superhero fantasy enables the young mutants to win their freedom, bringing hope back into *Logan*'s timeline.

The prominent sense of *Days of Future Past*'s alternate timeline being malleable while *Logan*'s future is fixed in a trajectory of decline indicates the films' worldviews. *Days of Future Past* upholds values of understanding and liberation that it aligns with the United States. *Logan*, conversely, presents US cities as irreversibly lost to corporate capitalism, the end point of a corrupt civilization that has robbed the US of freedom. Yet *Logan* moves toward a more optimistic conclusion, locating hope in untainted land outside of the US. The ways in which both films present their mutant protagonists further these distinct discourses.

MUTANT BODY POLITICS

The X-Men film series has been criticized for thematizing issues of social prejudice through a predominantly white male cast (see Zingsheim 2011; Brown 2016, 120–24; Smith 2016). As Jason Zingsheim outlines, in the initial trilogy's adaptation process, while many X-Men who hail from outside the US are not included, others are transformed into US citizens: Storm (Halle Berry) is seemingly African American rather than Kenyan, Colossus does not appear Russian, and Wolverine, although played by Australian Hugh Jackman and identified as Canadian, "displays no clear signs of Canadian cultural affiliations . . . [he is instead situated] within the US tradition of aggressive, violent, patriotic, White masculinity" (2011, 230). Meanwhile, Cocca identifies a trend whereby the Fox X-Men films adapt plot element from comics stories that focus on female characters but rework these to "center both quantitatively and qualitatively" (2016a, 81) on the series's central trio of white men: Wolverine, Xavier, and Magneto. This is evident, for example, in how blockbuster *Days of Future Past*'s adaptation of aspects of the "Days of Future Past" comic book storyline sees Wolverine, rather than Kitty, sent back in time, and has him bring together Xavier and Magneto. The hierarchical makeup of the main series X-Men films' team thus operates under similar logics to those that the previous chapter identified in *The Avengers*, its upper echelons negotiating between different models of white masculinity. Although superhero team narratives can offer little space for individual character development,[7] the centrality of Xavier and Magneto's ideological disagreement over relations between mutants and humans ensures that their subjectivities are explored in individual films and across the series. Meanwhile, Wolverine is the only team member who is fully decompressed in solo films. This privileged status, alongside the fact that he is the only character to be played consistently by the same actor and appears in more of Fox's films than any other mutant, situates Wolverine as a structuring node for Fox's X-Men films.

At stake in the alternate timeline narratives of *Days of Future Past* and *Logan* is whether they reinstate or revise the established order of Fox's X-Men films. In their alternation between familiarity and strangeness, they have the opportunity to either affirm or disrupt Wolverine's centrality. The presentation of mutant bodies provides a key site at which this process is negotiated.

A central concern of Fawaz's (2016) study of the "radical imagination" of postwar superhero comics is how this imagination manifests through the superhero body's mutability. For Fawaz, Silver Age superheroes' mutated bodies and disruptive powers articulate identity formations and political positions, particularly those of feminist and queer movements, that challenge normative structures. Shapeshifter Mystique provides a prime example of such a body that "refuse[s] to cohere into a unified image or physiology" (18). Yet the Fox films' treatment of Mystique (Rebecca Romijn in the initial trilogy) demonstrates how, rather than fulfilling her radical potential, she is presented as a source of anxiety that needs containing.

Dorian L. Alexander summarizes the most common aspects of Mystique's portrayal in the X-Men franchise: "An untrustworthy backstabber, a cunning and formidable adversary, slippery, unpredictable, and unforgivably ruthless . . . she remains the mutant femme fatale" (2018, 180). Mystique's morphable physique provides a literal manifestation of cultural constructions of femininity as duplicitous. Deploying her as a femme fatale situates her duplicity in a history of media representations of deceitful women who pose a threat to the patriarchal order. While, as analyzed in the previous chapter, Black Widow's duplicity situates her lower down the Avengers' hierarchy than her male teammates, Mystique's power to change form makes her a greater source of anxiety. The transformations of Mystique's body complement her shifts across the franchise and film series between villain and hero.

Mystique further disrupts limiting constructions of gender by shifting her body between feminine and masculine forms. As Alexander demonstrates, this invites a reading of the character as transsexual. Mystique's gender identity is not determined by her material body: when presenting a male body, she still holds a female identity (181–83). In Alexander's trans reading, Mystique's villainy echoes real world discourse "where transphobic association of transsexuality with purposefully deceiving 'decent folk' forces trans people into the role of villains" (189). Mystique's representation extends beyond the cultural construction of femininity as duplicitous and into the construction of trans people as deceitful. Alexander (186–90) develops their reading by exploring ways in which Mystique is presented as abject and uncanny, her body particularly taking on monstrous qualities in the initial trilogy. The subsequent films, beginning with *First Class*, attempt a more measured exploration of what Mystique's body represents, offering an explicit discourse about embracing her true self. After developing into the figurehead of a mutant revolution in *Apocalypse*, however, Mystique is killed by Jean Grey (Sophie Turner) in *Dark Phoenix*, the shapeshifter's radical trajectory cut short to further the vilification of another mutant woman.

Although Fawaz argues for the radical political potential of the mutable superhero body, Fox's X-Men films ultimately treat Mystique's unstable body as inferior to hard male bodies. Dyer (1997, 148–55) demonstrates that hard muscular bodies historically connote whiteness and assert white superiority. For instance, bodybuilding poses reference classical art depicting gods which has become bound to celebrations of whiteness. If the mutable body can be a vehicle for reimagining the sociopolitical landscape, the hard body is a means of inscribing white superiority.

Wolverine possesses a hard muscular body. The X-Men films' championing of this hard body asserts its physicality over the digital imaging used more prominently on villainous bodies, such as in Mystique's digital morphs. Yet Wolverine's regenerative abilities also give his body mutable qualities; in *Days of Future Past*, his body morphs via digital imaging to rapidly heal when wounded. In *Logan*, meanwhile, his body is deteriorating as its regenerative abilities wane. The different forms of hardness and mutability that Wolverine's body exhibits are central to the two films' negotiation of the X-Men franchise's politics.

WOLVERINE'S BODY

In Fox's X-Men films, Jackman's Wolverine helps maintain continuity amidst fragmentation. His hard physique is central to this stability, scenes in which a shirtless or naked Jackman showcases his musculature being a recurring trope. This stabilizing effect is created despite his body noticeably changing between films. The slim and well-toned body exhibited in 2000's *X-Men* grows over the years so that by 2013's *The Wolverine* Jackman exhibits a bodybuilder physique with bulging veins. Wolverine/Jackman's body remains stable as it bulks up since it is consistently treated as a superior male body and its musculature increasingly conforms to cultural expectations of what a live-action male superhero's body should look like. Daniel J. Connell (2020) explores how the preponderance and presentation of hypermuscular male bodies in twenty-first-century superhero blockbusters obscures the reality of how such bodies are constructed. The work of the actors' trainers and chefs, strategies put in place hours before shirtless scenes are shot such as dehydrating to shrink the skin around muscles, and potential postproduction enhancement of muscles by digital artists, are largely rendered invisible (28–29). The concealment of these processes projects the idea that increases to Jackman's musculature over the years are simply the natural result of his labor.

The stabilizing effect of Wolverine's musculature coheres with the diegetic premise of Wolverine's regenerative abilities slowing his aging. Wolverine's regenerative powers that diegetically rationalize his body's stability "reinscribe the singular, biological, and essential notion of traditional white maleness" (Shyminsky 2006, 398). Wolverine's superpower combines with the hidden processes through which Jackman's musculature is built to further the body's continual assertion of the naturalness of white male power. The iterative structure that Eco identifies in superhero narratives and its sociopolitical function of maintaining the status quo is thus inscribed onto Wolverine's body. In existing outside of the iterative structures of superhero seriality, the alternate timelines of *Days of Future Past* and *Logan* can potentially disrupt the stable seriality of Wolverine's body and its corresponding sociopolitical meanings.

The ways in which the two films use Wolverine's body to negotiate the series's continuity are established in their early uses of the trope of showcasing his body. That these scenes parallel each other in many details—both feature the superhero waking, popping out his claws, being shot, ridding his body of bullets, and looking at his body in the mirror—facilitates an instructive comparison.

In *Days of Future Past*, this scene does not occur in the alternate future. In this dystopia, Wolverine's only signs of aging are some wisps of grey hair; his body is covered by an armored costume, enabling the film to avoid exploring potential aging to his physique. After the older Wolverine's consciousness is sent back to his 1973 body, he wakes up naked, hard muscles situated in opposition to the thin woman's arm draped over him. Upon rising and inspecting himself in a mirror Wolverine notices the grey hairs gone from his temples, but the audience's attention is more clearly directed to his body, which is showcased in full from behind and from the torso upward in front. Sculped muscles and bulging veins proclaim this as a built male body in its prime. While this body is presented as spectacle and has just emerged from the bed in which Wolverine was having sex, narrative and presentational strategies are deployed that Neale (1983) outlines as disavowing the

Wolverine's naked body is showcased in *X-Men: Days of Future Past* (2014).

eroticization of male bodies in Hollywood cinema. These strategies include showing the body enduring pain and retaining the hero's status as active subject when gangsters enter the room and confront Wolverine. As the confrontation escalates Wolverine pops his claws. Unexpectedly, claws made of bone emerge from his knuckles, enforcing the temporal placement of this body on Wolverine's narrative continuity as before he was subjected to experiments that laced his bones with adamantium. The antagonists retaliate by shooting the hero multiple times in the chest. Wolverine winces in pain as he is shot and grunts through gritted teeth as, upon tensing his muscles, his body pushes out the bullets, wounds instantly healing. The malleability of Wolverine's body returns it to a state of hardness. Wolverine proceeds to skillfully dispatch the three gangsters. While Wolverine's strength in the alternate timeline goes unquestioned, the time travel premise is used to affirm his body's hardness, virility, and heroism. The film's use of alternates thus reinscribes the dominance of the hypermuscular white male body that is a key structuring element of the film series's continuity.

Alterations to Wolverine's familiar physical traits are much more pronounced in *Logan*. The ways in which these changes to what effectively constitutes the character's design map the timeline's strangeness are laid out in the opening sequence. The first shot shows the back seat of a limousine being shaken by an outside presence. The camera has to move down to find Logan being jolted awake: an unceremonious introduction to the former hero. This initial glimpse reveals scarring on Logan's cheek and a head of unkempt grey hair. These markers of his healing power fading and body aging distinguish this alternate Logan. The emphasis on bodily deterioration continues in a close-up on Logan's feet shuffling out of the car and limping as he approaches a group of thugs trying to steal the limousine's wheels. In the corresponding

Logan lies on the floor, gasping for breath, in *Logan* (2017).

scene from *Days of Future Past* Wolverine's muscular physique was proudly displayed as he confronted the gangsters; in *Logan*, his eyes droop, shirt and jacket are askew, and his words drawl out to be cut off mid-sentence as he is shot. Rather than standing firm and taking the bullet only to immediately push it back out, Logan is knocked to the ground. A mid-shot of him lying stretched across the widescreen frame, gasping for breath as blood seeps onto his shirt, is overlaid in the bottom right by the film's title, announcing that this image encapsulates the film's reimagining of the titular mutant.

Logan struggles back up and pops his claws only for one of them to stop halfway. As in *Days of Future Past*, the state of his claws locates him on a timeline, in this case providing further evidence of his powers dwindling. The ensuing fight is messy. Logan takes lots of blows and only wins by brutally murdering most of his foes—one manages to escape—in an animalistic rage, a starkly vicious performance of one of the character's famed "berserker rages." The proceeding melancholic piano theme mourns what Logan has become. The music continues as he enters a public restroom. Shirtless in front of a mirror, the camera slowly moves up Logan's bleeding body as he gasps while forcing out each bullet one at a time. His veins still bulge but the musculature now sports scars and his hands shake from the pain as he puts on a clean shirt after this grotesque ritual. The narrative positioning, presentation, and performance of this body resist erotic contemplation, framing it purely through discourses of violence and deterioration. Logan's body thus reflects the landscapes and timeline he inhabits: stable only in the sense of being set in a trajectory of decline. This timeline's situation in opposition to the iterative structures of superhero continuity is further evident in the ways in which this opening echoes while reworking the events of a scene from *The Wolverine*. In that previous film, the superhero is also losing his

Logan's body bleeds as he forces out bullets in *Logan* (2017).

regenerative powers, and after being shot struggles to retain consciousness while removing the bullets in the restroom of a train. Yet the bullet holes are the only wounds on his otherwise impeccable body and immediately after the scene he dispatches gangsters in a spectacular set-piece atop the train, affirming that despite the wounds he is still a superhero. *The Wolverine*, being set in the main series continuity, must revert Wolverine back to his stable superhero role, while *Logan*'s use of alternate timeline tropes facilitates interrogating this role by pushing him far from his assured superhero identity on his character spectrum.

The central aspects of the role that *Logan* interrogates are Wolverine's white masculinity and the figure of the Westerner that occupies a prominent place in his associative framework. Associations of the Westerner are also enforced and complicated by Jackman's star image. While playing gruff hero Wolverine made Jackman a Hollywood star, press coverage and other film roles further aligned him with the Westerner. An early piece of coverage in UK newspaper *Evening Standard* dubs Jackman "the Aussie Clint," describing him as having "the looks and swagger of a young Eastwood" (Rees 2001, 30). Comparisons between Jackman and an icon of the Western genre are capitalized on in film roles that explicitly adopt the iconography and characteristics of the Westerner, such as the duster-sporting eponymous hero of *Van Helsing* (Stephen Sommers 2004) and tough drover in *Australia* (Baz Luhrmann 2008). Neither of these characters are American and the drover allies with Aboriginal Australians, thereby revising the archetypal Westerner's US nationality and championing of whiteness even while Jackman's body connotes white superiority. *Logan* extends the revisionary approach to the figure of the Westerner from Jackman's earlier roles in its reflection on US identity and whiteness.

X-24 showcases a youthful physique with skin taut around muscles in *Logan* (2017).

Dyer demonstrates how the archetypical Westerner embodies white superiority. In the construction of whiteness as superior, enterprise is attributed to the white spirit and the most important vehicle for this enterprise is imperialism (1997, 30–32). The Western genre articulates this spirit by narrating strong white men conquering uncivilized Native Americans. Stylistically "it is in the visceral qualities of the Western—surging through the land, galloping about on horseback, chases, the intensity and skill of fighting, exciting and jubilant music, stunning landscapes—that enterprise and imperialism have had their most undeliberated, powerful appeal" (33). *Logan*, conversely, offers a mournful presentation of the US landscape and its central Westerner. Rather than celebrating the enterprise of the white man the film aligns it with corrupt civilization. Logan's deteriorating body and abrasive personality present the supposed natural superiority of whiteness, as previously emblematized by the stability of Wolverine's built body, and its irrepressible spirit, as a lie. Although, as discussed earlier, *Logan* makes a case for the value of genre fantasy, it also interrogates the Western genre by reframing the genre's classic iconography and themes, with Jackman's body providing a nexus for this revisionary approach.

Logan further problematizes white muscular masculinity in its presentation of X-24, who showcases a youthful physique with skin taut around muscles. Whereas the pronounced markers of Logan's aging, such as his scars, are primarily achieved through physical processes of makeup and prosthetics (Galas 2017), Jackman's appearance as X-24 is achieved by digitally de-aging the actor. In shots where Logan fights X-24, Jackman performs Logan while the clone is realized by digitally mapping a subtly de-aged Jackman's face onto the body of stunt double Eddie Davenport (Image Engine 2017). Holliday (2021–2022) discusses how *Logan*'s pitting of an aging star against a de-aged version of themself is a recurring trope in contemporary Hollywood, other examples being *Terminator: Genisys* (Alan Taylor 2015) and *Gemini Man* (Ang Lee 2019). In these narratives, the digitally de-aged body is typically situated diegetically as an artificial body, thus framing the fight as a collision between "old and young, past and present, presence and absence, authentic and artificial, profilmic and postproduction, virtual and material, and analog and digital" (235). These tensions map more broadly onto *Logan*'s negotiation of a bleak future via the past genre of the Western and the film's valorization of physicality over the highly digital worlds of other X-Men films. The film's favoring of physicality contributes to the vilification of X-24's digitized body. *Logan* thus resituates the hard male body as a source of threat and anxiety, while simultaneously continuing the superhero blockbuster's recurring use of the digital to identify villainous bodies. The hard male body now becomes that which is realized by digital technology, as foregrounded after X-24's assault on the Munson farm when the gaping wound on his face rapidly heals via a digital morph upon having a serum administered. In the film's valorization of the physical, the hard male body is positioned as a construct maintained by artificial means. The acknowledged artificiality of X-24's body furthers *Logan*'s exposure of the naturalness of the muscular white male body as a lie.

The differing qualities of harness and softness, stability and malleability, that Wolverine's body exhibits in *Days of Future Past* and *Logan* are interlocked with the films' uses of alternate timeline tropes. *Days of Future Past* harnesses the stabilizing function of Wolverine's body to reiterate familiar values that underpin Fox's X-Men films. Conversely, *Logan* disrupts this stability, its strange presentation of the hard male body's deterioration interrogating such values. *Days of Future Past* and *Logan* consolidate their distinct sociopolitical meanings in the endings given to their alternate timelines, particularly in their deployments of finality—through character deaths—and continuation.

WHO GETS A FUTURE?

Days of Future Past and *Logan* both prominently deploy the alternate timeline trope of character deaths, but the nature of these deaths, along with the films' relationship to the main series continuity, affect their meanings and wider impact on the X-Men franchise. *Days of Future Past* massacres a swath of characters while *Logan* builds up to the momentous death of its titular hero. The narrative framing of these deaths affects the textual afterlives of the deceased and those left alive. *Days of Future Past*'s presentation of time and space as malleable sets up an act of continuity maintenance that performs what Johnson (2017, 137–38) terms a "soft" reboot: resetting certain narrative elements without completely dismantling existing continuity. Through successfully averting the dystopian future, Wolverine also alters all events occurring in the prime timeline after 1973, ensuring that subsequent films are not obliged to maintain continuity with the initial trilogy. The film's closing moments, however, establish a framework for which characters should get a textual future. *Logan*'s depiction of the US in irreversible decline maps onto Logan's trajectory toward death, the film imagining an endpoint that limits the potential for its surviving characters to textually exist beyond the final scene. These deaths and futures have a racial dimension that is in dialogue with Fox's X-Men films' character and textual hierarchies.

Days of Future Past's alternate timeline features a more racially and ethnically diverse X-Men team than any previous X-Men film. The team includes Bishop (in comics of Aboriginal descent, here played by Black Frenchman Omar Sy), Warpath (in comics Apache, here played by BooBoo Stewart whose mixed descent includes Blackfoot heritage), Blink (in comics having purple skin and born in the Bahamas, here played by Bingbing), and Sunspot (in comics Brazilian, here played by Mexican Adan Canto). These characters had not been introduced to the franchise when the "Days of Future Past" comic book storyline was released, but Bishop became the time traveler in popular animated series *X-Men*'s (Fox Kids Network 1992–1997) adaptation of the storyline. Yet as with changes to the roles of female characters from the comic book storyline's narrative, *Days of Future Past* reduces Bishop's role from the animated series to privilege the film series's central white characters. After the dystopian future is averted, Wolverine wakes in a new timeline which golden tinted imagery codes as utopic. Wolverine walks around a pristine school, and a rush of restorative nostalgia for the initial film trilogy is offered as he encounters its X-Men—played by the original cast—alive and well. Amongst these, Storm is the only person of color.[8] The presence of Jean, Cyclops (James Marsden), and Xavier, who had died in the initial trilogy, indicates that the events of those three films have been undone while their racial structures have been reaffirmed. In this new timeline, Bishop, Warpath, Blink, and Sunspot are nowhere to be seen; they have been erased with the alternate timeline so that an order that privileges whiteness can be reinstated. It is not only characters that are resurrected but also Xavier's school in Westchester, thus locating this utopia in US suburbia, far from the Eastern locations where the X-Men hid in the dystopian timeline. *Days of Future Past*'s alternate timeline narrative reaffirms the established order.

Logan, conversely, utilizes its premise as an endpoint for Wolverine to challenge the established structures by which Fox's X-Men film series is sustained. Whereas in *Days of Future Past* the racially and ethnically diverse mutants of the future are sacrificed so that the white core of X-Men can be reinstated, in *Logan* it is Logan who is sacrificed so that the Latinx children can live. Although this sacrifice echoes white savior narratives, the children are not simply saved by the heroic white man's sacrifice; these young mutants prove vital to securing their own freedom, for instance collectively killing Pierce.

The presentation of Logan's death and its aftermath intervenes in conventions of superhero continuity and the Western genre. X-24 brutally kills Logan, the hard male body revitalizing itself by eliminating its deteriorating counterpart. This event testifies to the inescapable violence in which *Shane*'s remorseful gunslinger sees the Westerner as trapped. By killing Logan, X-24 supersedes him in embodying the Westerner's inherent violence. In the presentation of X-24, the film's reframing of the hard white male body that stabilizes the iteration of the X-Men films from natural and heroic to artificial and bestial thus culminates in asserting this body's role as an inherently destructive force that cannot change. These moves express a perspective comparable to Eco's: iterative superhero continuity only enforces the established order.

The iterative cycle is broken when Laura kills X-24 by shooting the weaponized clone with an adamantium bullet. Laura's recitation of the monologue from *Shane* in *Logan*'s final scene, as the children gather around Logan's grave, underscores the ways in which the film shows characters learning from genre while productively reframing it. Kent (2021) offers astute analysis of this use of the monologue. Whereas in *Shane*, the eponymous hero utters the words to articulate "the essential nature of masculine violence and the possibility that death is the logical resolution of this" (141), having Laura repeat the words reframes them "as an expression of Laura's grief at the departure of Logan, rather than as the tragic hero's resignation to his predetermined demise" (141). Crucially, unlike the hero in *Shane*, Laura does not go away alone to die, but leaves surrounded by peers to live (142). Laura has internalized the Western's moral teachings and used this knowledge to escape the trajectory of violence in which the traditional Westerner is trapped. Change to the established order is further evident in the film's dethroning of white masculinity. *Logan*'s reflection on genre conventions thus facilitates revisionism.

Broadly speaking, *Days of Future Past* and *Logan* invert the balancing of familiarity and strangeness in the trajectories of the comic book storylines whose plots they loosely adapt. "Days of Future Past" uses its alternate timeline to initiate shifts in the prime timeline that develop an exploration of Jewish identity; *Days of Future Past* reinstates the familiar hegemonic order for the film series going forward.[9] "Old Man Logan" moves from the strange premise of Logan as pacifist to returning him to a more familiar violent role; *Logan* has its titular character return to his familiar superhero role only to sever his cycle of violence and thus disrupt the established order. These inversions reveal that, even when a superhero blockbuster identifies a specific comics storyline as its source through strategies like its title and style, to understand its adaptive process one still needs to consider the wider network of intertextual forces with which it is dialogically engaged. Alternate timelines provide a stark diegetic manifestation of the negotiation of other incarnations, intertexts from elsewhere in popular culture, sociopolitical contexts, industrial trends, and innovation that is always at work when a new text is produced in a superhero franchise.

The narrative framing of both films' alternate timelines—*Days of Future Past*'s potential future that in being averted reboots the main series continuity and *Logan*'s imaginary endpoint—affects their impact on the wider franchise. *Days of Future Past*'s affirmative position on the future's mutability, expressed through its aestheticization of time as malleable, is undermined by the restoration of a familiar social order. Subsequent main series films largely continue to perpetuate this order. In *Apocalypse* and *Dark Phoenix*, Storm (Alexandra Shipp) is the only Black character on a roster of white and blue (played by white actors) X-Men while Jean and Mystique gain central roles only for the former to become psychologically unstable and kill the latter. Xavier and Magneto remain central although, with *Logan* widely publicized as Jackman's last outing as Wolverine, his stabilizing presence only features in one sequence in *Apocalypse*—for which he appears, characteristically, shirtless—and not at all in *Dark Phoenix*. None of the mutants who were introduced in *Days of Future Past*'s alternate timeline return in *Apocalypse* or *Dark Phoenix*.

In linking the Westerner's inherent violence to the iterative structure of superhero continuity, which in Fox's X-Men films is inscribed into the hard white male body, *Logan* critiques the film series's underpinning structures but limits its ability to rework them. Bringing an end to this cycle in an alternate timeline largely forecloses the possibility of its young mutants featuring in future films. As Connell outlines, Laura's role in the film's third act "denotes a changing of the guard, a move away from the hypermasculine extremes of previous outings. The trouble with this notion is that this is a bubble: there is no series, no sequel, and no actual change ... there is every chance we might not see Laura—our true change in the environment—again" (2020, 30–31). *Logan*'s closing shot of Wolverine's grave proclaims this the final resting place for both Jackman's iteration of the character and this timeline. The young mutants have successfully crossed the border into Canada, but the exploration of spaces outside US cities where utopia could be cultivated ends in these woodlands. While the film decenters white masculinity and critiques contemporary US values, the narrative framework through which it expresses these meanings restricts their potential to impact other X-Men films.

This is not to say, however, that the constitution of the X-Men franchise remains static. Like all superhero franchises, it is a fluid and contested space, and imaginary stories have power to affect its composition despite forces that limit their reach. Although, at the time of this writing, Keen has not had another starring role as Laura, the character has become increasingly central to X-Men comics in the two decades since her 2003 debut in animated television series *X-Men: Evolution* (Kids' WB 2000–2003). Kent (2021, 143) traces how in 2016 Laura first took the mantle of Wolverine in the 616 comics universe and has since featured in many prominent stories both in place of and alongside Logan's Wolverine, frequently featuring on the main X-Men team. Along with these steps to draw Laura into the center of X-Men comics, white masculinity was decentered in Fox's final X-Men film, *The New Mutants*, which focuses on Cheyenne girl Dani Moonstar (Blu Hunt) who develops a romantic relationship with Scottish girl Rahne Sinclair (Maisie Williams). A thread can also be traced from *Days of Future Past*, with *The New Mutants* featuring a new incarnation of Sunspot (Henrique Zaga). Meanwhile, Blink (Jamie Chung) and Warpath's brother, John Proudstar (Blair Redford), have central roles in Fox's live-action television series *The Gifted* (Fox 2017–2019). The status of *The New Mutants* and *The Gifted* in the X-Men film series's hierarchy, however, is telling. Both are bracketed off from the main series X-Men films, with the flagship team alluded to only in dialogue. Medium-budget *The New Mutants* is placed in closer proximity by featuring loose intertextual links to other Fox X-Men films[10] while *The Gifted* is situated in a universe where the X-Men have disappeared. As with the MCU, textual and media hierarchies privilege the biggest budget blockbusters and are interlocked with racial hierarchies. The core of primarily white X-Men are reserved for Fox's main series films, while lower stake films and television shows give characters of color more prominent roles.

The change to the X-Men films' industrial management that occurred when Disney gained the franchise's cinematic licensing rights upon purchasing Fox in 2019, and the corresponding end to the Fox films, brings about the potential for reorganizing the franchise when the X-Men are introduced into the MCU. Yet in doing so the X-Men will enter the MCU's hierarchical structures in which, as with the Fox films, changes to the racial and gendered formations struggle under the entrenched power of white masculinity. At the time of this writing, Disney has shown no inclination to continue the adventures of the young mutants from either *Logan* or *The New Mutants*. In 2022, however, it was announced that Jackman would reprise the role of Wolverine in a third Deadpool film—the one Fox series that Disney is currently continuing—which was subsequently titled *Deadpool & Wolverine* (Shawn Levy 2024). Jackman's highly publicized return to the role affirms his incarnation of Wolverine's continuing centrality to the X-Men franchise, which is starkly literalized in *Deadpool & Wolverine*'s premise identifying Wolverine as the "anchor being" whose existence ensures his universe's stability. Following Logan's death, the universe Deadpool inhabits (which is situated as the one from *Logan*) starts deteriorating, prompting Deadpool to recruit a Wolverine from another timeline. The proceeding multiversal adventure features cameo appearances from iterations of characters from Marvel's cinematic past, including Keen's Laura. Despite *Deadpool & Wolverine*'s intertextual engagement with *Logan*, however, Wolverine is recentered, his team up with Deadpool at the narrative's core. The film climaxes with the duo short circuiting a machine set to destroy all timelines by using their bodies to create a new circuit between the machine's twin power sources of matter and antimatter. As the matter and antimatter surge through Wolverine's veins, their annihilatory collision causes his costume to explode off his chest, showcasing the superhero's sculpted muscles bulging as they strain to save the multiverse. Although knowingly hyperbolizing the treatment of Jackman's body in earlier X-Men films, *Deadpool & Wolverine*'s parodic treatment of the character is ultimately complicit in upholding Wolverine, and the model of white masculinity that he embodies, as a stabilizing factor for the X-Men franchise.

As my analysis of *Days of Future Past* and *Logan* has shown, in these cinematic realizations of alternate timelines, differing degrees of mutability and stability in the presentation of spaces and bodies map familiarity and strangeness. Whereas previous chapters elucidated how tensions between the digital and physical, alongside the hybridization of superhero conventions with other genres, can be deployed in superhero blockbusters to construct meanings within individual films and across multiple films that share a diegetic universe, I have demonstrated that these and other factors can also be used to distinguish timelines. The superhero blockbuster's adaptive strategies are thus reworked and developed in the construction of alternate timelines that can maintain, reinvigorate, or interrogate film series and fictional universes.

CONCLUSION

CRISIS ON THE DC EXTENDED UNIVERSE

In the twenty-first century, the superhero genre has risen to a newfound prominence in Hollywood but has not cast off its comic book roots. Along with reworking narrative and stylistic elements from networks of texts in a range of media that includes decades of comic books, superhero blockbusters metamorphose superhero comic books' aesthetic strategies, while adapting their methods for managing vast fictional universes and multiverses. Through doing so, the superhero blockbuster develops its own set of motifs and tropes, yet these maintain dialogue with comic book aesthetics. The approach that I have developed in this book illuminates the central role of style and form in managing the textual networks that superhero texts construct in franchises, universes, and multiverses. Understanding how superhero blockbusters organize these networks is vital when interrogating the films' adaptive strategies, style, and meanings.

As has also been demonstrated, superhero blockbusters' adaptive strategies harness and refine qualities of the Hollywood blockbuster paradigm that *Superman: The Movie* helped establish in the 1970s. Superhero blockbusters foreground special effects spectacle while employing it in the negotiation of their textual networks. Cutting-edge special effects reenvision popular superheroes and the universes they inhabit in fantastic new ways. This showcases the technologies while pushing blockbuster incarnations of superheroes to the center of their franchises and provides ways to express, in metamorphosed form, common themes of franchises and the genre, such as when Spider-Man's dynamic digital body conveys his bond with New York and rearticulates the superhero genre's fascination with the urban metropolis in a post-9/11 America. In the twenty-first century, digital filmmaking technologies produce such special effects while providing tools to de-age actors, facilitating the exploration of cinematic universes across time and space. If *The Movie* tested strategies of serialized blockbuster production in the 1970s, in the twenty-first century the MCU expanded blockbusters' modes of seriality into a shared universe model while Fox's X-Men films began envisioning alternate timelines. Both techniques adapt storytelling strategies from superhero comics books, in doing so intensifying the Hollywood blockbuster's pursuit of textual multiplication by mapping ways to manage serial storytelling across series, universes, and multiverses.

The complex forms of intertextuality evident in these fictional constructs incorporate while modifying traditional forms of Hollywood intertextuality. Stars' personas are placed in dialogue with the franchise characters that they play, having the potential to amplify or reframe these characters' associations along with shaping their wider role in their fictional universe. Genre's traditional function of identifying groups of texts that can be read in relation to one another while being distinguished from other textual groupings is refocused in a system in which franchises and universes perform these functions. The Hollywood blockbuster's genre hybridity is, in superhero blockbusters, deployed to offer familiar points of reference that map distinguishing features of characters, universes, and timelines. Furthermore, points of overlap between genres can be foregrounded to harmonize the pluralities of characters and universes, for example linking together various qualities from Superman's spectrum of possible roles or constructing continuity between Iron Man and Thor's respective associations with modern warfare and fantasy. These strategies provide means for consolidating the textual networks that Hollywood blockbusters seek to maintain. With the twenty-first-century superhero blockbuster boom currently in its third decade, appreciation of superhero blockbusters' adaptive and intertextual strategies is crucial to understanding their role in sustaining and developing Hollywood's blockbuster filmmaking paradigm.

As superhero franchises, universes, and multiverses expand and multiply in blockbuster films, they undergo crises along the way. Many of these involve commercial or critical failings that lead to narrative continuity being rebooted. Meanwhile, corporate acquisitions and changing licensing rights can reshape a Hollywood studio's superhero output. At the time of this writing, a fourth blockbuster iteration Superman is being planned, Spider-Man is on his third, and the MCU is slowly incorporating the X-Men. The MCU's expansion has not, however, gone unimpeded, with the MCU's increasing signs of faltering leading, in November 2023, to the headline of a widely discussed *Variety* article by Tatiana Siegel declaring "Marvel in Crisis." Siegel joins Robinson, Gonzalez, and Edwards (2023) in identifying significant problems for Marvel Studios emerging after the "Infinity Saga." For instance, Robinson, Gonzalez, and Edwards (422–26), in their book chronicling the MCU, outline factors including the accusations of assault and harassment against Kang actor Jonathan Majors (for which he was found guilty of two counts), the loss of other key MCU stars and the characters they played for a range of reasons, and pressure from Disney for an increased quantity of texts prompting lapses in quality that negatively impacted certain films both critically and commercially.

One of the most prominent crises of the superhero blockbuster boom occurred in DC Studios' effort to sustain a shared cinematic universe, the DC Extended Universe (DCEU), which is rife with dislocation.[1] For example, the DCEU's approach to certain franchises has changed course, as occurred with the reworking of the eponymous team from *Suicide Squad* (David Ayer 2016) in *The Suicide Squad* (James Gunn 2021), while all-star ensemble film *Justice League* branched into two distinct versions, the 2017 theatrical cut and *Justice League: The Snyder Cut* (Zack Snyder 2021). Eventually, the crisis became terminal, and via the tried-and-tested means of an alternate timeline narrative, *The Flash* (Andrés Muschietti 2023) performed an act of universe management that paved the way for a new cinematic iteration of DC's universe in what has officially been named the DC Universe (DCU). This streamlined name reflects the streamlining of unwieldly continuity that has frequently occurred in comic book crossover events, with *The Flash* particularly drawing narrative influence from crossover event *Flashpoint*. The framework for analyzing superhero blockbusters developed in this book is primed for examining both the DCEU's distinct features and the ways in which its films participate in the superhero blockbuster's established strategies, motifs, and tropes. I now end the book by demonstrating that the analytical tools I have developed are both pliable and incisive, facilitating continued examination of superhero blockbusters as filmmakers take distinct approaches and navigate crises, by applying these tools to analysis of the DCEU.

REESTABLISHING SUPERMAN AND HIS UNIVERSE

The DCEU began by anchoring itself in a new incarnation of DC's longest running superhero, Superman, in solo film *Man of Steel*. It then took something on an inverse approach to the MCU by, rather than introducing other key superheroes in solo films, fast-tracking to ensemble film *Batman v*

Superman strains to regain control of his flight, framed by a backdrop of Metropolis presented upside down, in *Man of Steel* (2013).

Superman. This distinct composition still, however, performs the reconfiguration of individual franchises and management of the universe's continuity seen in other superhero blockbusters.

Man of Steel seek to launch actor Henry Cavill's Superman into the center of the network of texts in various media and iterations that comprise the Superman franchise. Distancing itself from previous Superman films, *Man of Steel* refocuses the franchise around its dark pole, channeling post-9/11 sentiment into a model of emotionally withdrawn and aggressive masculinity. Romance is downplayed while violence is amplified. One of the only strategies that *Man of Steel* retains from *Superman: The Movie* is framing flight penetrating through the depth of cinematic space. Yet assertions of superior spectacle in the flight sequences where the superhero bursts forcefully rather than gliding elegantly through the air, bolstered in 3D versions of the film which augment cinematic depth and showcase Superman's power by having him at times breach negative parallax, seek to push aside the Reeve films. These claims to enhanced spectacle culminate in *Man of Steel*'s climactic aerial battle between Superman and Zod (Michael Shannon). The choreography comprises an onslaught of movement as Superman and Zod launch physical assaults on each other, their bodies alternating between firing and tumbling through Metropolis's sky, the virtual camera rushing tirelessly to keep up. In 3D versions, each throws or punches the other deep into positive parallax. This chaotic tumult, realized through digital special effects, showcases trajectories of movement absent from *The Movie*'s flight scenes alongside increased violence.

Upon Zod throwing Superman through multiple skyscrapers, a shot frames the superhero head-on as he careens through an open plan office. This hurtling trajectory ends on a slowed image in which Superman strains to regain control of his flight, framed by a backdrop of the city presented upside down. While recalling the upside-down presentation of the city when Superman's flight was showcased in *The Movie*, this shot's contents and narrative context underscore key differences between the films. Shards of glass rain upward in the upside-down composition. The city's topsy-turviness is no longer an expression of thrilling freedom but of chaotic danger, skyscrapers becoming foci of destruction and tragedy. It is no leap to read this as an articulation of post-9/11 fear of attacks on Western cities, with Zod filling the role of terrorist.

Cavill's Superman's positioning at a violent point on the character's spectrum that is anchored in the post-9/11 context, along with this incarnation's conceptualization of the American way, are underscored when he kills Zod. When Superman has Zod in a headlock, the Kryptonian terrorist directs his laser vision at a human family. Superman grimaces as, rather than letting civilians die, he snaps Zod's neck, then drops to his knees and screams in anguish. Brown outlines how Superman's actions express that "the world has changed, and after 9/11 American values have changed along with it" (2016, 101), thereby echoing the Bush administration's justification for the "war on terror." In dialogue with contemporary sociopolitical contexts, the American way is reframed as regretful but necessary violence.

Batman v Superman accelerates the expansion of the universe established in *Man of Steel*, maintaining its rooting in discourses of aggressive masculinity while depicting the first encounters between Bruce Wayne/Batman (Ben Affleck), Clark/Superman, and Diana Prince/Wonder Woman (Gal Gadot). *Batman v Superman* performs processes of compression and franchise management to establish its new incarnation of Batman. The traumatic events that instigated Bruce's transformation into Batman are compressed into the opening title sequence, which shows his parents' murder, their funeral, and Bruce falling into a cave inhabited by bats. This economic retelling of Batman's origin assumes audience familiarity with these events, which in cinema were most recently retold in 2005's *Batman Begins*. Meanwhile, particular images gesture to specific texts from the Batman franchise, such as close-ups on Martha Wayne's (Lauren Cohan) pearl necklace being stretched and broken as she is murdered, which recreate the imagery of panels from *The Dark Knight Returns* #1 (June 1986). The DCEU's history and relations to a network of texts are outlined in familiar motifs.

As has become evident throughout this book, in superhero blockbusters spaces and bodies have complex connotative functions, while providing sites through which franchises, universes, and timelines are negotiated. In

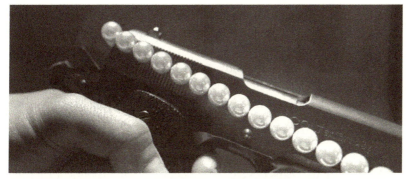

Martha Wayne's pearl necklace is stretched by her attacker in *Batman v Superman: Dawn of Justice* (2016).

Martha Wayne's pearl necklace is stretched by her attacker in *The Dark Knight Returns* #1 (1986).

Batman v Superman, the *Daily Planet* offices and the Batcave provide Clark's and Bruce's home environments. Unlike the screwball comedy-infused *Daily Planet* offices of *The Movie*, in *Batman v Superman* the newspaper offices are a space for solemn sociopolitical discourse, affirming the DCEU's reconfiguration of the Superman franchise around the dark pole. Meanwhile, an armored costume on display in the Batcave has the words "HAHAHA joke's on you BATMAN" scrawled across in yellow spray paint. The words and "HAHAHA" motif indicate that they were written by supervillain Joker, while the more subtle "R" on the costume that they cover confirms that this costume belonged to Batman sidekick Robin. This image does not just signify Joker's presence in the universe but also gives him a specific history; it points to "A Death in the Family," a comic book story from *Batman* #426–29 (December 1988–January 1989) in which Joker kills Robin, therefore suggesting that this event also happened in the DCEU. Through the way it interlocks with another text from the Batman franchise, this grim detail rationalizes why Affleck's Batman has become so aggressive. The *Daily Planet* offices and the Batcave are representative of Superman and Batman's respective cities, Metropolis and Gotham, which the characters come to embody. As Jason Bainbridge explains, "Metropolis is often referred to [by comic book creators] as New York by day and Gotham as New York by night" (2010, 163). Metropolis typically affirms the modern city's dazzling wonders; Gotham discloses the city's dark underside. While Gotham performs its familiar role in *Batman v Superman*, Metropolis has given way to a disillusionment that weighs on Clark/Superman. *Batman v Superman*'s compression of these sentiments into discrete internal spaces and its superheroes compares to the strategy through which superheroes embody different values in Marvel Studios' all-star ensemble films. Placing the two visions of the modern city and their corresponding superheroes in relation to one another also participates in the superhero genre's ongoing thematization of the wonders and fears of urban experience.

The presentation and ontology of superheroes' bodies situates them within their franchises and in relation to other superheroes and supervillains. Affleck's and Cavill's profilmic musculature is showcased in separate scenes where the characters are shirtless. Their physiques are pointedly larger than other performers who have previously played Batman and Superman, implicitly positioning these incarnations of the characters as superior. For example, in *Batman Begins* Christian Bale's Bruce effortlessly executes rapid press-ups, but Affleck's Bruce trumps this by undertaking pull-ups with a boulder chained to his legs. While Bruce trains to maintain his muscle, Clark's musculature is the result of his alien biology, which also grants him superpowers that are hailed as godlike in the film. Both physiques, however, continue the tradition in which hard muscular bodies assert white superiority, as discussed in chapter four. Their distinct narrative framing represents a clash between different embodiments of white American masculinity: Superman's innate power, which upholds the American way, and Batman's discipline over both his body and capitalist enterprise. It is Batman's enterprise and intellect that grants him the upper hand in the battle between the two after he shoots Superman with a shell he designed made from kryptonite, a material that is deadly to Kryptonians. The physical

Doomsday's bones grow out of his skin and he uncontrollably emits krackle in *Batman v Superman: Dawn of Justice* (2016).

blows Batman subsequently exchanges with Superman demonstrate that his maintenance of strong masculinity allows him to engage in physical battle with godlike beings.

Superhero blockbusters' recurring explorations of different kinds of capitalism represent one way in which they endeavor to express sociopolitical meanings. The films' aesthetic strategies manifest and shape these meanings. In *Batman v Superman*, Bruce's entrepreneurial capitalism functions comparably to Iron Man's in the MCU, facilitating his development of weapons of war that elevate him to godlike status. *Batman v Superman*'s villain, Lex Luthor (Jesse Eisenberg), is presented as another kind of entrepreneurial capitalist. Lex's jittery demeanor recalls Eisenberg's performance as Mark Zuckerberg in *The Social Network* (David Fincher 2010), affirming his status as a young and reckless twenty-first-century entrepreneurial capitalist. Doomsday, a hypermasculine creature that Lex creates from his own and Zod's DNA, embodies the instability attributed to Lex's form of capitalism. Lex's scrawny physique is all intellect and no brawn. Doomsday inverts this structure, manifesting a monstrous body with no intellect. Doomsday's body defies criteria of perceptual realism by transcending abilities of terrestrial beings, the creature effortlessly propelling his bulky form through the air. A mid-shot in which bones grow out of Doomsday's skin while he uncontrollably emits jagged red krackle encapsulates how his physical and conceptual qualities connote the subconscious of a dangerous and unstable psyche. As is often the case in superhero blockbusters, a villain's overtly digital form signifies a disconnect from humanity. Superman defeats Doomsday by stabbing this monster with Batman's kryptonite spear. This act, by which Superman sacrifices himself, champions Superman's nobility and physical strength while justifying the deadly weaponry developed through the entrepreneurial capitalist's intelligence, thus affirming the film's perspective that an entrepreneurial capitalism that combines strength of mind and body can be a force for elevating humanity.

Each of this book's chapters has touched on ways that superhero blockbusters exhibit awareness of, yet struggle to renegotiate, the marginal position of women in the genre. In *Batman v Superman*, Wonder Woman is not granted her own space but rather gestures outward to the universe's diegetic history and textual future. These gestures often depend on audience knowledge of the Wonder Woman franchise. For example, a photo marked "Belgium, November 1918" shows Wonder Woman standing alongside soldiers in World War I, encapsulating her status as ageless demigoddess and warrior while indicating that this story will be explored in a subsequent film.

Without a discrete space to inhabit in *Batman v Superman*, Diana/Wonder Woman's body becomes the primary means of establishing her role in the universe. The scarlet dress in which Diana is first seen has a thick metallic circle around the neck, while the sequined texture of the silver dress in which she is next seen recalls chainmail. Both dresses feature cutaway areas that display parts of her body, including cleavage, back, and her shoulder and collar bones. These designs gesture to the partially armored qualities of her superhero costume, which covers her chest, wrists, and lower legs in protective metal, while leaving the rest of her skin bare. Diana/Wonder Woman's costumes connote her diegetic and textual history as a warrior, indicating physical strength that situates her alongside the male superheroes, while simultaneously sexualizing her slender, feminine physique. Wonder Woman's power is showcased in the battle against Doomsday. She arrives just in time to protect Batman's human body from Doomsday's laser vision, absorbing the blast with her wrist-covering bracelets and then using them to fire a shockwave that shunts the monster back. These actions demonstrate her power that exceeds the human. The accompanying musical theme of racing chords played on an electric cello resonates like a battle cry from the past transposed to the present. These initial impressions are affirmed as Wonder Woman fights alongside the godlike Superman, battling Doomsday with a sword and shield. While this climactic battle certifies Wonder Woman's position of power in the DCEU, however, her associations of historical war underscore how she is removed from the film's central discourses on masculinized structures in the contemporary US city.

In expanding the DCEU in an ensemble film in which the new incarnations of two of its three superheroes had not been introduced in solo films, *Batman v Superman* refocuses aspects of universe management. In its compressed introductions of Batman and Wonder Woman, audience knowledge

Wonder Woman in *Batman v Superman: Dawn of Justice* (2016).

of the characters' wider franchises is heavily called on. Hierarchical continuity is foregrounded over narrative continuity by placing a superhero versus superhero battle at the film's core. In the character hierarchy that emerges, Wonder Woman is situated lower down than the film's headline male duo, whose values come to underpin the universe.

OVERHAULING A WORLD OF MEN

The masculinized structure for the DCEU established in *Batman v Superman* is broadly reflective of superhero blockbusters' gendered underpinnings. In DC Studios granting Wonder Woman a solo film in the universe's early stages, however, filmmakers had the opportunity to decompress the longest-running female superhero and have her intervene in the DCEU's underpinning structures. *Wonder Woman*, the DCEU's fourth film, thematizes its superhero's placement in masculinized structures in a narrative in which the demigoddess leaves her native island of Themyscira and travels to what the Amazons who inhabit Themyscira dub the "world of men." In being set during World War I, Wonder Woman delivers on *Batman v Superman*'s promise of expanding the universe's history. Yet Taylor and Glitsos (2023) outline how, as with *Captain Marvel*, this premise represents another instance of a female superhero's solo film being set in the past, thus containing its feminist themes in a closed moment. Despite being unable to directly interrogate the DCEU's masculinized structures, however, *Wonder Woman* reframes common gendered tropes of the superhero genre, which effectively represents another "world of men," while gesturing to the wider DCEU.

The Wonder Woman franchise historically reworks the superhero genre's gendered logics, taking the quality of physical strength typically ascribed as masculine and combining it with feminine compassion. Noah Berlatsky (2015) explores how Wonder Woman cocreator psychologist William Moulton Marston, who wrote Wonder Woman comics under the penname Charles Moulton from her debut in *All-Star Comics* #8 (January 1942) until his death in 1947, imbued the character with his psychological theories, particularly his conviction that a utopian society would be based on loving, strong women inducing others into submission. In Marston's stories, Wonder Woman's compassion and use of physical violence are not opposed qualities; rather, love is "the quintessence of force. . . . Love turns people into superior, more erotically invested state cogs, who will socialize better, produce better, and if need be, fight better" (Berlatsky 2015, 100). While subsequent Wonder Woman creators typically distance the stories from Marston's views on dominance and submission, which were interlaced with eroticism, the binding of conventionally masculine and feminine qualities has remained a defining feature of Wonder Woman's character spectrum.

This combination is underscored in the ways in which classical gods are placed central to Wonder Woman's associative framework. While the superhero genre is rooted in discourses of urban modernity, with Superman's powers recurringly compared to the accomplishments of industrialization like locomotives and skyscrapers, Wonder Woman was introduced in *All-Star Comics* #8 as being "as lovely as Aphrodite—as wise as Athena—with the speed of Mercury and the strength of Hercules." Although removed from the modern technologies claimed by the male superhero, Wonder Woman's alignment with both female and male figures from Greek and Roman mythology attributes to her a mixture of qualities coded feminine and masculine. The opening page of *Wonder Woman* #1 (June 1942) clearly demarcates the balance of these qualities. One of the figures whose powers Wonder Woman possesses is in each corner. Aphrodite and Athena are at the top, Hercules and Mercury at the bottom, thus reflecting the ordering in the worded description and mapping a hierarchy in which the women are above the men. Meanwhile, Wonder Woman is placed nearer Aphrodite and Athena, again suggesting the primacy of the goddesses and superiority of the feminine. Cocca notes that from *Sensation Comics* #17 (May 1943) and *Wonder Woman* #5 (July 1943), Wonder Woman's introduction was amended to "'beautiful *as* Aphrodite, wise *as* Athena, stronger *than* Hercules, and swifter *than* Mercury,' leaving no doubt as to her equality with the female gods and supremacy over the male gods" (2016b, 26, Cocca's emphasis). This modification further refines the hierarchy of gendered qualities.

Wonder Woman's association with myth complements her alignment with nature. Her home environment, fictional island Themyscira (renamed from

The opening page of *Wonder Woman* #1 (1942) situates Wonder Woman in relation to Aphrodite, Athena, Hercules, and Mercury.

Paradise Island in the 1987 comic book relaunch), combines the two while offering a distinct example of the superhero genre's recurring efforts to conceptualize utopia. Justin Hall identifies the Golden Age comic book representation of Paradise Island "as a traditional separatist utopia . . . Marston, made it very clear that the Amazons were running a society better than men

Themyscira in *Wonder Woman* (2017).

ever could, away from patriarchal oppression" (Fawaz, Hall, and Kinsella 2017, 9–10). The film's presentation of Themyscira adapts this construction. Curtis outlines how the film's Themyscira foregrounds intersectionality "in the prominence of women of color and the suggestion of the Amazons' lesbianism" (2020, 934). The Amazons that populate Themyscira represent a range of body types, races, and ages.[2] The film complements the island's social organization with representational strategies that, following Dyer, evoke utopia as a feeling and, following Bukatman, encapsulate utopia as unrestricted movement. The island is rich in vegetation, the verdant landscape showcased in all its splendor as the differing shades of green gleam in bright sunlight. The first time we see the island, a young Diana runs freely through it, playfully evading her tutor. The passage of time is inscribed into the environment, with statues corroding and foliage spreading, yet the persistent copresence of leaf and stone creates a sense of balance. Themyscira's utopia founded on femininity and nature is shown to be long-established and maintained over time.[3]

Through the contrast Themyscira provides to the world of men, the latter is constructed as dystopian. Themyscira's bright greens and blue sky provide a stark contrast to the dank shades in which the film presents the world of men. The contrast is made strikingly apparent after US soldier Steve Trevor (Chris Pine) washes up on Themyscira's shore. As the camera proceeds to drift through the invisible wall that conceals Themyscira from the surrounding world to reveal pursuing German boats, the resplendent hues shift into a dark and foreboding seascape. The world of men's washed-out palette recalls the coloring of *Man of Steel* and *Batman v Superman*. Thus, although *Wonder Woman*'s events are contained in the universe's past, the critique the film mounts of the world of men and its gender inequalities gestures to the universe's present and the structures by which it is governed.

As in *Batman v Superman*, the world of men in *Wonder Woman* is in the thrall of violent masculinity. *Wonder Woman* aligns this violence with deception and places it in opposition to peace and truth. This arrangement rejects the superhero genre's recurring alignment of femininity with duplicity, as seen in the figures of Black Widow and Mystique, and instead aligns femininity with truth. Wonder Woman's association with truth is encapsulated in her lasso. The superhero initially gained a "magic lasso" that compelled people to obey her every command in *Sensation Comics* #6 (June 1942). After the character was relaunched following *Crisis on Infinite Earths*, the weapon was reconceptualized as a "lasso of truth" in *Wonder Woman* vol. 2 #2 (March 1987), its power of control over others now modified to simply compelling them to honesty. This modification repositioned Wonder Woman on her spectrum, away from a figure that induced submission to a point where she more purely embodies truth. The film, both in its utilization of the lasso's "post-Crisis" function and thematization of truth and deception, positions its incarnation of Wonder Woman as an embodiment of truth. Conversely, the world of men is permeated by lies; Steve's occupation as a spy makes deception his trade, while god of war Ares, in disguise as the unassuming Sir Patrick Morgan (David Thewlis), has been stoking the war through manipulation.

Yet *Wonder Woman*'s critique of values celebrated in *Batman v Superman* by ascribing them to the world of men and reframing them is complicit in promoting aspects of these values. If Superman stands for truth and binds it to the American way in his famous worded identifier, Wonder Woman often similarly valorizes US nationality. Berlatsky demonstrates that early Wonder Woman comics, which situate the superhero in World War II, construct a formulation in which "the Nazis embody war; therefore, fighting the Nazis is fighting on behalf of peace. Or, more broadly, masculinity embodies war; therefore, fighting on behalf of an America that Marston sees as feminine means fighting on behalf of peace" (2015, 84). These comics promote America's war effort by reframing the country as feminine. Although resituating Wonder Woman in World War I, the film similarly aligns masculinity with war and deception while ultimately redeeming the Allied Powers. Steve, despite being a spy, comes to represent the conventionally feminine quality of love and affirms Wonder Woman's understanding of love. During the film's climax, Steve demonstrates his righteousness in an act of sacrifice, hijacking a plane set to drop gas bombs on London and blowing it up mid-air. As Ares implores Wonder Woman to concede to humanity's inherent evil by killing the creator of the deadly gas, Dr. Maru (Elena Anaya), Wonder Woman recalls her last conversation with Steve, wherein he proclaimed his love for her. Amidst the destruction all around her, Wonder Woman smiles, informs

Ares that he is wrong about humanity and spares Maru. As she pushes forward to defeat Ares, Wonder Woman declares her belief in love. Wonder Woman is empowered by love for humanity and romantic love, both of which Steve showed her throughout the film and defined his final actions. Love and the pursuit of peace thus supersede deception and war as the American spy's defining qualities, affirming the DCEU's celebration of US national identity even while reframing the values by which it is underpinned.

Despite strategies that bracket *Wonder Woman* off from the DCEU's governing structures, it is still able to mount critiques of the wider universe. Yet, as has been seen throughout this book, the means through which superhero blockbusters negotiate the textual networks in which they are situated and thus inherently sustain, in this case both the Wonder Woman franchise and DCEU, result in critiques of these networks being laced with complicity. Subsequent texts can once again renegotiate underpinning structures, with all-star ensemble films having a privileged status in managing their universe's hierarchical continuity.

A HIERARCHY OF JUSTICE

Justice League teams established DCEU superheroes Wonder Woman, Batman, and Superman with Arthur Curry/Aquaman (Jason Momoa), Victor Stone/Cyborg (Ray Fisher), and Barry Allen/Flash (Ezra Miller). In forming an all-star superhero team of which only half of its characters had previously starred in DCEU films, *Justice League* deploys different organizational logics to the MCU's all-star films, although these are pursued using familiar strategies. Meanwhile, the DCEU's extratextual crisis, stimulated by *Justice League*'s commercial failure and subsequent release of the *Snyder Cut*, meant that there was no *Justice League* sequel, so characters subsequently introduced to the universe were not able to directly enter DC's flagship team's hierarchy.

Justice League's character hierarchy is in ways distinct from while in other ways reflects that seen in Marvel Studios' Avengers films. Wonder Woman's success at intervening in the DCEU's underpinning structures in her solo film is evidenced in her role as co-team leader; alongside Batman, she assembles the Justice League. Despite this authoritative role, as the only female character on a team of heterosexual men she is at times objectified by her teammates, particularly in the theatrical cut where, for instance, Flash's adolescent lusting over her is amplified in a gag that sees him momentarily fall in battle with his face pressed against her breasts. In *Justice League*'s compression of Wonder Woman, the ways in which her resistance to masculinized structures are largely elided result in her at times being relegated to sexualized object. Conversely, Superman's masculinity is presented solely as strength. Following his sacrifice in *Batman v Superman*, the Kryptonian superhero is absent for most of *Justice League*. Upon his resurrection he is shirtless, but rather than be objectified by his soon-to-be-teammates, Superman actively engages in combat with them in the film's only superhero versus superhero battle. Placing Superman's shirtless body against bodies that wear armored costumes (Wonder Woman, Batman, Flash, and Aquaman's) and Cyborg's cybernetic body foregrounds his inherent power. As he easily defeats all the other superheroes simultaneously, the white male dominance that his muscular physique asserts is foregrounded. Whiteness, a quality that the film's strongest superhero shares with co-team leaders Wonder Woman and Batman, becomes a unifying quality in the hierarchy's upper echelons. Aquaman, played by mixed-race actor Jason Momoa whose portrayal of the character embodies Māori identity through means such as his tattoos (Dagbovie-Mullins and Berlatsky 2021, 7), and Black superhero Cyborg negotiate the hierarchy's lower levels with white speedster Flash.

With Aquaman, Cyborg, and Flash having not been fully introduced in previous films, the distribution of spaces and genre fractals in their associative frameworks become crucial to establishing the characters. Like Wonder Woman, who embodies Themyscira but has taken up residence in Paris, Aquaman is situated apart from the other team members' US home environments and coded as foreign. Bruce first locates Aquaman in Iceland and we later see Aquaman's ancestral environment of the kingdom of Atlantis, whose mythical qualities parallel Themyscira's. Cyborg and Flash both inhabit US cities but are distinguished by genre fractals. Science fiction and horror tropes are prominent in the presentation of Cyborg as a modernized Frankenstein's monster, while cinematic time travel motifs circulate the Flash. For example, when Flash exhibits his superspeed blue sparks fire all around him, this krackle recalling the electrical fissures that the time-travelling DeLorean emits in *Back to the Future* (Robert Zemeckis 1986).[4] *Justice League* also deploys techniques used to represent Quicksilver's superspeed in *Days of Future Past*, metamorphosing comic book strategies that present physics-defying powers by rupturing comics' spatiotemporal conventions through instead interlacing the cinematic image's typically discrete qualities of movement and stillness. This strategy is most pronounced in the *Snyder Cut* when Barry saves Iris West (Kiersey Clemons)—his longstanding love interest in the Flash franchise—from a car crash. Yet rather than the liberation expressed when Quicksilver moves through near-frozen space, the *Snyder Cut* evokes sadness at Barry's disconnect from the world. As time slows around Barry, Rose Bett's "Song to the Siren" begins playing, the mournful tune and lyrics expressing romantic longing for somebody who captivates the singer from afar underscore the wistfulness in Barry's eyes as he gazes at the woman he is about the save: a gaze that for him is sustained, yet for her is imperceptible. Once the film's temporal flow returns to normal, Barry kneels over the rescued Iris, who now returns his gaze, yet he cannot find the words to express his feelings and speeds off again.

As with Barry, the *Snyder Cut* similarly expands Victor's backstory, giving him more depth and emotional weight. Yet unlike Aquaman and Flash, Cyborg is not subsequently given a solo film that would further decompress the character. The negotiation of hierarchical continuity in superhero universes, while managed in all-star ensemble texts, also plays out in dialogue between solo texts and all-star texts. This dialogue cannot be enacted if a character is not given a solo text or if all-star ensemble texts stop being produced.

For example, the lack of subsequent Justice League films restricts *Black Adam*'s ability to renegotiate the racial underpinnings of the universe's hierarchical continuity by situating its Middle Eastern superhero in relation to the universe's flagship superheroes. Although themes of racial identity are explored in solo film *Aquaman* (Jaume Collet-Serra 2022), which in decompressing its titular hero after *Justice League* explores the mixed-race superhero's heritage (see Dagbovie-Mullins and Berlatsky 2021, 6–10), *Aquaman* does not explicitly renegotiate its superhero's place in the universe's character hierarchy. *Black Adam*, meanwhile, centers issues of national identity in presenting its setting of fictional Middle Eastern country Kahndaq under occupation from imperialist organization Intergang. The casting of Dwayne Johnson as Black Adam is representative of the increasing prominence of multiracial actors playing protagonists in Hollywood blockbusters that capitalize on their racial ambiguity (see Beltrán 2005), in this case by having an actor of Black Nova Scotian and Samoan descent play a Middle Eastern character. In harnessing Johnson's immense star power, *Black Adam* endeavors to situate its eponymous hero in relation to the DCEU's top-tier superheroes, particularly Superman. Yet the lack of direct interaction between Black Adam and Superman leaves allusion as the primary means though which Black Adam can be compared to the DCEU's embodiment of white US masculinity.

While the Justice League do not participate in *Black Adam*'s action—the titular hero is instead pitted against the Justice Society, in their DCEU debut—the flagship all-star team are present in image and evoked in Black Adam's appearance and movement. Teenager Amon Tomaz (Bodhi

Black Adam flies toward the camera in *Black Adam* (2022).

Sabongui) adorns his bedroom with posters and memorabilia of the Justice League. When Black Adam abruptly wakes in this room, a bolt of lightning fired from his hands in reaction to a dream scorches the head off a Superman poster, clearly identifying Superman as Black Adam's primary target in the DCEU's character hierarchy. The film's action sequences affirm this link through a series of intertextual gestures to Superman. For Black Adam's first and climactic fights he dons capes that billow behind him as he floats and his flight is realized in ways that are pointedly reminiscent of Cavill's Superman: he bursts though the air, at times framed using the head-on propulsion motif, and engages in a tumultuous aerial battle with Hawkman (Aldis Hodge) that recalls Superman and Zod's fight in *Man of Steel*. The comparison constructed between Black Adam and Superman is certified in a mid-credit scene in which Cavill's Superman finally makes a brief appearance. After he descends from the sky, cape billowing, Superman emerges from smoke to a swell of John Williams's *Superman: The Movie* score. The presence of this score indicates a shift in the DCEU's positioning of *The Movie* in the Superman franchise, intertwining Reeve's and Cavill's incarnations, rather than placing them as oppositions. The composition of the DCEU's hierarchical continuity, meanwhile, is signaled to also be disrupted when Superman says, "We should talk, Black Adam," to which his newfound counterpart responds with a wry smile, suggesting that he intends to do more than simply talk. Yet as the credits resume, the superhero versus superhero battle is deferred. With the DCEU's crisis subsequently becoming terminal, this deferral seems indefinite. The universe's collapse—for a range of reasons that include *Black Adam*'s commercial underperformance—deny the Middle Eastern superhero a chance to dethrone the embodiment of the American way.

The interlinked strategies of compression, hierarchization, and continuity maintenance used to manage superhero universes are all present in the

DCEU, albeit reconfigured and in ways constrained by its textual organization. The ways in which this organization affects the strategies shape the sociopolitical meanings of individual films and their ability to impact the wider universe. As the DCEU's crisis intensified, continuity maintenance was employed in the more extreme form of using an alternate timeline narrative to bracket off the universe's continuity.

A FLASH TOUR OF DC'S CINEMATIC PAST

The DCEU deploys some distinct uses of alternate timeline narratives. In *Batman v Superman* and the *Snyder Cut*, Batman has dreams of a post-apocalyptic future. This future foregrounds many common tropes of alternate timelines, including distinct stylization in its bronzed palette, cityscapes in ruin, redesigns of superheroes such as having Batman wearing goggles and a duster coat over his costume, and the radical reframing of characters, most prominent in Batman having teamed up with archenemy Joker and being hunted by Superman. *The Flash* takes a different approach to its alternate timeline. After Barry travels back in time to alter the past, the resulting new timeline's strangeness is gradually revealed.

Similarly to how comic book crossover events that steer the course of the uni/multiverse seek to encompass that uni/multiverse, *The Flash* endeavors to encompass not just the DCEU but also previous screen incarnations of its characters. An opening sequence features Affleck's Batman and Gadot's Wonder Woman, situating these incarnations of the characters in the prime timeline that Barry leaves upon creating an alternate timeline. As Barry trains a younger version of himself in the alternate timeline, Zod's invasion of Earth begins. While this event is essentially the DCEU's genesis point, it reveals just how strange the new timeline is when Barry discovers that there are no superheroes to stop Zod. In Barry's proceeding efforts to assemble a team of superheroes, he first locates Batman. Yet rather than Affleck's Batman, for this timeline Michael Keaton reprises the role from blockbusters *Batman* (Tim Burton 1989) and *Batman Returns* (Tim Burton 1992).

While Keaton's Batman is familiar from earlier films but strange to the DCEU, the next recruit leans more into strangeness. In seeking Superman, Barry discovers that years ago an alien landed in Russia, where they are now being held captive. Upon liberating the Kryptonian, Barry finds not Superman but a new incarnation of Supergirl (Sasha Calle). This incarnation draws on alternate timeline comic book story *Superman: Red Son*'s premise and furthers the reimagining of the universe through changing the Kryptonian who landed in Russia to Supergirl. Crucially, Supergirl is no longer secondary to Superman but replaces him as the first and only heroic Kryptonian to land on Earth. Along with reconfiguring the Superman franchise's and DCEU's gendered structures, casting Latina actor Calle as Supergirl also intervenes in their racial underpinnings. Yet the radical potential of this reenvisioning of one of DC's foundational superheroes is blunted when Calle's Supergirl is ultimately shown to be an insufficient replacement for Cavill's Superman. Whereas Cavill's Superman's aggressive masculinity was equipped to defeat Zod, Calle's Supergirl is killed by Zod. This defeat occurs over and over, with the two Barrys' efforts to travel back in time to the start of the battle leading only to recurring failure, the alternate timeline trope of unceremonious superhero deaths deployed in the repetition of Batman and Supergirl's demises. Calle's Supergirl's fate is thus comparable to that of Bishop, Warpath, Blink, and Sunspot in *Days of Future Past*; she is introduced in an alternate timeline only to affirm the familiar through her death. In this case, she affirms the need for Superman, the white male savior without whom the timeline is doomed.

The Flash broadens its array of character incarnations through its presentation of a multiverse. Combinations of motion and stasis are deployed to depict Flash's superpowers that grant him the ability to navigate timelines, but the relative motion and stasis of bodies more broadly provides a central motif in how the film negotiates its multiverse of DC characters' screen incarnations. Those who actively participate in the film's action, namely Keaton's Batman, are granted new degrees of mobility. Keaton's Batman, in being brought into a twenty-first-century superhero blockbuster, gains heightened agility, his movements no longer constrained by a rubber costume but invigorated by a digital body. This agility is showcased as he grapples with a Kryptonian giant, flipping around the alien's upper body to evade its strikes and plant explosives. Meanwhile, incarnations who inhabit colored globes that demarcate their universes in the Speed Force—a plane Barry can enter where moments and multiplicities of time manifest spatially—are held largely in stasis. The presentation of these globes and their contents metamorphoses a motif in which superhero comic books visually represent a multiverse as overlapping globes, as seen in the overlapping Earths on the cover of *Crisis on Infinite Earths* #1 (discussed and reproduced in chapter three). While such static images in comic books represent an infinite multiverse, in the moving images of cinema, *The Flash* incorporates stasis to connote the status of particular incarnations in the multiverse. Within his globe, George Reeves's Superman is shown in black and white in his familiar fists on hips post, moving only to turn around so that he can look upon a version of the Golden Age Flash (Jason Ballantine [uncredited]);[5] Christopher Reeve's

Christopher Reeve's Superman and Helen Slater's Supergirl stare at a tear in their universe's sky in *The Flash* (2023).

Superman and Helen Slater's Supergirl (from the 1984 film) glide down to a rooftop only to stand staring at a tear in their universe's sky; and Adam West's Batman (from the 1960s television series) is preserved in a single pose like a statue. Unlike Keaton's agile digital body, these digital recreations that de-age, and in the cases of Reeves, Reeve, and West resurrect, actors' bodies, do so to render them as static monuments. This presentation expresses reverence for the actors' portrayals, in many cases also acting as a tribute to real life death, thus manifesting another way to add to the means by which, as Mulvey (2006) explores, digital technology reveals the cinematic image's inherent stillness and its corresponding encapsulation of pastness and death. The digital de-aging and resurrection of these past incarnations testifies to how such technologies provide twenty-first-century superhero blockbusters new tools for negotiating superhero franchises.

The relative stasis of these incarnations contained in their universe's globes situates them in the past but in doing so manifests what Andrew J. Friedenthal (2019, 23) identifies as a key theme of the DC comic book multiverse: legacy. Enshrining the legacy of fictional history is a function that alternate timeline narratives can perform that is interconnected with continuity maintenance. In preserving past versions of characters in discrete universes, their importance to their franchises and the wider multiverse is acknowledged while their narrative continuity is neatly bracketed off. The act of restorative nostalgia that is performed in *The Flash*'s reconstruction of these past incarnations seeks to restore their place in their franchises. The memorializing presentation situates Reeve's Superman in the past while indicating that his legacy lives on, continuing to inform new incarnations of Superman. Nostalgia thus continues to be a strategy that superhero blockbusters deploy as they adapt vast networks of texts that go back decades, while one must be attentive to the kind of nostalgia being offered and how its negotiation of past texts shapes a film's meanings.

The superhero blockbuster is now itself a well-established tradition, as evidenced in how *The Flash* expresses nostalgia for earlier examples. Although the DCEU began, in *Man of Steel*, by pushing *The Movie* and Reeve's Superman to the periphery of the Superman franchise, as the universe draws to a close Reeve's Superman is embraced and presented as a defining point in the legacy of not just the Superman franchise and DC multiverse but also the superhero blockbuster. *The Flash* ends with the DCEU fractured; Flash changes the past again to form a new timeline that is separate from the DCEU's prime timeline, both of which can be bracketed off to make way for the DCU.[6] Yet *The Flash*'s emphasis on legacy attests to the fluidity of superhero franchises, universes, and multiverses. In these constructs, as visually manifested in *The Flash*'s Speed Force, past and present exist simultaneously, texts maintaining an ongoing dialogue with one another that manifests in narrative and stylistic strategies. DC Studios' future superhero blockbusters, and any other superhero blockbuster that adapts a long-running superhero property, will be shaped through this dialogue.

In the above analysis of the DCEU, I only alluded to aspects of the industrial, economic, and behind the scenes factors contributing to the universe's crisis, to allow focus on the films' textuality. The analytical framework developed in this book provides a foundation for analyzing superhero blockbusters as production and reception contexts shift, and as superhero blockbusters engage with emerging filmmaking trends and cultural contexts. Analyzing the aesthetics of superhero blockbusters' adaptive practices reveals nuanced and often paradoxical meanings, while illuminating the ways in which these meanings are formed. The cinematic metamorphosis of aesthetic strategies developed in comic books inflects the adaptation of meanings that circulate individual superhero franchises, universes, and multiverses, along with the genre more broadly. Superhero blockbusters' interactions with networks of texts stimulate the pluralities of meanings that they generate, the films constantly reflecting on, combining, and rearranging elements of past texts. The adaptation of narrative strategies and models of serialization from superhero comic books further shapes superhero blockbusters' meanings. Close attention to these complex adaptive practices is crucial when analyzing the films from a genre that helped establish the Hollywood blockbuster as we know it today and, in the twenty-first century, has intensified its contributions to popular film culture.

NOTES

INTRODUCTION: SUPERHERO BLOCKBUSTERS AS ADAPTATIONS

1. Liefeld is seen to have incited and to exemplify a trend in 1990s superhero comics for hyperbolized gendered bodies (see Bukatman 2003, 59–66; Jeffery 2016, 158–59).

2. Aaron Taylor notes that the perceived oversaturation of superhero films in the twenty-first century is not due to the quantity of superhero films produced, which is relatively low compared to many other popular genres, but to superhero films' increasing dominance of box office takings and high level of media exposure (2019, 92–93).

3. *Action Comics* #1 was published by National Allied Publications who, after various corporate maneuvers and name changes, became DC Comics. In this book, to avoid confusion, I adopt Ian Gordon's rationale for "refer[ring] to the corporation that controls Superman as DC, or DC Comics. Using 'DC' is a convenience that covers the many names and different corporate structures that have controlled Superman" (2017, 8–9).

4. The definition of comic book cinema is disputed within this literature. I do not seek to intervene in the debate over what constitutes "comic book cinema," since I am concerned with the specific category of the superhero blockbuster.

5. Of the studies discussed, Collins (1991) pays the closest attention to aesthetic strategies.

TRUTH, JUSTICE, AND THE CINEMATIC WAY: *SUPERMAN: THE MOVIE*, THE FIRST SUPERHERO BLOCKBUSTER

1. In this chapter, when naming incarnations by medium and format (e.g. "the radio serial" or "the television series") I am referring to the incarnations listed here.

2. Siegel and Shuster had previously printed a story titled "The Reign of the Super-Man" in their self-published fanzine *Science Fiction: The Advance Guard of Future Civilization* (January 1933). The story, presented as prose written by Siegel (under the pseudonym Herbert S. Fine) and illustrated by Shuster, featured a very different character referred to as "the Superman," who had powers of telepathy and precognition, which he used for villainy (see Regalado 2015, 89–94).

3. Superman comic book stories that deploy this description almost word for word include those printed in *Action Comics* #15 (August 1939), *Action Comics* #17 (October 1939),

Action Comics #18 (November 1939), *Action Comics* #19 (December 1939), *Action Comics* #22 (March 1940), and *Action Comics* #24 (May 1940).

4. For the final two Fleischer Studios cartoons and the first of the eight Famous Studios cartoons, the opening was changed to "Faster than a speeding bullet! More powerful than a locomotive! Able to soar higher than any plane!" For the remaining Famous Studios cartoons, it was changed again to "Faster than a streak of lightning! More powerful than the pounding surf! Mightier than a roaring hurricane!"

5. The only alteration in wording is "planet" instead of "world."

6. This describes the opening as seen in the first two seasons. In subsequent seasons different footage is used for the train.

7. Lois's surname is not provided until *Action Comics* #2 (July 1938).

8. The first usage of the word "meek" to describe Clark is in *Action Comics* #6 (November 1938).

9. This is particularly the case with the Fleischer cartoons.

10. When demanded, Reeves can provide vocal distinction. In "Superman Week" (1955), Clark/Superman fakes a television interview between his two identities by delivering Clark's voice, in an off-screen recording, in a more nasal tone.

11. Scott Higgins provides average budgets for serials as between $140,000 and $180,000 for Republic and Columbia (who produced the Superman serials) and between $175,000 and $250,000 for Universal; "This was roughly equivalent to a stand-alone programmer from the respective studios, but stretched across triple the running time" (2016, 6).

12. For the first season, roughly $15,000 per episode (Grossman 1977, 64).

13. For a survey of Golden Age Superman stories in which Superman acts as a "champion of the oppressed," see Wright (2001, 11–13).

14. "The Superman Super-Spectacular!" in *Action Comics* #309 (February 1964) and "Superman's Mission for President Kennedy" in *Superman* #170 (July 1964).

15. This team up first occurred in *Justice League of America* #21–22 (August 1963 and September 1963).

16. The fact that Clark has just spent twelve years in the Fortress of Solitude diegetically rationalizes his antiquated attire.

17. Burke argues that the imagery that the comics panels fades into recalls film serials, while Morton argues that it approximates television.

18. The motif is also used in the end credits, which are presented similarly to the opening credits.

19. This instance of direct address metamorphoses a trope deployed in many previous incarnations, in which stories end with Clark clearly implying to Lois that he is Superman. This joke is often shared with the audience via Clark winking to them, which Gordon (2017, 150–51) traces back to the Fleischer Studios cartoons.

20. Examples include *Back to the Future Part II* and *Part III* (Robert Zemeckis 1989 and 1990) and *Pirates of the Caribbean: Dead Man's Chest* and *At World's End* (Gore Verbinski 2006 and 2007). For the *Lord of the Rings* trilogy (Peter Jackson 2001, 2002, and 2003), all instalments, not just the sequels, were shot back-to-back, suggesting the studio's confidence in the cast, crew, and appeal of source material.

21. Aaron Taylor finds that approximately twenty-three of the 232 films serials produced between 1930 and 1956, almost 10 percent, feature "superheroic or masked-avenger types" (2019, 94).

22. Lois recites the lyrics in spoken word, with John Williams's score in the background. The song was later released as a single sung by Maureen McGovern.

23. Featuring in *Superman: The Man of Steel* #18–19 (December 1992–January 1993), *Justice League America* #69 (December 1992), *Superman* vol. 2 #74–75 (November 1992–December 1992), *The Adventures of Superman* #497 (December 1992), and *Action Comics* #684 (December 1992).

24. There are, however, inconsistencies between the narratives of *Superman II* and *Returns*, which Gordon (2017, 86) outlines.

DIGITAL POWER AND MORAL RESPONSIBILITY: *SPIDER-MAN* AND THE MARVEL SUPERHERO IN THE TWENTY-FIRST CENTURY

1. At the time of this writing, *Spider-Man* has grossed $403,706,375 domestically and $821,708,551 worldwide; *Spider-Man 2* $373,585,825 domestically and $783,976,453 worldwide; *Spider-Man 3* $336,530,303 domestically and $894,983,373 worldwide (Box Office Mojo).

2. For example, Andreas Rauscher (2010) argues that digital effects are a key factor that facilitated the new wave of superhero adaptations in the 2000s, while Brown maintains that "the current dominance of the superhero film genre is a direct result of post-9/11 anxieties" (2016, 62).

3. To avoid confusion with other Spider-Man texts, when referring to these films individually I call them *Spider-Man 1*, *Spider-Man 2*, and *Spider-Man 3*. I refer to them collectively as the *Spider-Man* trilogy.

4. The most prominent exception is Billy Batson, although when he transforms into superhero Captain Marvel, he gains the body of a grown man.

5. I will often refer to movements created by a virtual camera simply as camera movements. Aylish Wood (2007, 166) determines that, since virtual cameras perform the same basic movements as physical cameras (tracks, pans, zooms, etc.), it is appropriate to discuss them using the same terminology.

6. While the trilogy is set in New York, some scenes were shot in other US cities, such as Los Angeles or Chicago, and others on sets. Therefore, throughout the trilogy, whether scenes feature heavy CGI, more discreet digital compositing, or no digital manipulation at all, the film's indexical relationship to New York is always potentially masqueraded.

7. A stunt double's body is also used in certain scenes. However, the films seek to hide this body's existence, whereas the digital body and Maguire's body declare their presence.

8. Straczynski's run spans *The Amazing Spider-Man* vol. 2 #30–58 (June 2001–November 2003) and, after the series was renumbered from the 500th anniversary issue, *The Amazing Spider-Man* #500–545 (December 2003–January 2008). Although Straczynski cowrote some issues with other writers, and various artists worked on the run, I refer to the run as Straczynski's since he was the constant creative voice throughout his tenure.

9. The 616 universe encompasses the majority of Marvel's comic books. Other universes are given other numbers.

10. This eight includes the Thing, who is a white man transformed into a rock monster, but not Vision, who is an android.

11. Peter/Spider-Man helps Jennifer again, investigating the abduction of other homeless children, in *The Amazing Spider-Man* vol. 2 #40–42 (June 2002–August 2002).

12. This diegetic narrative is again interlinked with the complementary extratextual narrative about the special effects advancing from film to film.

13. The intertextual dialogue through which this worded identifier developed can be traced back way before Spider-Man's inception. In one notable instance that demonstrates the words and ideas reverberating through superhero lore, Eben Kent (Edward Cassidy) says to Clark in chapter one of the first Superman film serial, "Because of these great powers, your speed and strength, your x-ray vision and super sensitive hearing, you have a great responsibility." Ben Saunders outlines how, outside of the superhero genre, variations "can be found in a range of more "respectable" sources, from the medieval-era writings of Christine de Pisan to the modern wartime speeches of Franklin Delano Roosevelt. Stan Lee himself, however, cites the influence of the Bible—specifically Luke 12:48: 'For unto whomsoever much is given, of him shall be much required.'" (2011, 73).

14. This shot also features the symbiote crawling over Peter's bedside table, indicating another presence that Peter has overlooked.

15. The high degree of agency Peter gains within the *Bugle* offices while bonded with the symbiote is central to his entrepreneurial ascension. Peter ruthlessly exposes Eddie's fraudulent practices and demands a staff job from Jonah, for which he names his own wage.

16. In the case of Doctor Octopus, upon being cured Otto regains control over the digitally realized mechanical appendages.

17. Monica Flegel and Judith Leggatt (2021, 72) note the most significant early examples as a Latino Iron Man and African American Nick Fury.

EARTH'S MIGHTIEST SUPERHERO BLOCKBUSTERS: NETWORKED SERIALITY IN THE MARVEL CINEMATIC UNIVERSE

1. Joanna Robinson, Dave Gonzales, and Gavin Edwards (2023, 121) identify the first public use of the name Marvel Cinematic Universe as occurring in 2010, when President of Marvel Studios Kevin Feige uttered it while promoting *Iron Man 2* (Jon Favreau 2010).

2. Mark J. P. Wolf (2012, 268–80) outlines how creators and fans of imaginary worlds construct "circles of authorship" and "levels of canonicity," while Johnson (2013, 140–49) explores hierarchical organization of industries that contribute to media franchises.

3. It is beyond the scope of this chapter to analyze all the MCU's transmedial expansions, merchandise, and tie-ins. I have selected some of the most prominent and representative for discussion.

4. These efforts include Disney making the "IMAX Enhanced" versions of certain films, which are unavailable on physical home video formats, available on Disney+. Furthermore, Marvel Studios stopped producing the "One-Shot" short films that were previously

exclusively included on MCU DVDs and Blu-Rays. The new Disney+ category of "Marvel Studios Special Presentation" acts as something of a midpoint between the MCU's short films, feature films, and television series, revamping the televisual format of the holiday special to provide more MCU texts exclusive to the streaming platform.

5. Prior to this, the only character from a Marvel Television series to appear in an MCU film was Edwin Jarvis (James D'Arcy), a central character in *Agent Carter*, who appeared briefly in *Endgame*.

6. At the time of this writing, the only MCU production for Disney+ to star characters who have headlined a film series is *The Guardians of the Galaxy Holiday Special* (James Gunn 2022), a Marvel Studios Special Presentation that proves the rule of such characters not starring in serialized television shows.

7. At the time of this writing, Kang's MCU future is unstable, following Marvel Studios dropping Majors in December 2023 after the actor was found guilty of misdemeanor assault and harassment.

8. For one of the numerous appearances of this advertisement, see the back cover of *Avengers vs. X-Men* #1 (June 2012).

9. Flanagan, McKenny, and Livingstone (2016, 84) see the encompassing architecture of MCU feature films more broadly as the action-adventure genre.

10. See, for example, Henry Jenkins's (2006, 84–86) analysis of post-9/11 Captain America comics.

11. Robinson, Gonzales, and Edwards (253–61 and 264–68) demonstrate that Marvel Studios' early efforts to feature female superheroes in films were stifled by certain members of the Creative Committee of Marvel Entertainment (a group of executives and comics creators who sought to ensure coordination between Marvel's different divisions, which disbanded in 2015) who believed toys based on female characters did not sell. This specific industrial context contributes to the MCU's participation in the superhero genre's recurring marginalization of female characters.

12. Loki's sex is changeable in both Norse mythology and Marvel comics.

13. *Captain Marvel*'s positive portrayal of S.H.I.E.L.D. participates in the Captain Marvel franchise's recurring promotion of the military-industrial complex, which Cocca (2021) explores in detail.

14. Scarlet Witch is Eastern European, whereas Vision is an android who speaks with a British accent.

15. This meaning is, however, undermined by the recurring jokes about Thor's physique throughout the film.

THE STRANGEST CONTINUITY OF ALL: ALTERNATE TIMELINES IN FOX'S X-MEN FILMS

1. Following Brown's (2019) discussion of Batman's multiplicities, I use the word "prime" to describe that which is designated as the main timeline and universe. In Marvel comics, this is the 616 universe.

2. For a more detailed account of Magneto's changing characterization in the period, see Nicholaus Pumphrey (2014).

3. I am thankful to Rafael Alves Azevedo for highlighting this link for me.

4. For example, Kristin Thompson (2019) finds that 3D box office share in the US and Canada peaked in 2010 at 21 percent and by 2016 had fallen to 14 percent.

5. Kent identifies the "glaring absence" (126) of the Mexican girls whose bodies have been exploited as a significant limitation in the film's exploration of this theme.

6. *Buck and the Preacher* (Sidney Poitier 1972) was a landmark Western in terms of reframing these concerns of the genre in such racial terms.

7. Team comic books can circumvent this by having issues focused on individual characters or smaller groups within the team.

8. Beast is blue-skinned but played by white actor Kelsey Grammer.

9. It should be noted that, following Jewish identity becoming a core aspect of Magneto's associative framework in 1980s comics, Fox's X-Men films at times foregrounded it, most notably by depicting his experiences in the Holocaust in 2000's *X-Men* and 2011's *X-Men: First Class*. These associations thus inform *Days of Future Past*'s depiction of Magneto.

10. The facility in which *The New Mutants* is set is run by the Essex Corporation, which is also referenced in *Apocalypse* and *Deadpool 2*. Furthermore, Dani has a vision that reuses footage from *Logan* of mutants being experimented on at Alkali-Transigen's research facility, suggesting that the Essex Corporation is behind the experiments at both facilities. The name Essex Corporation indicates that it is run by Nathaniel Essex, a.k.a. supervillain Mister Sinister.

CONCLUSION: CRISIS ON THE DC EXTENDED UNIVERSE

1. DC's production company for the first two DCEU films, *Man of Steel* and *Batman v Superman*, was DC Entertainment. Subsequent films were produced by DC Films, which in 2023 changed its name to DC Studios. All these companies are subsidiaries of Warner Bros. Discovery. For simplicity, I refer to the DCEU's production company as DC Studios in this conclusion.

2. Although Cocca (2020, 51) does a quantitative analysis of characters and dialogue in the Themyscira scenes and finds that in these metrics whiteness is favored.

3. The linking of nature and Wonder Woman's power is affirmed in sequel *Wonder Woman 1984* (Patty Jenkins 2020) when she learns to fly. The head-on propulsion motif is used various times in this sequence, thus intertextually comparing her to Superman. Yet rather than placing a city behind her, the backdrop is solely soft clouds and blue sky, binding her liberated movement not to the metropolis but to the natural world.

4. Solo film *The Flash* further elaborates this intertextual link through numerous allusions to *Back to the Future*.

5. This version of Golden Age Flash, civilian identity Jay Garrick, had not featured in a previous screen incarnation.

6. At the time of this writing, *Aquaman and the Lost Kingdom* (James Wan 2023) is designated as the last DCEU film.

BIBLIOGRAPHY

Aaron, Jason, Adam Kubert, and Morry Hollowell. June 2012. "The Invincible Iron Man vs. Magneto." *AVX: Vs* #1. New York: Marvel Comics.

Alexander, Dorian L. 2018. "Faces of Abjectivity: The Uncanny Mystique and Transsexuality." In *Gender and the Superhero Narrative*, edited by Michael Goodrum, Tara Prescott, and Philip Smith, 180–204. Jackson: University Press of Mississippi.

Altheide, David L. 2010. "Fear, Terrorism and Popular Culture." In *Reframing 9/11: Film, Popular Culture and the "War on Terror,"* edited by Jeff Birkenstein, Anna Froula, and Karen Randell, 11–22. New York: Continuum.

Avery, Fiona, J. Michael Straczynski, John Romita Jr., et al. September 2003. "Unintended Consequences." *The Amazing Spider-Man* vol. 2 #55. New York: Marvel Comics.

Avery, Fiona, J. Michael Straczynski, John Romita Jr., et al. October 2003. "The Revolution Within." *The Amazing Spider-Man* vol. 2 #56. New York: Marvel Comics.

Bainbridge, Jason. 2010. "'I am New York'—Spider-Man, New York City and the Marvel Universe." In *Comics and the City: Urban Space in Print, Picture and Sequence*, edited by Jörn Ahrens and Arno Meteling, 163–79. New York: Continuum.

Barnhardt, Adam. 2021. "New Disney+ Listing Seemingly Removes Agents of SHIELD From MCU Continuity." *Comicbook*, May 4, 2021. https://comicbook.com/marvel/news/disney-plus-agents-of-shield-removed-continuity-legacy-listing/.

Bates, Cary, Curt Swan, and Joe Giella. June 1978, reprinted 2000. "Superman Takes a Wife." *Action Comics* #484. In *Superman in the Seventies*, edited by Michael Wright, 201–22. New York: DC Comics.

Bazin, André. 2005. *What Is Cinema? Volume 1*, edited and translated by Hugh Gray. Berkeley: University of California Press.

Bechdel, Alison. 2006. *Fun Home: A Family Tragicomic*. London: Jonathan Cape.

Beltrán, Mary. 2005. "The New Hollywood Racelessness: Only the Fast, Furious, (and Multiracial) Will Survive." *Cinema Journal* 44 (2): 50–67.

Bendis, Brian Michael, Bill Jemas, Mark Bagley, et al. October 2000–August 2011. *Ultimate Spider-Man* #1–160. New York: Marvel Comics.

Bendis, Brian Michael, David Marquez, Olivier Coipel, et al. July 2016–February 2017. *Civil War II* #0–8. New York: Marvel Comics

Bendis, Brian Michael, Jason Aaron, John Romita Jr., et al. May 2012–December 2012. *Avengers vs. X-Men* #0–12. New York: Marvel Comics.

Bendis, Brian Michael, Leinil Francis Yu, Mark Morales, et al. November 2008. "Secret Invasion (Part VI)." *Secret Invasion #6*. New York: Marvel Comics.

Bendis, Brian Michael, Sara Pichelli, Justin Ponsor, et al. November 2011–December 2013. *Ultimate Comics: Spider-Man #1–28*. New York: Marvel Comics.

Berlatsky, Noah. 2015. *Wonder Woman: Bondage and Feminism in the Marston/Peter Comics, 1941-1948*. New Brunswick: Rutgers.

Berger, Richard. 2008. "'Are There Any More at Home Like You?': Rewiring *Superman*." *Journal of Adaptation in Film & Performance* 1 (2): 87–101.

Binder, Otto, and Al Plastino. May 1959, reprinted 2002. "The Supergirl from Krypton!" *Action Comics #252*. In *Superman in the Fifties*, edited by Nick J. Napolitano, 93–100. New York: DC Comics.

Bluestone, George. 1957. *Novels into Film*. Berkeley: University of California Press.

Bolter, Jay David, and Richard Grusin. 2000. *Remediation: Understanding New Media*. Cambridge: MIT Press.

Box Office Mojo. http://www.boxofficemojo.com/. Accessed September 2023.

Boym, Svetlana. 2007. "Nostalgia and Its Discontents." *Hedgehog Review* 9 (2): 7–18.

Brinker, Felix. 2017. "Transmedia Storytelling in the 'Marvel Cinematic Universe' and the Logics of Convergence-Era Popular Seriality." In *Make Ours Marvel: Media Convergence and a Comics Universe*, edited by Matt Yockey, 207–33. Austin: University of Texas Press.

Brooker, Will. 2012. *Hunting the Dark Knight: Twenty-First Century Batman*. London: IB Tauris.

Brown, Jeffrey A. 2016. *The Modern Superhero in Film and Television: Popular Genre and American Culture*. New York: Routledge.

Brown, Jeffrey A. 2019. *Batman and the Multiplicity of Identity: The Contemporary Comic Book Superhero as Cultural Nexus*. New York: Routledge.

Brownie, Barbara, and Danny Graydon. 2016. *The Superhero Costume: Identity and Disguise in Fact and Fiction*. London: Bloomsbury.

Bukatman, Scott. 2003. *Matters of Gravity: Special Effects and Supermen in the 20th Century*. Durham: Duke University Press.

Burke, Liam. 2015. *The Comic Book Film Adaptation: Exploring Modern Hollywood's Leading Genre*. Jackson: University Press of Mississippi.

Burke, Liam. 2018. "'A Bigger Universe': Marvel Studios and Transmedia Storytelling." In *Assembling the Marvel Cinematic Universe: Essays on the Social, Cultural and Geopolitical Domains*, edited by Julian C. Chambliss, William L. Svitavsky, and Daniel Fandino, 32–51. Jefferson: McFarland.

Byrne, John, Dick Giordano, and Tom Ziuko. October 1986. "From Out the Green Dawn." *The Man of Steel #1*. New York: DC Comics.

Cardwell, Sarah. 2002. *Adaptation Revisited: Television and the Classic Novel*. Manchester: Manchester University Press.

Carroll, Lewis, and John Tenniel. 1865 and 1871, reprinted 1993. *Alice's Adventures in Wonderland and Through the Looking Glass*. Hertfordshire: Wordsworth.

Carroll, Noël. 1982. "The Future of Allusion: Hollywood in the Seventies (and Beyond)." *October* 20: 51–81.

Claremont, Chris, Bill Sienkiewicz, and Glynis Wein. November 1984, reprinted 2008. "Slumber Party!" *The New Mutants* #21. In *The New Mutants Classic Vol. 3*, edited by Mark D. Beazley, 72–110. New York: Marvel Publishing.

Claremont, Chris, Bill Sienkiewicz, and Glynis Oliver. October 1985, reprinted 2009. "Saturday Night Fight." *The New Mutants* #32. In *The New Mutants Classic Vol. 4*, edited by Mark D. Beazley, 150–72. New York: Marvel Publishing.

Claremont, Chris, Dave Cockrum, Bob Wiacek, et al. September 1982, reprinted 2020. "Gold Rush!" *The Uncanny X-Men* #161. In *The Uncanny X-Men Omnibus Vol. 3*, edited by Cory Sedlmeier, 180–203. New York: Marvel Worldwide.

Claremont, Chris, Dave Cockrum, Josef Rubinstein, et al. October 1981. "And the Dead Shall Bury the Living!" *The Uncanny X-Men* #150. In *The Uncanny X-Men Omnibus Vol. 2*, edited by Cory Sedlmeier, 504–43. New York: Marvel Worldwide.

Claremont, Chris, John Byrne, Terry Austin, et al. January 1981, reprinted 2020. "Days of Future Past." *The Uncanny X-Men* #141. In *The Uncanny X-Men Omnibus Vol. 2*, edited by Cory Sedlmeier, 252–74. New York: Marvel Worldwide.

Claremont, Chris, John Byrne, Terry Austin, et al. February 1981, reprinted 2020. "Mind Out of Time." *The Uncanny X-Men* #142. In *The Uncanny X-Men Omnibus Vol. 2*, edited by Cory Sedlmeier, 276–98. New York: Marvel Worldwide.

Claremont, Chris, John Romita Jr., Dan Green, et al. December 1985, reprinted 2014. "The Trial of Magneto!" *The Uncanny X-Men* #200. In *The Uncanny X-Men: The Trial of Magneto*, edited by Ed Hammond, 122–62. Tunbridge Wells: Panini.

Cocca, Carolyn. 2014. "The 'Broke Back Test': A Quantitative and Qualitative Analysis of portrayals of women in mainstream superhero comic books, 1993–2013." *Journal of Graphic Novels and Comics* 5 (4): 411–28.

Cocca, Carolyn. 2016a. "Containing the X-Women: De-powering and De-queering Female Characters." In *The X-Men Films: A Cultural Analysis*, edited by Claudia Bucciferro, 79–91. Lanham: Rowman & Littlefield.

Cocca, Carolyn. 2016b. *Superwomen: Gender, Power, and Representation*. New York: Bloomsbury.

Cocca, Carolyn. 2021. *Wonder Woman and Captain Marvel: Militarism and Feminism in Comics and Film*. London: Routledge.

Collins, Jim. 1991. "Batman: The Movie, Narrative: The Hyperconscious." In *The Many Lives of the Batman: Critical Approaches to a Superhero and His Media*, edited by Roberta E. Pearson and William Uricchio, 164–81. New York: Routledge.

Comerford, Chris. 2023. *Cinematic Digital Television: Negotiating the Nexus of Production, Reception and Aesthetics*. Abingdon: Routledge.

Connell, Daniel J. 2020. "The Simulacrum of Hypermasculinity in Comic Book Cinema." In *Toxic Masculinity: Mapping the Monstrous in Our Heroes*, edited by Esther De Dauw and Daniel J. Connell, 19–33. Jackson, University Press of Mississippi.

Constable, Catherine. 2015. *Postmodernism and Film: Rethinking Hollywood's Aesthetics*. New York: Wallflower Press.

Conway, Gerry, Gil Kane, John Romita Sr., et al. June 1973, reprinted 2009. "The Night Gwen Stacy Died." *The Amazing Spider-Man* #121. In *The Amazing Spider-Man: The Night Gwen Stacy Died*, edited by Ed Hammond, 6–26. Tunbridge Wells: Panini.

Coogan, Peter. 2006. *Superhero: The Secret Origin of a Genre*. Austin: MonkeyBrain Books.
Cronin, Brian. 2020. "What Was DC's First 'Imaginary Story'?" *Comic Book Resources*, April 10, 2020. https://www.cbr.com/dc-comics-superman-imaginary-story-lois-lane/.
Curtis, Neal. 2020. "*Wonder Woman* and *Captain Marvel*: The (Dis)Continuity of Gender Politics." *Journal of Popular Culture* 53 (4): 926–45.
Dagbovie-Mullins, Sika A. and Eric L. Berlatsky. 2021. "Introduction." In *Mixed Race Superheroes*, edited by Sika A. Dagbovie-Mullins and Eric L. Berlatsky, 1–24.
Darowski, Joseph J. 2014. "When Business Improved Art: The 1975 Relaunch of Marvel's Mutant Heroes." In *The Ages of the X-Men: Essays on the Children of the Atom in Changing Times*, edited by Joseph J. Darowski, 37–45. Jefferson: McFarland.
Denison, Rayna. 2015. "American Superheroes in Japanese Hands: Superhero Genre Hybridity as Superhero Systems Collide in *Supaidāman*." In *Superheroes on World Screens*, edited by Denison and Mizsei-Ward, 53–72. Jackson: University Press of Mississippi.
DiPaolo, Marc. 2011. *War, Politics and Superheroes: Ethics and Propaganda in Comics and Film*. North Carolina: McFarland & Company.
Dove-Viebahn, Aviva. 2023. "Fantasies of White Feminism: The Human as 'Other' in *Captain Marvel*." *Feminist Media Studies* 24 (5): 1156–1170.
Drucker, Aaron. 2012. "Spider-Man: MENACE!!! Stan Lee, Censorship and the 100-Issue Revolution." In *Web-Spinning Heroics: Critical Essays on the History and Meaning of Spider-Man*, edited by Robert Moses Peaslee and Robert G. Weiner, 90–100. Jefferson: McFarland & Company.
Dyer, Richard. 1997. *White*. London: Routledge.
Dyer, Richard. 2002. *Only Entertainment*, 2nd ed. London: Routledge.
Eco, Umberto. 1972. "The Myth of Superman," translated by Natalie Chilton. *Diacritics* 2 (1): 14–22.
Elliott, Kamilla. 2003. *Rethinking the Novel/Film Debate*. Cambridge: Cambridge University Press.
Falconer, Duncan. 2008. "A Hall of Mirrors II: The Prismatic Age." *Mindless Ones*, August 3, 2008. http://mindlessones.com/2008/08/03/a-hall-of-mirrors-ii-prismatic-age/.
Fawaz, Ramzi. 2016. *The New Mutants: Superheroes and the Radical Imagination of American Comics*. New York: New York University Press.
Fawaz, Ramzi, Justin Hall, and Helen M. Kinsella. 2017. "Discovering Paradise Islands: The Politics and Pleasures of Feminist Utopias, a Conversation." *Feminist Review* 116: 1–21.
Feasey, Rebecca. 2008. *Masculinity and Popular Television*. Edinburgh: Edinburgh University Press.
Feil, Ken. 2005. *Dying for a Laugh: Disaster Movies and the Camp Imagination*. Middletown: Wesleyan University Press.
Finger, Bill, E. Nelson Bridwell, and Al Pastino. July 1964, reprinted 1999. "Superman's Mission for President Kennedy." *Superman* #170. In *Superman in the Sixties*, edited by Dale Crain, 180–89. New York: DC Comics.
Flanagan, Martin. 2012. "'Continually in the Making': Spider-Man's New York." In *Web-Spinning Heroics: Critical Essays on the History and Meaning of Spider-Man*, edited by Robert Moses Peaslee and Robert G. Weiner, 40–52. Jefferson: McFarland & Company.

Flanagan, Martin, Mike McKenny, and Andy Livingstone. 2016. *The Marvel Studios Phenomenon: Inside a Transmedia Universe*. New York: Bloomsbury.

Flegel, Monica, and Judith Leggatt. 2021. *Superhero Culture Wars: Politics, Marketing, and Social Justice in Marvel Comics*. London: Bloomsbury.

Fox, Gardner, Carmine Infantino, Joe Giella, et al. September 1961, reprinted 2016. "Flash of Two Worlds!" *The Flash* #123. In *The Flash: The Silver Age Volume 2*, edited by Jeb Woodard, 165–90. Burbank: DC Comics.

Fox, Gardner, Everett E. Hibbard, Sheldon Moldoff, et al. December 1940, reprinted 1991. "The First Meeting of the Justice Society of America." *All-Star Comics* #3. In *All Star Comics Archives Volume 1*, edited by Michael Charles Hill, 13–57. New York: DC Comics.

Fox, Gardner, Mike Sekowsky, and Bernard Sachs. August 1963, reprinted 2002. "Crisis on Earth-One." *Justice League of America* #21. In *Crisis on Multiple Earths*, edited by Nick J. Napolitano, 5–30. New York: DC Comics.

Fox, Gardner, Mike Sekowsky, and Bernard Sachs. September 1963, reprinted 2002. "Crisis on Earth-Two." *Justice League of America* #22. In *Crisis on Multiple Earths*, edited by Nick J. Napolitano, 31–56. New York: DC Comics.

Fox, Gardner, Mike Sekowsky, Bernard Sachs, et al. March 1960, reprinted 2016. "Starro the Conqueror." *The Brave and the Bold* #28. In *The Justice League of America: The Silver Age Volume 1*, edited by Scott Nybakken, 6–32. Burbank: DC Comics.

Freeman, Matthew. 2013. "Woman on Top: Postfeminism and the Transformation Narrative in *Lois & Clark: The New Adventures of Superman*." In *Examining Lois Lane: The Scoop on Superman's Sweetheart*, edited by Nadine Farghaly, 189–210. Lanham: Scarecrow Press.

Friedenthal, Andrew J. 2019. *The World of DC Comics*. New York: Routledge.

Frye, Northrop. 1973. *Anatomy of Criticism: Four Essays*. Princeton: Princeton University Press.

Fussfeld Cohen, Orit. 2014. "The New Language of the Digital Film." *Journal of Popular Film and Television* 42 (1): 47–58.

Galas, Marj. 2017. "How a Makeup Artist Helped Hugh Jackman Look His Worst in 'Logan.'" *Variety*, April 7, 2017. https://variety.com/2017/artisans/production/makeup-hugh-jackman-logan-x-men-1202023528/.

Gibbs, John, and Douglas Pye. 2005. "Introduction." In *Style and Meaning: Studies in the Detailed Analysis of Film*, edited by John Gibbs and Douglas Pye, 1–15. Manchester: Manchester University Press.

Gilmore, James N. 2014. "Will You Like Me When I'm Angry? Discourses of the Digital in *Hulk* and *The Incredible Hulk*." In *Superhero Synergies: Comic Book Characters Go Digital*, edited by James N. Gilmore and Matthias Stork, 11–26. Lanham: Rowman & Littlefield.

Glut, Don, Rick Hoberg, Dave Hunt, et al. August 1978, reprinted 2018. "What If Jane Foster Had Found—the Hammer of Thor?" *What If?* #10. In *What If? Classic: The Complete Collection Vol. 1*, edited by Mark D. Beazley, 326–60. New York: Marvel Worldwide.

Goldsmith, Ben, Susan Ward, and Tom O'Regan. 2010. *Local Hollywood: Global Film Production and the Gold Coast*. Queensland. University of Queensland Press.

Gordon, Ian. 2017. *Superman: The Persistence of an American Icon*. New Brunswick: Rutgers University Press.

Gray, Jonathan. 2010. *Show Sold Separately: Promos, Spoilers, and Other Media Paratexts*. New York: New York University Press.

Gribbin, Sean. 2023. "Runaways Is the First Marvel Series Removed from Disney+." *Comic Book Resources*, May 27, 2023. https://www.cbr.com/marvel-runaways-removed-disney-plus/.

Grossman, Gary. 1976. *Superman: Serial to Cereal*. New York: Popular Library.

Gunning, Tom. 1986. "The Cinema of Attraction: Early Film, Its Spectator, and the Avant-Garde." *Wide Angle* 8 (3–4): 63–7.

Gunning, Tom. 2007. "Moving Away from the Index: Cinema and the Impression of Reality." *Differences: A Journal of Feminist Cultural Studies* 18 (1): 29–52.

Hall, Sheldon. 2002. "Tall Revenue Features: The Genealogy of the Modern Blockbuster." in *Genre and Contemporary Hollywood*, edited by Steve Neale, 11–26. London: British Film Institute.

Hamilton, Edmond, Curt Swan, and George Klein. February 1964, reprinted 2018. "The Superman Super-Spectacular!" *Action Comics* #309. In *Action Comics 80 Years of Superman: The Deluxe Edition*, edited by Paul Levitz, 159–73. Burbank: DC Comics.

Hassler-Forest, Dan. 2012. *Capitalist Superheroes: Caped Crusaders in the Neoliberal Age*. Winchester: Zero Books.

Hatfield, Charles, Jeet Heer, and Kent Worcester (editors). 2013. *The Superhero Reader*. Jackson: University Press of Mississippi.

Henderson, Stuart. 2014. *The Hollywood Sequel: History & Form, 1911–2010*. Basingstoke: Palgrave Macmillan.

Herbert, Daniel. 2017. *Film Remakes and Franchises*. New Brunswick: Rutgers.

Hickman, Jonathan, Esad Ribić, and Ive Svorcina. July 2015–March 2016. *Secret Wars* #1–9. New York: Marvel Comics.

Higgins, Scott. 2016. *Matinee Melodrama: Playing with Formula in the Sound Serial*. New Brunswick: Rutgers University Press.

Holland, Jeanne. 2012. "It's Complicated: *Spider-Man 2*'s Reinscription of 'Good' and 'Evil' in Post-9/11 America." *Journal of American Culture* 35 (4): 289–303.

Holliday, Christopher. 2019. "Review: *Spider-Man: Far from Home*." *Fantasy/Animation*. https://www.fantasy-animation.org/current-posts/2019/7/5/review-spider-man-far-from-home-jon-watts-2019.

Holliday, Christopher. 2021–2022. "Retroframing the Future: Digital De-Aging Technologies in Contemporary Hollywood Cinema." *Journal of Cinema and Media Studies* 61 (5): 210–37.

Hutcheon, Linda. 1989. *The Politics of Postmodernism*. London: Routledge.

Hutcheon, Linda. 1998. "Irony, Nostalgia and the Postmodern." *University of Toronto English Library*. http://www.library.utoronto.ca/utel/criticism/hutchinp.html.

Ioannidou, Elisavet. 2013. "Adapting Superhero Comics for the Big Screen: Subculture for the Masses." *Adaptation* 6 (2): 230–38.

Image Engine, 2017. "Logan Case Study." *Image Engine*, March 1, 2017. https://image-engine.com/case-studies/logan/.

Jameson, Fredric. 1991. *Postmodernism; or, The Cultural Logic of Late Capitalism*. Durham: Duke University Press.

Jameson, Fredric. 1988. "Postmodernism and Consumer Society." In *Postmodernism and Its Discontents: Theories, Practices*, edited by E. Ann Kalpan, 13–29. London: Verso.

Jeffery, Scott. 2016. *The Posthuman Body in Superhero Comics: Human, Superhuman, Transhuman, Post/Human*. New York: Palgrave.

Jeffries, Dru. 2017. *Comic Book Film Style: Cinema at 24 Panels Per Second*. Austin: University of Texas Press.

Jenkins, Henry. 2006. "Captain America Sheds His Mighty Tears: Comics and September 11." In *Terror, Culture, Politics: Rethinking 9/11*, edited by Daniel J. Sherman and Terry Nardin, 69–102. Bloomington: Indiana University Press.

Jenkins, Henry. 2009. "'Just Men in Tights': Rewriting Silver Age Comics in an Era of Multiplicity." In *The Contemporary Comic Book Superhero*, edited by Angela Ndalianis, 16–43. New York: Routledge.

Jess-Cooke, Carolyn. 2009. *Film Sequels: Theory and Practice from Hollywood to Bollywood*. Edinburgh: Edinburgh University Press.

Johns, Geoff, Andy Kubert, Sandra Hope, et al. July 2011–October 2011. *Flashpoint* vol. 2 #1–5. New York: DC Comics.

Johnson, Derek. 2013. *Media Franchising: Creative License and Collaboration in the Culture Industries*. New York: New York University Press.

Johnson, Derek. 2017. "Battleworlds: The Management of Multiplicity in the Media Industries." In *World Building: Transmedia, Fans, Industries*, edited by Marta Boni, 129–42. Amsterdam: Amsterdam University Press.

Jurgens, Dan, Jerry Ordway, Louise Simonson, et al. December 1992–January 1993, reprinted 1993. "The Death of Superman." *Superman: The Man of Steel* #18–19, *Justice League America* #69, *Superman* vol. 2 #74–75, *The Adventures of Superman* #497, and *Action Comics* #684. In *The Death of Superman*, edited by Bob Kahan. New York: DC Comics.

Jurgens, Dan, John Byrne, Tery Austin, et al. December 1996. "The Wedding Album." *Superman: The Wedding Album* #1. New York: DC Comics.

Jurgens, Dan, Lee Weeks, Scott Hanna, et al. December 2015–July 2016, reprinted 2016. *Superman: Lois and Clark* #1–8. In *Superman: Lois and Clark*, edited by Paul Santos. Burbank: DC Comics.

Kent, Miriam. 2021. *Women in Marvel Films*. Edinburgh: Edinburgh University Press.

King, Geoff, 2000. *Spectacular Narratives: Hollywood in the Age of the Blockbuster*. London: I. B. Tauris.

King, Geoff. 2002. *New Hollywood Cinema: An Introduction*. London: I. B. Tauris.

Kitses, Jim. 1969. *Horizons West: Directing the Western from John Ford to Clint Eastwood*. London: British Film Institute.

Klock, Geoff. 2002. *How to Read Superhero Comics and Why*. New York: Continuum.

Koh, Wilson. 2009. "Everything Old Is Good Again: Myth and Nostalgia in *Spider-Man*." *Continuum: Journal of Media and Cultural Studies* 23 (5): 735–47.

Lacassin, Francis, 1972. "The Comic Strip and Film Language." *Film Quarterly* 26 (1): 11–23.

Leaver, Tama. 2012. "Artificial Mourning: The *Spider-Man* Trilogy and September 11th." In *Web-Spinning Heroics: Critical Essays on the History and Meaning of Spider-Man*, edited by Robert Moses Peaslee and Robert G. Weiner, 154–64. Jefferson: McFarland & Company.

LeBel, Sabine. 2009. "'Tone Down the Boobs, Please!': Reading the Special Effect Body in Superhero Movies." *Cineaction* 77: 56–67.

Lee, Peter. 2012. "Have Great Power, Greatly Irresponsible: Intergenerational Conflict in 1960s *Amazing Spider-Man*." In *Web-Spinning Heroics: Critical Essays on the History and Meaning of Spider-Man*, edited by Robert Moses Peaslee and Robert G. Weiner, 29–39. Jefferson: McFarland & Company.

Lee, Stan, Jack Kirby, and Dick Ayers. September 1963, reprinted 2009. "The Coming of The Avengers." *The Avengers* #1. In *The Avengers Volume 1*, edited by Cory Sedlmeier, 1–22. New York: Marvel Publishing.

Lee, Stan, and Jack Kirby. March 1964, reprinted 2009. "Captain America Joins . . . the Avengers!" *The Avengers* #4. In *The Avengers Volume 1*, edited by Cory Sedlmeier, 73–96. New York: Marvel Publishing.

Lee, Stan, Jack Kirby, and Paul Reinman. September 1963, reprinted 2009. "X-Men." *The X-Men* #1. In *Marvel Masterworks: The X-Men Vol. 1*, edited by Cory Sedlmeier, 1–23. New York: Marvel Publishing.

Lee, Stan, John Romita Sr., and Mike Esposito. August 1967, reprinted 2011. "In the Clutches of the Kingpin!" *The Amazing Spider-Man* #51. In *Marvel Masterworks: The Amazing Spider-Man Volume 6*, edited by Cory Sedlmeier, 1–21. New York: Marvel Comics

Lee, Stan, and Steve Ditko. August 1962, reprinted 1997. "Spider-Man!" *Amazing Fantasy* #15. In *Marvel Masterworks Volume 1: The Amazing Spider-Man Nos 1–10 and Amazing Fantasy No. 15*, edited by Bob Budiansky, 1–13. Exeter: Pedigree Books.

Lee, Stan, and Steve Ditko. February 1964, reprinted 1997. "The Man Called Electro!" *The Amazing Spider-Man* #9. In *Marvel Masterworks Volume 1: The Amazing Spider-Man Nos 1–10 and Amazing Fantasy No. 15*, edited by Bob Budiansky, 201–23. Exeter: Pedigree Books.

Lee, Stan, and Steve Ditko. September 1965, reprinted 2012. "The Menace of the Molten Mole Man!" *The Amazing Spider-Man* #28. In *Marvel Masterworks: The Amazing Spider-Man Volume 3*, edited by Cory Sedlmeier, 171–91. New York: Marvel Worldwide.

Lefèvre, Pascal. 2007. "Incompatible Visual Ontologies?: The Problematic Adaptation of Drawn Images." In *Film and Comic Books*, edited by Ian Gordon, Mark Jancovich, and Matthew P. McAllister, 1–12. Jackson: University Press of Mississippi.

Leitch, Thomas. 2007. *Film Adaptation and Its Discontents: From Gone with the Wind to the Passion of the Christ*. Baltimore: John Hopkins University Press.

Leitch, Thomas. 2008. "Adaptation, the Genre." *Adaptation* 1 (2): 106–20.

Lennard, Dominic. 2012. "Wonder Boys." In *Shining in Shadows: Movie Stars of the 2000s*, edited by Murray Pomerance, 12–31. New Brunswick: Rutgers University Press.

Lessing, Gotthold Ephraim. 1766, reprinted 2003. "Laocoon: An Essay on the Limits of Painting and Poetry." In *Classics and Romantic German Aesthetics*, edited by J. M. Bernstein, translated by W. A. Streel, 25–129. Cambridge: Cambridge University Press.

Lobdell, Scott, Mark Waid, Roger Cruz, et al. February 1995–June 1995, reprinted 2021. "Age of Apocalypse." *X-Men Alpha* #1, *Amazing X-Men* #1–4, *Astonishing X-Men* #1–4, *Factor X* #1–4, *Gambit and the X-Ternals* #1–4, *Generation Next* #1–4, *Weapon X* #1–4, *X-Calibre* #1–4, *X-Man* #1–4, and *X-Men Omega* #1. In *X-Men: Age of Apocalypse Omnibus*, edited by Mark D. Beazley, unpaginated. New York: Marvel Worldwide.

Lowther, George. 1942, reprinted 1995. *The Adventures of Superman*. Bedford: Applewood Books.

Maggin, Elliott S., Curt Swan, and Bob Oksner. June 1974, reprinted 2000. "Make Way for Captain Thunder." *Superman* #276. In *Superman in the Seventies*, edited by Michael Wright, 9–28. New York: DC Comics.

Mankiewicz, Tom, and Robert Crane. 2012. *My Life as a Mankiewicz: An Insider's Journey through Hollywood*. Lexington: University Press of Kentucky.

Manovich, Lev. 2001. *The Language of New Media*. Cambridge: MIT Press.

Marston, William Moulton, and Harry G. Peter. January 1942, reprinted 2016. "Introducing Wonder Woman." *All-Star Comics* #8. In *The Golden Age Wonder Woman Omnibus Volume 1*, edited by Suzannah Rowntree, 11–19. Burbank: DC Comics.

Marston, William Moulton, and Harry G. Peter. June 1942, reprinted 2016. "Summons to Paradise." *Sensation Comics* #6. In *The Golden Age Wonder Woman Omnibus Volume 1*, edited by Suzannah Rowntree, 90–103. Burbank: DC Comics.

Marston, William Moulton, and Harry G. Peter. June 1942, reprinted 2016. "Who Is Wonder Woman?" *Wonder Woman* #1. In *The Golden Age Wonder Woman Omnibus Volume 1*, edited by Suzannah Rowntree, 147. Burbank: DC Comics.

Marston, William Moulton, and Harry G. Peter. July 1943, reprinted 2016. "Battle for Womanhood." *Wonder Woman* #5. In *The Golden Age Wonder Woman Omnibus Volume 1*, edited by Suzannah Rowntree, 516–31. Burbank: DC Comics.

Marston, William Moulton, and Harry G. Peter. May 1943, reprinted 2016. "Riddle of the Talking Lions." *Sensation Comics* #17. In *The Golden Age Wonder Woman Omnibus Volume 1*, edited by Suzannah Rowntree, 473–86. Burbank: DC Comics.

Marz, Ron, Derec Aucoin, Darryl Banks, et al. August 1994. "Forced Entry." *Green Lantern* vol. 3 #54. New York: DC Comics.

Matthews, Jolie C., and Dustin Tran. 2023. "Still Never at the Top: Representation of Asian and Black Characters in Sony/Marvel Studios' *Spider-Man* trilogy." *Critical Studies in Media Communication* 40 (4): 199–212.

McCloud, Scott. 1994. *Understanding Comics: The Invisible Art*. New York: HarperPerennial.

McGowan, Matthew, and Jeremy Short. 2012. "Spider-Management: A Critical Examination of the Business World of Spider-Man." In *Web-Spinning Heroics: Critical Essays on the History and Meaning of Spider-Man*, edited by Robert Moses Peaslee and Robert G. Weiner, 113–18. Jefferson: McFarland & Company.

McSweeney, Terence. 2014. *The "War on Terror" and American Film: 9/11 Frames Per Second*. Edinburgh: Edinburgh University Press.

McSweeney, Terence. 2018. *Avengers Assemble: Critical Perspectives on the Marvel Cinematic Universe*. London: Wallflower.

Meikle, Kyle. 2019. *Adaptations in the Franchise Era: 2001–16*. New York: Bloomsbury.

Metz, Christian. 1974. *Film Language: A Semiotics of Cinema*, translated by Michael Taylor. New York: Oxford University Press.

Millar, Mark, Dave Johnson, Andrew Robinson, et al. June 2003–August 2003. *Superman: Red Son* #1–3. New York: DC Comics.

Millar, Mark, Steve McNiven, Dexter Vines, et al. July 2006–January 2007. *Civil War* #1–7. New York: Marvel Comics.

Millar, Mark, Steve McNiven, Dexter Vines, et al. August 2008–November 2009, reprinted 2014. "Old Man Logan." *Wolverine* vol. 3 #66–72 and *Wolverine: Old Man Logan Giant-Size*. In *Wolverine: Old Man Logan*, edited by Mark D. Beazley. New York: Marvel Worldwide.

Miller, Frank, and Klaus Janson. June 1986, reprinted 2002. "The Dark Knight Returns." *The Dark Knight Returns* #1. In *Batman: The Dark Knight Returns*, edited by Dale Crain, 8–54. London: Titan Books.

Minett, Mark, and Bradley Schauer. 2017. "Reforming the 'Justice' System: Marvel's *Avengers* and the Transformation of the All-Star Team Book." In *Make Ours Marvel: Media Convergence and a Comics Universe*, edited by Matt Yockey, 39–65.

Mittermeier, Sabrina. 2021. "Avengers: Endgame (Review)." *Science Fiction Film and Television* 14 (3): 423–29.

Molotiu, Andrei. 2012. "Abstract Form: Sequential Dynamism and Iconostasis in Abstract Comics and Steve Ditko's *Amazing Spider-Man*." In *Critical Approaches to Comics: Theories and Methods*, edited by Matthew J. Smith and Randy Duncan, 84–100. New York: Routledge.

Morrison, Grant. 2011. *Supergods: Our World in the Age of the Superhero*. London: Jonathan Cape.

Morton, Drew. 2016. *Panel to the Screen: Style, American Film, and Comic Books During the Blockbuster Era*. Jackson: University of Mississippi Press.

Mulvey, Laura. 2006. *Death 24x a Second: Stillness and the Moving Image*. London: Reaktion.

Ndalianis, Angela. 2009a. "Enter the Aleph: Superhero Worlds and Hypertime Realities." In *The Contemporary Comic Book Superhero*, edited by Angela Ndalianis, 270–90. New York: Routledge.

Ndalianis, Angela. 2009b. "The Frenzy of the Visible in Comic Book Worlds." *Animation: An Interdisciplinary Journal* 4 (3): 237–48.

Neale, Steve. 1983. "Masculinity as Spectacle: Reflections on Men and Mainstream Cinema." *Screen* 24 (6): 2–16.

Neale, Steve. 2000. *Genre and Hollywood*. London: Routledge.

North, Dan. 2008. *Performing Illusions: Cinema, Special Effects and the Virtual Actor*. London: Wallflower Press.

O'Neil, Denny, Curt Swan, and Murphy Anderson. January 1971, reprinted 2000. "Superman Breaks Loose." *Superman* #233. In *Superman in the Seventies*, edited by Michael Wright, 163–77. New York: DC Comics.

Online Marvel Database. https://marvel.fandom.com/wiki/. Accessed September 2023.

Parody, Clare. 2011. "Franchising/Adaptation." *Adaptation* 4 (2): 210–18.

Pedler, Martyn. 2009. "The Fastest Man Alive: Stasis and Speed in Contemporary Superhero Comics." *Animation* 4 (3): 249–63.

Perkins, V. F. 1972. *Film as Film: Understanding and Judging Movies*. Harmondsworth: Penguin.

Potter, Greg, George Pérez, Bruce Patterson, et al. March 1987, reprinted 2015. "A Fire in the Sky!" *Wonder Woman* vol. 2 #2. In *Wonder Woman by George Pérez Omnibus*, edited by Scott Nybakken, 45–67. Burbank: DC Comics.

Pratt, Henry John. 2012. "Making Comics into Film." In *The Art of Comics: A Philosophical Approach*, edited by Aaron Meskin and Roy T. Cook, 147–64. Chichester: Wiley-Blackwell.

Prince, Stephen. 1996. "True Lies: Perceptual Realism, Digital Images, and Film Theory." *Film Quarterly* 49 (3): 27–37.

Proctor, William. 2017. "Schrödinger's Cape: The Quantum Seriality of the Marvel Multiverse." In *Make Ours Marvel: Media Convergence and a Comics Universe*, edited by Matt Yockey, 319– 345. Austin: University of Texas Press.

Pumphrey, Nicholaus. 2014. "From Terrorist to Tzadik: Reading Comic Books as Post-Shoah Literature in Light of Magneto's Jewish Backstory." In *The Ages of the X-Men: Essays on the Children of the Atom in Changing Times*, edited by Joseph J. Darowski, 91–104. Jefferson: McFarland.

Purse, Lisa. 2011. *Contemporary Action Cinema*. Edinburgh: Edinburgh University Press.

Purse, Lisa. 2013. *Digital Imaging in Popular Cinema*. Edinburgh: Edinburgh University Press.

Rauscher, Andreas. 2010. "The Marvel Universe on Screen: A New Wave of Superhero Movies?" In *Comics as a Nexus of Cultures: Essays on the Interplay of Media, Disciplines and International Perspectives*, edited by Mark Berninger, Jochen Ecke and Gideon Haberkorn, 21–32. Jefferson: McFarland & Company.

Rees, Jasper. 2001. "Meet the Aussie Clint." *Evening Standard*, July 11, 2001.

Regalado, Aldo J. 2015. *Bending Steel: Modernity and the American Superhero*. Jackson: University Press of Mississippi.

Ressner, Jeffrey. 2012. "The Traditionalist." *DGA Quarterly*. https://www.dga.org/Craft/DGAQ/All-Articles/1202-Spring-2012/DGA-Interview-Christopher-Nolan.aspx.

Reynolds, Richard. 1994. *Super Heroes: A Modern Mythology*. Jackson: University Press of Mississippi.

Robinson, Joanna, Dave Gonzales, and Gavin Edwards. 2023. *MCU: The Reign of Marvel Studios*. London: Headline.

Rossen, Jake. 2008. *Superman vs. Hollywood: How Fiendish Producers, Devious Directors, and Warring Writers Grounded an American Icon*. Chicago: Chicago Review Press.

Rucka, Greg, Mike Perkins, Paul Mounts, et al. September 2019–September 2020. *Lois Lane* vol. 2 #1–12. Burbank: DC Comics.

Russell, Vanessa. 2009. "The Mild-Mannered Reporter: How Clark Kent Surpassed Superman." In *The Contemporary Comic Book Superhero*, edited by Angela Ndalianis, 216–32. New York: Routledge.

Saunders, Ben. 2011. *Do The Gods Wear Capes? Spirituality, Fantasy, and Superheroes*. London: Continuum.

Schatz, Thomas. 1981. *Hollywood Genres: Formulas, Filmmaking and the Studio System*. Philadelphia: Temple University Press.

Schatz, Thomas. 1993. "The New Hollywood." In *Film Theory Goes to the Movies*, edited by Jim Collins, Hilary Radner and Ava Preacher Collins, 8–36. New York: Routledge.

Schatz, Thomas. 2009. "New Hollywood, New Millenium." *Film Theory and Contemporary Hollywood Movies*, edited by Warren Buckland, 19–46. New York: Routledge.

Sconce, Jeffrey. 2002. "Irony, Nihilism and the New American 'Smart' Film." *Screen* 34 (4): 349–69.

Scott, Suzanne. 2013. "Who's Steering the Mothership? The Role of the Fanboy Auteur in Transmedia Storytelling." In *The Participatory Cultures Handbook*, edited by Aaron Delwiche and Jennifer Jacobs Henderson, 43–52. New York: Routledge.

Shone, Tom. 2004. *Blockbuster: How Hollywood Learned to Stop Worrying and Love the Summer*. New York: Free Press.

Shooter, Jim, Michael Zeck, John Beatty, et al. May 1984–April 1985, reprinted 2011. *Marvel Super Heroes Secret Wars* #1–12. In *Marvel Super Heroes Secret Wars*, edited by Mark D. Beazey. New York: Marvel Publishing.

Shyminsky, Neil. 2006. "Mutant Readers, Reading Mutants: Appropriation, Assimilation, and the X-Men." *International Journal of Comic Art* 8 (2): 387–405.

Siegel, Jerry (as Herbert S. Fine) and Joe Shuster. January 1933. "The Reign of the Super-Man." *Science Fiction: The Advance Guard of Future Civilization* 3: unpaginated.

Siegel, Jerry, and Joe Shuster. June 1938, reprinted 2013. "Superman, Champion of the Oppressed!" *Action Comics* #1. In *Superman: The Golden Age Omnibus Volume 1*, edited by Rowena Yow, 14–26. New York: DC Comics.

Siegel, Jerry, and Joe Shuster. July 1938, reprinted 2013. "Revolution in San Morte Pt. 2." *Action Comics* #2. In *Superman: The Golden Age Omnibus Volume 1*, edited by Rowena Yow, 28–41. New York: DC Comics.

Siegel, Jerry, and Joe Shuster. November 1938, reprinted 2013. "Superman's Phoney Manager." *Action Comics* #6. In *Superman: The Golden Age Omnibus Volume 1*, edited by Rowena Yow, 80–92. New York: DC Comics.

Siegel, Jerry, and Joe Shuster. August 1939, reprinted 2013. "Superman and the High Seas." *Action Comics* #15. In *Superman: The Golden Age Omnibus Volume 1*, edited by Rowena Yow, 230–42. New York: DC Comics.

Siegel, Jerry, and Joe Shuster. October 1939, reprinted 2013. "The Return of the Ultra-Humanite." *Action Comics* #17. In *Superman: The Golden Age Omnibus Volume 1*, edited by Rowena Yow, 317–29. New York: DC Comics.

Siegel, Jerry, and Joe Shuster. November 1939, reprinted 2013. "Superman's Super Campaign." *Action Comics* #18. In *Superman: The Golden Age Omnibus Volume 1*, edited by Rowena Yow, 331–43. New York: DC Comics.

Siegel, Jerry, and Joe Shuster. December 1939, reprinted 2013. "Superman and the Purple Plague." *Action Comics* #19. In *Superman: The Golden Age Omnibus Volume 1*, edited by Rowena Yow, 345–56. New York: DC Comics.

Siegel, Jerry, and Joe Shuster. March 1940, reprinted 2013. "Europe at War, Part 1." *Action Comics* #22. In *Superman: The Golden Age Omnibus Volume 1*, edited by Rowena Yow, 420–32. New York: DC Comics.

Siegel, Jerry, and Joe Shuster. May 1940, reprinted 2013. "Carnahan's Heir." *Action Comics* #24. In *Superman: The Golden Age Omnibus Volume 1*, edited by Rowena Yow, 501–13. New York: DC Comics.

Siegel, Jerry, and Joe Shuster. January 1945, reprinted 2020. "The Origin of Superboy." *More Fun Comics* #101. In *Superboy: A Celebration of 75 Years*, edited by Reza Lokman, 8–12. Burbank, DC Comics.

Siegel, Jerry, and Kurt Schaffenberger. August 1960. "Mr. and Mrs. Clark (Superman) Kent!" *Superman's Girlfriend Lois Lane* #19. New York: National Comics.

Siegel, Tatiana. 2023. "Crisis at Marvel: Jonathan Majors Back-Up Plans, 'The Marvels' Reshoots, Reviving Original Avengers and More Issues Revealed." *Variety*, November 1, 2023. https://variety.com/2023/film/features/marvel-jonathan-majors-problem-the-marvels-reshoots-kang-1235774940/.

Simon, Joe, and Jack Kirby. March 1941, reprinted 2019. *Captain America Comics* #1. In *Timely's Greatest: The Golden Age Simon & Kirby Omnibus*, edited by Cory Sedlmeier, 169–234. New York: Marvel Worldwide.

Simone, Gail. 1993. "Women in Refrigerators." *Women in Refrigerators*. http://www.lby3.com/wir/.

Singer, Marc. 2018. *Breaking the Frames: Populism and Prestige in Comics Studies*. Austin: University of Texas Press.

Smith, Andrew A. 2012. "J. Jonah Jameson—Hero or Villain? Spider-Man's Nemesis Hard to Pigeonhole." In *Web-Spinning Heroics: Critical Essays on the History and Meaning of Spider-Man*, edited by Robert Moses Peaslee and Robert G. Weiner, 101–12. Jefferson: McFarland & Company.

Smith, Clancy. 2014. "Days of Future Past: Segregation, Oppression and Technology in X-Men and America." In *The Ages of the X-Men: Essays on the Children of the Atom in Changing Times*, edited by Joseph J. Darowski, 63–76. Jefferson, McFarland: 2014.

Smith, Jason. 2016. "Mutating Minorities: White Racial Framing and Group Positioning." In *The X-Men Films: A Cultural Analysis*, edited by Claudia Bucciferro, 179–92. Lanham: Rowman & Littlefield.

Spiegelman, Art. 1986. *Maus: A Survivor's Tale*. New York: Pantheon.

Spiegelman, Art, and Chip Kidd. 2001. *Jack Cole and Plastic Man: Forms Stretched to their Limits*. San Francisco: Chronicle Books.

Stam, Robert. 2000. "Beyond Fidelity: The Dialogics of Adaptation." In *Film Adaptation*, edited by James Naremore, 54–76. London: Athlone Press, 2000.

Starlin, Jim, Jim Aparo, Mike DeCarlo, et al. December 1988–January 1989. "A Death in the Family." *Batman* #426–29. New York: DC Comics.

Straczynski, J. Michael, John Romita Jr., Scott Hanna, et al. September 2001. "All Fall Down." *The Amazing Spider-Man* vol. 2 #33. New York: Marvel Comics.

Straczynski, J. Michael, John Romita Jr., Scott Hanna, et al. December 2001. "Stand Tall." *The Amazing Spider-Man* vol. 2 #36. New York: Marvel Comics.

Straczynski, J. Michael, John Romita Jr., Scott Hanna, et al. January 2002. "Interlude." *The Amazing Spider-Man* vol. 2 #37. New York: Marvel Comics.

Straczynski, J. Michael, John Romita Jr., Scott Hanna, et al. June 2002. "Sensitive Issues." *The Amazing Spider-Man* vol. 2 #40. New York: Marvel Comics.

Straczynski, J. Michael, John Romita Jr., Scott Hanna, et al. July 2002. "Looking Back." *The Amazing Spider-Man* vol. 2 #41. New York: Marvel Comics.

Straczynski, J. Michael, John Romita Jr., Scott Hanna, et al. August 2002. "A Strange Turn of Events." *The Amazing Spider-Man* vol. 2 #42. New York: Marvel Comics.

Tasker, Yvonne. 1993. *Spectacular Bodies: Gender, Genre and the Action Cinema*. London: Routledge.

Taylor, Aaron. 2017. "Playing Peter Parker: Spider-Man and Superhero Film Performance." In *Make Ours Marvel: Media Convergence and a Comics Universe*, edited by Matt Yockey, 268–96. Austin: University of Texas Press.

Taylor, Aaron. 2019. "Genre and Superhero Cinema." In *Comics and Pop Culture: Adaptation from Panel to Frame*, edited by Barry Keith Grant and Scott Henderson, 92–109. Austin: University of Texas Press.

Taylor, James C. 2022. "Postmodern Parody in Superhero Cinema." In *The Superhero Multiverse: Readapting Comic Book Icons in Twenty-First-Century Film and Popular Media*, edited by Lorna Piatti-Farnell, 87–104. Lanham: Lexington.

Taylor, Jessica, and Laura Glitsos. 2023. "'Having It Both Ways': Containing the Champions of Feminism in Female-Led Origin and Solo Superhero Films." *Feminist Media Studies* 23 (2): 656–70.

Thompson, Kristin. 2019. "3D in 2019: RealDvided?" *Observations on Film*, February 12, 2019. http://www.davidbordwell.net/blog/2019/02/12/3d-in-2019-realdvided/.

Tye, Larry. 2012. *Superman: The High-Flying History of America's Most Enduring Hero*. New York: Random House.

Vu, Ryan. 2016. "Marvel Cinematic Universality." *Science Fiction Film and Television* 9 (1): 125–31.

Ware, Chris. 2000. *Jimmy Corrigan: The Smartest Kid on Earth*. New York: Pantheon.

Weetch, Owen, 2016. *Expressive Spaces in Digital 3D Cinema*. London: Palgrave.

Wein, Len, Dave Cockrum, Glynis Wein. May 1975, reprinted 2020. "Second Genesis!" *Giant-Size X-Men #1*. In *The Uncanny X-Men Omnibus Vol. 1*, edited by Mark D. Beazley and Cory Sedlmeier, 10–46. New York: Marvel Worldwide.

Weiner, Robert G., and Robert Moses Peaslee. 2012. "Introduction." In *Web-Spinning Heroics: Critical Essays on the History and Meaning of Spider-Man*, edited by Peaslee and Weiner, 4–19. Jefferson: McFarland & Company.

Wertham, Fredric. 1954. *Seduction of the Innocent*. New York: Rinehart & Company.

Whedon, Joss, John Cassaday, and Laura Martin. July 2008. "Gone." *Giant-Size Astonishing X-Men #1*. New York: Marvel Comics.

Wolf, Mark J. P. 2012. *Building Imaginary Worlds: The Theory and History of Subcreation*. New York: Routledge.

Wolfman, Marv, George Pérez, Dick Giordano, et al. April 1985–March 1986, reprinted 2000. *Crisis on Infinite Earths #1–12*. In *Crisis on Infinite Earths*, edited by Rick Taylor and Jim Spivey. New York: DC Comics.

Wood, Aylish. 2007. *Digital Encounters*. London: Routledge.

Wright, Bradford W. 2001. *Comic Book Nation: The Transformation of Youth Culture in America*. Baltimore: Johns Hopkins University Press.

X-Men Films Wiki. https://xmenmovies.fandom.com/wiki/X-Men_Movies_Wiki. Accessed September 2023.

Yockey, Matt. 2008. "Somewhere in Time: Utopia and the Return of Superman." *Velvet Light Trap* 61: 26–37.

Yockey, Matt. 2017. "Introduction: Excelsior! or, Everything that Rises Must Converge." In *Make Ours Marvel: Media Convergence and a Comics Universe*, edited by Matt Yockey, 1–38. Austin: University of Texas Press.

Yost, Chris, Eric Pearson, Luke Ross, et al. April 2012–June 2012. *The Avengers Prelude: Fury's Big Week #1–4*. New York: Marvel Comics

Zeller-Jacques, Martin. 2012. "Adapting the X-Men: Comic-Book Narratives in Film Franchises." In *A Companion to Literature, Film, and Adaptation*, edited by Deborah Cartmell, 143–58. Chichester: Blackwell.

Zingsheim, Jason. 2011. "X-Men Evolution: Mutational Identity and Shifting Subjectivities." *Howard Journal of Communications* 22 (3): 223–39.

INDEX

Page numbers in *italics* refer to figures.

3D cinema, 191–92, 194, 217
9/11: in cinema, depiction and response, 74, 98–103, 106; in comics, depiction and response, 96–98, 241n10; press coverage, 110; US sentiment after, 74, 157, 214, 217–18

Action Comics #1 (June 1938): cover, *36*, *37*, 58, 79, 81, 132; genesis of superhero genre, 8, 26, 77; Lois Lane, 42–43; relationship between Superman and Clark Kent, 42–43, 46–47, *48*; seriality, 127; sociopolitical meanings, 38–39; style and form, *16*, 17–18, 37–38, 42–43, 46–47, *48*, 57; Superman's powers, 26, 38
Action Comics #2 (July 1938), 238n7
Action Comics #6 (November 1938), 238n8
Action Comics #252 (May 1959), 187
Action Comics #484 (June 1978), 53
adaptation theory: comparing comics and film form, 14–21; fidelity criticism, 14–15; interrogating the word/image binary, 21–25; medium-specificity, 14–15; poststructuralist, 26–29
Adventures of Superman (first run syndication 1952–1958), 37, 39, 40–41, *44*, *45*, 49–50, 51, 52, 56
Adventures of Superman, The (Lowther and Shuster 1942), 37
Adventures of Superman, The (WOR/MBS/ABC 1940–1951), 37, 39, 40, 47; "Clan of the Fiery Cross" (1946), 51

Agent Carter (ABC 2015–2016), 135–36, 137, 159, 241n5
Agents of S.H.I.E.L.D. (ABC 2013–2020), 135–36, 137
"Age of Apocalypse" (February 1995–June 1995), 180, *181–82*, 185
ages of superhero comics, defining, 9–10
Alice in Wonderland (Geronimi, Jackson, and Luske 1951), 24
Alice's Adventures in Wonderland (Carroll and Tenniel 1865), 22–24
All-Star Comics #3 (December 1940), 130
All-Star Comics #8 (January 1942), 224
all-star team comics, 130–32, 140
Altered States (Ken Russell 1980), 61
alternate timeline: definition, 172; designation in Fox's X-Men films, 186–87; dystopia, 195, 197; history of use in superhero comics, 172–73; nostalgia and legacy, 233–35; sociopolitical implications, 173–75, 183, 209–13; spatiotemporal malleability, aesthetics of, 189–94; spatiotemporal rigidity, aesthetics of, 197–98; style and narrative strategies in X-Men comics, 176–85; superhero deaths, 185, 208–10; Wolverine's body and continuity, 202–8
Alyn, Kirk, *45*, 49, 53
Amazing Fantasy #15 (August 1962): cover 79–81, *80*, 132; relationship between Spider-Man and Peter Parker, 81, *82*, 94

259

Amazing Spider-Man, The (Webb 2012), 120, 124, 125
Amazing Spider-Man, The, #9 (February 1964), 79
Amazing Spider-Man, The, #28 (September 1965), 81
Amazing Spider-Man, The, #51 (August 1967), 96
Amazing Spider-Man, The, #121 (June 1973), 124
Amazing Spider-Man, The, vol. 2 #33 (September 2001), 88–89
Amazing Spider-Man, The, vol. 2 #36 (December 2001), 96, 97, 98
Amazing Spider-Man, The, vol. 2 #37 (January 2002), 98
Amazing Spider-Man, The, vol. 2 #40–42 (June 2002–August 2002), 240n11
Amazing Spider-Man, The, vol. 2 #55–56 (September 2003–October 2003), 98
Amazing Spider-Man 2, The, (Webb 2014), 123, 125
Ant-Man, 130
Ant-Man and the Wasp: Quantumania (Reed 2023), 138
Aquaman (Wan 2018), 230
Aquaman and the Lost Kingdom (Wan 2023), 242n6
Aquaman/Arthur Curry, 228–30
Atom Man vs Superman (Bennet 1950), 37, 45
Aunt May, 107–8, 125–26
Australia (Luhrmann 2008), 206
Avengers: comics, 130, *131*, 132, 145; Marvel Cinematic Universe, 127, 134–42, 145–59, 162–67
Avengers, The (Whedon 2012), 127, 135–36, 167; character hierarchy, 147–58, 163, 165, 200; compression of characters, 145–47; merchandise and tie-in promotions, 139, 147; superhero versus superhero battles, 147–52; Thanos, 134–35, 164
Avengers, The #1 (September 1963): character introductions, 145; cover, *131*, 132; story, 130

Avengers, The #4 (March 1964), 142
Avengers: Age of Ultron (Whedon 2015), 135, 152, 163
Avengers: Endgame (Russo brothers 2019), 21, 126, 135, 164–67, 241n5
Avengers: Infinity War (Russo brothers 2018), 135, 162, 164
Avengers Prelude, The: Fury's Big Week (April 2012–June 2012), 135–36
Avengers vs. X-Men (May 2012–December 2012), 148
AVX: Vs #1 (June 2012), 148–49

Back to the Future (Zemeckis 1986), 229
Batman (ABC 1966–1968), 42, 234
Batman (Burton 1989), 232
Batman Begins (Nolan 2005), 29, 198, 218, 220
Batman/Bruce Wayne, 27, 29, 42, 73, 218–23, 228–29, 232–34
Batman Returns (Burton 1992), 232
Batman v Superman: Dawn of Justice (Snyder 2016), 75, 216, 218–23, 226–27, 229, 232
Beast, 242n8
Bingbing, Fan, 193
Bishop, 209, 233
Black Adam, 230–31
Black Adam (Collet-Serra 2022), 230–31
Black Panther (Coogler 2018), 163
Black Panther/T'Challa, 163–64, 166, 167
Black Panther: Wakanda Forever (Coogler 2022), 169
Black Widow (Shortland 2021), 169
Black Widow/Natasha Romanoff: *The Avengers*, 146–47, 150–52, 155, 164, 201, 227; *Avengers: Endgame*, 165, 167; solo film, 169
Blink, 191, 193, 209, 212, 233
Boym, Svetlana, 104–6, 107, 142
Brando, Marlon, 60, 74
Brave and the Bold, The #28 (March 1960), 132
Bringing Up Baby (Hawks 1938), 55
Brooker, Will, 26, 27, 29, 42, 72–73, 198

INDEX

Brown, Jeffrey A., 11, 146, 173, 200, 218, 239n2, 241n1
Buck and the Preacher (Poitier 1972), 242n6
Bukatman, Scott: hypermasculinity, 151; kaleidoscopic perception, 61–62, 83; superheroes and the city, 64, 69, 100; utopia as movement, 71, 98, 156, 195, 226
Burke, Liam: comics form, 20; comics formats, 7; comics style in cinema, 13, 14, 22, 86, 149; "golden age of comic book filmmaking," 30; intertextuality in superhero comics, 26; Marvel Cinematic Universe, 128; nostalgia, 32; Spider-Man, 102, 124; *Superman: The Movie*, 59, 238n17
Bush, George W., 74, 110, 114, 218
Byrne, John, 171, 176–77

Cable, 186
Campbell, Bruce, 116
capitalism: critical presentation of, 108–13, 116–17, 119, 144, 196–97; positive presentation of, 119, 145, 150, 153, 157, 167, 220–22; and postmodern film, 106
Captain America: Civil War (Russo brothers 2016), 135, 163
Captain America Comics #1 (March 1941), 142, *143*
Captain America/Steve Rogers: *The Avengers*, 145–46, 152–54, 155, *156*, 157–58; *Avengers: Endgame*, 164–67; *Avengers: Infinity War*, 164; *Captain America: Civil War*, 163; *Captain America: The First Avenger*, 141–42, 144; *Captain America: The Winter Soldier*, 159; comics, 142, *143*
Captain America: The First Avenger (Johnston 2011), 141–42, 144, 152
Captain America: The Winter Soldier (Russo brothers 2014), 159, 163
Captain Marvel (Boden and Fleck 2019), 159–62, 165, 167, 223, 241n13
Captain Marvel/Billy Batson, 239n4
Captain Marvel/Carol Danvers: comics, 159; Marvel Cinematic Universe, 138, 159–62, 166–67

Cassaday, John, 85
CGI. *See* digital imaging
cinema of attractions, 11
Civil War (July 2006–January 2007), 132
Civil War II (July 2016–February 2017), 159
Claremont, Chris, 171
Cloak & Dagger (Freeform 2018–2019), 136
Cocca, Carolyn, 146, 200, 224, 241n13, 242n2
Cockrum, Dave, 171
Collins, Jim, 27, 29, 52, 237n5
Collyer, Bud, 47
Colossus, 200
comic books, 3–4
Comics Code, 51, 79
comics form: comparing to film form, 16–21; image ontology, 18–19, 85–86, 133; juxtaposition of styles and signs, 79–81; movement, 47; page layout, 17, 147–48; spatiotemporal plasticity, 17, 88–89, 189–90; written words, 19–21
Constable, Catherine, 12, 106
Coogan, Peter, 26; ages of superhero comics, 9–10; definition of superhero, 8–9
Crisis on Infinite Earths (April 1985–March 1986), 132–34, 173, 227, 233
crossover events, comic book, 130, 132–34, 140, 155
Cyborg/Victor Stone, 228–30
Cyclops, 180, 209

Daredevil, 137
Daredevil (Netflix 2015–2018), 136
Dark Knight Returns, The, #1 (June 1986), 218, *219*
Dark Knight trilogy (Nolan 2005, 2008, and 2012), 29, 42, 194, 198
Dark Phoenix (Kinberg 2019), 186, 202, 211
"Days of Future Past" (January 1981–February 1981), 170, 187, 200, 209; creative team, 176; impact on prime timeline, 180, 183, 210–11; premise, 176; presentation of alternate timeline, 176–80; superhero deaths, 185
DC Extended Universe: alternate timelines, 232–35; compression in ensemble films,

218–23, 228–30; critiquing the universe's masculinized structures, 223–28; establishing and expanding the universe, 216–33; hierarchical continuity, 220–23, 228–32
Deadpool, 3–5, 186, 213
Deadpool (Miller 2016), 186
Deadpool 2 (Leitch 2002), 3–5, 186, 242n10
Deadpool & Wolverine (Levy 2024), 213
"Death in the Family, A" (December 1988–January 1989), 220
"Death of Superman" (December 1992–January 1993), 73, 185
Defenders, The (Netflix 2017), 136
digital imaging, 119, 199–200, 217; bodies, 85, 88, 89–95, 122–24, 202, 208, 221, 233; de-aging, 160–61, 207–8, 215, 243; krackle, 149–50, 190–91, 221, 229; resurrection, 234; space, 98–100; spatiotemporal manipulation, 192–94, 229–30; theorizing, 83–91
disaster movies, 67
Disney+, 135, 137–38, *139*, 168–69, 240n4, 241n6
Ditko, Steve, 81, 100
Doctor Octopus, 92, 99, 100–102, 122, 240n16
Doctor Strange, 123, 164
Doctor Strange and the Multiverse of Madness (Raimi 2022), 137
Domino, 3–5
Doomsday, 221–22
Downey, Robert, Jr., 152–53
Dyer, Richard: utopia, 69–72, 156, 226; whiteness, 102, 202, 207

Eco, Umberto, 41, 174–75, 185, 203, 210
Eisenberg, Jesse, 221
Electro, 122
Elliott, Kamilla, 15–16, 22–25, 29, 35
Eternals (Zhao 2021), 168
Evans, Chris, 152–53

Falcon and the Winter Soldier, The (Disney+ 2021), 168–69
Falcon/Sam Wilson, 164, 168–69

Fantastic Four (Story 2005), 152
Fantastic Four: Rise of the Silver Surfer (Story 2007), 152–53
Fawaz, Ramzi, 171, 173–74, 201, 202
Feige, Kevin, 138, 240n1
femininity/females: agency of characters, 114–19, 125–26; leading television shows, 75, 135–36, 138, 159; merchandise, 147; postfeminism, 73, 160; representation of superheroes in ensemble films, 146–47, 150–52, 165, 166–67, 222–23, 228–29; sexualization of female superheroes, 4, 147, 228–29; spectatorship, 68; superheroes' costumes, 4, 162, 222; superheroes in alternate timelines, 175, 232–33; superheroes in solo films, 159–63, 169, 223, 226–28; superheroes' powers, 4, 146, 150–52, 201–2, 222–24, 227–28
Flash, The (Muschietti 2023), 216, 232–35
Flash #123 (September 1961), 52, 172–73
Flash/Barry Allen, 228–30, 232–33, 235
"Flash of Two Worlds!," 52, 172–73
Flashpoint (July 2011–October 2011), 173, 216
Fleischer/Famous Studios Superman cartoons, 37, 39, 40, 41, 44–45, 47, 49, 50–51, 53, 56, 67, 238n4, 238n19
Flerken, 161
franchise (media), defining, 27–29
Fury, Nick, 135–36, 160–61, 240n17

Garfield, Andrew, 120, 123
Gemini Man (Lee 2019), 208
genre hybridity, 66–72, 141, 146–47, 215
Giant-Size Astonishing X-Men #1 (July 2008), *84*, 85
Giant-Size X-Men #1 (May 1975), 171
Gifted, The (Fox 2017–2019), 212
Godfather, The (Coppola 1972), 60
Goose the Flerken, 161
Gordon, Ian, 26, 27, 36, 50, 74, 237n3, 238n19, 239n24
Grant, Cary, 55–56
graphic novel, defining, 7–8
Green Goblin/Harry Osborn, 95, 113, 114–15, 118

Green Goblin/Norman Osborn, 83, 92, 99, 104, 111–13, 117
Green Lantern, 115
Green Lantern vol. 3 #54 (August 1994), 115
Grey, Jean, 202, 209, 211
Guardians of the Galaxy, 164, 241n6
Guardians of the Galaxy Holiday Special, The (Gunn 2022), 241n6
Gunning, Tom: cinema of attractions, 11; realism and movement, 87, 90

Hassler-Forest, Dan, 38–39, 74, 104, 106
Hawkeye (Disney+ 2021), 137
Hawkeye/Clint Barton: comics, 176; Marvel Cinematic Universe, 137, 146, 155
Hawkman, 231
Hiddleston, Tom, 151
His Girl Friday (Hawks 1940), 56
Holland, Tom, 120
Holliday, Christopher, 122, 160–61, 207–8
horror, 7, 66, 79, 152, 229
Hulk/Bruce Banner: comics, 130; Marvel Cinematic Universe, 21, 138, 145, 151–52, 154, 155, 158; merchandise, 139
Hutcheon, Linda, 104, 105–6, 108, 142, 144

"imaginary" stories, 172–76, 212. *See also* alternate timeline
Incredible Hulk, The (CBS 1977–1982), 21
Incredible Hulk, The (Leterrier 2008), 145, 152
Iron Fist (Netflix 2017–2018), 136
Iron Man (Favreau 2008), 140–41, 144–45, 149, 152–53, 173
Iron Man 2 (Favreau 2010), 144–45, 240n1
Iron Man 3 (Black 2013), 144–45, 159, 163
Iron Man/Tony Stark: *The Avengers*, 145–46, 147–50, 151, 152–58; *Avengers: Endgame*, 163–65, 167; *Avengers: Infinity War*, 163; *Captain America: Civil War*, 163; comics, 130, 145, 148, 152, 159, 240n17; solo films, 140–41, 144–45, 159, 163; as Spider-Man's mentor, 122, 126

Jackman, Hugh, 200, 202–3, 206, 211, 213
Jameson, Fredric, 104–6, 111

Jameson, J. Jonah, 104, 109–11, 117, 122, 240n15
Jaws (Spielberg 1975), 11, 65
Jeffries, Dru, 3, 13, 14
Jenkins, Henry, 174, 241n10
Jessica Jones (Netflix 2015–2019), 136, 159
Johnson, Derek, 27–28, 142, 209, 240n2
Johnson, Dwayne, 230
Joker, 42, 219–20, 232
Jones, Michelle, *123*, *124*, 125
Justice League (Snyder 2017), 216, 228–30
Justice League of America: cinema, 228–30; comics, 52, 131–32
Justice League: The Snyder Cut (Snyder 2021), 216, 228–30, 232
Justice Society of America: cinema, 230; comics, 52, 130

Kang the Conqueror, 138, 216, 241n7
Kennedy, John F., 51
Kent, Miriam, 115, 125, 162, 195, 196, 210, 212
King, Geoff, 11, 60, 64–65, 68
King Kong (Cooper and Schoedsack 1933), 152
Kirby, Jack, 81
Kubert, Adam, 180

Lane, Lois: comics, 42–43, 53, 75, 172, 175, 238n7; *Lois and Clark*, 73; *Superman Returns*, 74; *Superman: The Movie*, 54, 55, 56–58, 67–72
Last Tango in Paris (Bertolucci 1972), 60
Laura/Wolverine: cinema, 187, 195–96, 198–99, 210, 211–12, 213; comics, 212
Lefèvre, Pascal, 14, 17–21, 83, 176
Leitch, Thomas, 14, 29
Liefeld, Rob, 4, 237n1
Lizard, The, 122
Logan (Mangold 2017), 185–87, 213; criticism of Donald Trump, 195–96; dystopia, 195, 197; impact on X-Men franchise, 211–12; Logan's death, 208–9, 210–11; premise, 187; profilmic, emphasis on, 197–98; "realism," 198–99; spatiotemporal rigidity, 197–98; story settings, 194–200, 212; Western genre,

194–99, 206–8, 210–11; Wolverine's body, 204–5, 207–8
Lois and Clark: The New Adventures of Superman (ABC 1993–1997), 73
Lois Lane vol. 2 (September 2019–September 2020), 75
Loki: comics, 130, *131*, 132, 241n12; Marvel Cinematic Universe, 150–52, 158
Loki (Disney+ 2021–2023), 138
Luke Cage (Netflix 2016–2018), 136, 163
Luthor, Lex, 67, 221

Madureira, Joe, 180
Magik, 190
Magneto: cinema, 191, 193–94, 200–201, 211, 242n9; comics, 148–49, 180, 183
Maguire, Tobey, 94–95, 117
Mangold, James, 197
Man of Steel (Snyder 2013), 75, 216–18, 226, 231, 235
Man of Steel, The #1 (October 1986), 72
Marston, William Moulton (pseud. Charles Moulton), 224, 227
Marvel Cinematic Universe: characterization in solo films, 140–45, 159–62; compression in ensemble films, 145–47, 163–67; in crisis, 215–16; hierarchical continuity in phases two and three, 158–67; merchandise, 139, 147; shared universe model of seriality, 127–29; television shows, 135–38, 159, 168–69, 173, 241n5; textual hierarchy, 134–40, 159, 167–69
Marvels, The (DaCosta 2023), 138
Marvel Studios: Assembled (Disney+ 2021), 138
Marvel superhero, key characteristics of, 78–81, 130, 170
Marvel Super Heroes Secret Wars (May 1984–April 1985), 132
masculinity/males: adolescent, 74; centrality to superhero genre, 95, 171, 175, 200, 213; in crisis, 50; feminized, 151–52; patriarchy, 74, 108–11; physical strength and muscles, 43, 151, 153–54, 164, 202–8, 221, 229; violent, 75, 200, 217–18, 227; white, 108, 171, 200, 206–8, 210–13, 220, 230
McCloud, Scott, 7, 19, *20*, 86
McNiven, 179
McSweeney, Terence, 106, 141, 157
military-industrial complex, 144–45, 146, 153, 157, 159, 161, 241n13
Miller, Mark, 179
Moonstar, Dani, 212, 242n10
More Fun Comics #101 (January 1945), 187
Morlun, 88, *89*
Morton, Drew, 13–14, 22, 59, 238n17
Ms. Marvel (Disney+ 2022), 138
Multiverse: continuity maintenance and compression, 52, 133–34, 172–73, 234–35; DC Extended Universe, 232–35; as governing system, 128, 130; Marvel Cinematic Universe, 169, 213; sociopolitical implications, 173–76. *See also* alternate timeline
Mulvey, Laura, 192, 234
musical genre, 68–72
Mysterio, 123, 183
Mystique, 187, 194, 201–2, 227

Ndalianis, Angela, 27, 172, 189
Neale, Steve, 10, 203–4
New Hollywood, 11–13, 65–67, 72, 76, 127
New Mutants, The (Boone 2020), 186, 190, 212–13, 242n10
New Mutants, The #21 (November 1984), 190
New Mutants, The #32 (October 1985), 190
New York: alternate timelines, 177, 188–89; *Amazing Spider-Man* films, 124; Fox X-Men films, 188–89; Marvel Cinematic Universe, 136, 145, 154, 156, 164; Marvel comics, 85, 96, 98, 145, 177, 187; MCU *Spider-Man* films, 120–21, 123–24; relationship to Gotham and Metropolis, 220; *Spider-Man* trilogy, 83, 85, 95, 98–103, 108, 120–22; *Superman: The Movie*, 64
Nightcrawler, 190–91
nostalgia: *Captain America: The First Avenger*, 141–42; *The Flash*, 234–35; mise-en-scene in *Spider-Man*, 106–13,

119; for the *Spider-Man* trilogy, 122; for *Superman: The Movie*, 74, 234–35; in *Superman: The Movie*, 58, 67, 76; theorizing, 104–6; *X-Men: Days of Future Past*, 209
Novels into Film (Bluestone 1957), 15

"Old Man Logan" (August 2008–November 2009), 187; creative team, 179; Logan's characterization, 179, 183, 185, 211; premise, 176; Western genre, 179–80, 185
Olsen, Jimmy, 54

Phastos, 168
Plastic Man (Jack Cole), 10
Proudstar, John, 212
Pryde, Kitty, 176, *177–78*, 178–79, 183, 200
Punisher, The (Netflix 2017–2019), 136, 159
Purse, Lisa, 11, 83, 85, 93–94, 99

Quicksilver, 191–94, 229

race: Black superheroes, representation of, 4–5, 124–25, 163–64, 169; diversity in superheroes, 96, 162–64, 168–69, 171, 200, 209–12, 229, 230–31, 233; diversity in supporting characters, 96–98, 100–103, 124–25, 162, 197; racialized violence, 196–97; whiteness, 95, 102–3, 113, 175, 202–4, 206–8, 209–10, 220, 229, 242n2
Reeve, Christopher, 54–58, 234–35
Reeves, George, *44*, 45, 49, 52, 53, 55, 233–34, 238n10
remediation, 13–14
Reynolds, Richard, 8, 130, 171
Right Stuff, The (Kaufman 1983), 160
Robertson, Joe "Robbie," 96, 98, 116
Robin, 79, 220
romance, 68–72, 73, 227–28
Romita, John, Jr., 88, 171
Runaways (Hulu 2017–2019), 136, 137

Sandman, 93, 99, 122
Scarlet Witch/Wanda Maximoff, 137, 163, 164, 167, 241n14

Schatz, Thomas, 9–10, 12, 65–68, 137
science fiction, 68, 74, 141, 164, 194, 229
Secret Invasion #6 (November 2008), 155
Secret Wars (July 2015–March 2016), 173
Seduction of the Innocent (Wertham 1954), 7
Sensation Comics #6 (June 1942), 227
Sensation Comics #17 (May 1943), 224
Shane (Stevens 1953), 196–97, *198*, 199, 210
Shang-Chi and the Legend of the Ten Rings (Cretton 2021), 168
shared universe, comic book, 129–34
She-Hulk: Attorney at Law (Disney+ 2022), 138, *139*
She-Hulk/Jennifer Walters, 138, *139*
S.H.I.E.L.D., 136, 141, 153, 157, 159, 160–61, 241n13
Shuri, 169
Sienkiewicz, Bill, 190
Sinclair, Rahne, 212
Smallville (WB/CW 2001–2011), 73–74
Social Network, The (Fincher 2010), 221
Some Like It Hot (Wilder 1959), 118–19
Space Odyssey, A (Kubrick 1968), 61
Spider-Man (ABC 1967–1970), 83, 109–10
Spider-Man (Raimi 2002), 5; commercial success, 77; digital imaging, 83, 89–92, 98; nostalgia, 105–13; presentation of Spider-Man's powers, 89–91, 119
Spider-Man 2 (Raimi 2004): commercial success, 77; digital imaging, 92, 98–100; interaction between Spider-Man and multicultural citizenry, 100–103; Mary Jane Watson, 114–15; Peter's impoverishment, 114; presentation of Spider-Man's powers, 91, 115, 119
Spider-Man 3 (Raimi 2007): commercial success, 77; digital imaging, 92–95, 99–100; Mary Jane Watson, 115–19, 120; presentation of Spider-Man's powers, 99, 120
Spider-Man: Far from Home (Watts 2019), 121–23, 125
Spider-Man: Homecoming (Watts 2017), 120–21, 122
Spider-Man: Into the Spider-Verse (Persichetti, Ramsay, and Rothman 2018), 124–25

Spider-Man/Miles Morales, 124–25
Spider-Man: No Way Home (Watts 2021), 123–24, 125, 137
Spider-Man/Peter Parker: Amazing Spider-Man films, 120, 122–25; bond with New York, 85–86, 100–103, 120–22, 123, 214; comics, 78–83, 85, 88–89, 96–98, 104, 113, 124–25, 132; Marvel Cinematic Universe, 120–26, 164, 166; relationship between Spider-Man and Peter, 81, 82, 94–95; Spider-Man trilogy, 77, 85–86, 88, 91–96, 98–104, 106–24, 128, 141–42, 156. See also individual titles
Stacy, Gwen, 99, 117, 123–25
Stam, Robert, 14, 26
Starro, 132
Star Wars (Lucas 1977), 65
stereoscopic cinema. See 3D cinema
Storm, 185, 200, 209, 211
Straczynski, J. Michael, 96, 239n8
Suicide Squad (Ayer 2016), 216
Suicide Squad, The (Gunn 2021), 216
Sunspot, 209, 212, 233
Supaidāman (TV Tokyo 1978–1979), 83, 92
Superboy, 187
Supergirl: cinema; 232–33, 234; comics, 187; television, 75
Supergirl (CBS/CW 2015–2021), 75
Supergirl (Szwarc 1984), 72, 127, 233
superhero, defining, 9; versus superhero battle, 130, 147–52, 220–21, 223, 229, 230–31
Superman (Bennet and Carr 1948), 37, 45, 240n13
Superman #233 (January 1971), 47, 48
Superman #276 (June 1974), 39
Superman/Clark Kent: and the American way, 40–41, 51–52, 58, 75, 218, 227; as "champion of the oppressed," 38, 50, 238n13; cinematic future, 215; comics, 8, 16, 17–18, 26, 36–39, 42–43, 46–47, 50, 51, 53, 56–57, 68, 72–73, 75, 79, 81, 127, 132, 172, 175, 187; DC Extended Universe, 75, 216–23, 229, 230–35; film serials, 37, 45, 49, 56, 240n13; and industrialization, 38–39, 40–41, 67, 224; newspaper strip, 37; novelization, 37; relationship between Superman and Clark, 41–52, 53, 54–58, 141; Superman Returns, 72, 74–75; television, 37, 39, 40–41, 44, 45, 49–50, 51, 52, 73–74. See also Fleischer/Famous Studios Superman cartoons; and individual titles
Superman II (Lester and Donner 1980), 72
Superman III (Lester 1983), 72
Superman IV: The Quest for Peace (Furie 1987), 72
Superman: Lois and Clark (December 2015–July 2016), 75
Superman: Red Son (June 2003–August 2003), 174, 232
Superman Returns (Singer 2006), 72, 74–75
Superman's Girlfriend Lois Lane #19 (August 1960), 172
Superman: The Movie (Donner 1978): and the American way, 58; cinematic spectacle, 58–65, 67–72, 83; genre hybridity, 67–72, 141; impact on Superman franchise, 72–76, 231, 233–35; Lois Lane, 54, 55, 56–58, 67–72; merchandise, 66; Metropolis, 61–64; nostalgia, 58, 104; presentation of Superman's flight, 56, 61–64, 69–72, 90, 91, 92, 156, 188, 217; relationship between Superman and Clark Kent, 54–58; score, 66, 73, 231, 239n22; seriality, 65–66, 72, 127; teaser trailer, 34–35; utopia, 69–72
Superman: The Wedding Album (December 1996), 73, 175

Tasker, Yvonne, 5, 11
Terminator: Genisys (Taylor 2015), 208
Thanos, 134–35, 158, 164–67
Themyscira, 223, 224–26, 229, 242n2
This Is Cinerama (Todd, Todd, Thompson, and Rickey 1952), 59
Thor (Branagh 2011), 140–41
Thor/Jane Foster, 175
Thor: Love and Thunder (Waititi 2022), 175
Thor Odinson: The Avengers, 145, 147–50, 151, 154, 155, 158; Avengers: Endgame,

INDEX

165, 167, 241n15; *Avengers: Infinity War*, 162, 164; comics, 130, 175; *Thor*, 140–41; *Thor: Ragnarok*, 162
Thor: Ragnarok (Waititi 2017), 21, 162
Through the Looking Glass, and What Alice Found There (Carroll and Tenniel 1871), 22–24
Top Gun (Scott 1986), 160
trans people, representation of, 201–2
Trask, Dr. Bolivar, 187, 189, 193–94, 196
Trevor, Steve, 226–28
True Lies (Cameron 1994), 160
Trump, Donald, 75, 195–96

Ultimate Comics: Spider-Man (November 2011–December 2013), 124–25
Ultimate Spider-Man (December 2000–August 2011), 124
Uncanny X-Men, The, #141 (January 1981), 170, 177–79, 183. *See also* "Days of Future Past" (January 1981–February 1981)
Uncanny X-Men, The, #142 (February 1981), 170, *184*, 185. *See also* "Days of Future Past" (January 1981–February 1981)
Uncanny X-Men, The, #150 (October 1981), 183
Uncanny X-Men, The, #161 (September 1982), 183
Uncanny X-Men, The, #200 (December 1985), 183
Uncle Ben, 89, 104, 107–8, 113, 114
urban experience, 38–39, 61–64, 68–69, 85–86, 187–88, 214, 218, 220
utopia, 69–72, 98, 102–3, 107–9, 156, 195, 209, 212, 225–26

Van Helsing (Sommers 2004), 206
Venom/Eddie Brock, 93, 116, 240n15
Vietnam War, 58, 79, 189
Vision, 163, 164, 241n14
Vulture, 122

Wakanda, 163–64
WandaVision (Disney+ 2021), 137
"war on terror," 110, 114, 140, 159, 218

Warpath, 209, 212, 233
Wasp, 130
Watson, Mary Jane, 114–19, *120*
West, Adam, 234
Western genre, 179–80, 194–99, 206–8, 210–11
What If? (comic book series), 172–73, 175
What If . . . ? (Disney+ 2021–), 173
What If? #10 (August 1978), 175
White, Perry, 51, 54
"With great power comes great responsibility," 81, 108, 126, 240n13
Wolverine, The (Mangold 2013), 186, 202, 205–6
Wolverine/Logan: body, presentation of, 202–8, 213; centrality to X-Men films, 201, 202–3, 213; cinema, 191, 195–96, 198–99, 200–201, 202–11, 213; comics, 176, 179, *181–82*, 183–85, 212; death, 208–9, 210–11, 213; deterioration of powers, 195, 202, 204–6; nationality, 200; Westerner, links to, 179, 185, 206–7, 210
Wolverine: Old Man Logan Giant-Size (November 2009), 176, 185. *See also* "Old Man Logan" (August 2008–November 2009)
Wolverine vol. 3 #66–72 (August 2008–June 2009), 176, 180, 183, 185. *See also* "Old Man Logan" (August 2008–November 2009)
women in refrigerators, 115, 125
Wonder Woman (Jenkins 2017), 223, 226–28
Wonder Woman #1 (June 1942), 224, *225*
Wonder Woman #5 (July 1943), 224
Wonder Woman 1984 (Jenkins 2020), 242n3
Wonder Woman/Diana Prince: cinema, 218, 222–23, 226–29, 232; comics, 224–25, 227
Wonder Woman vol. 2 #2 (March 1987), 227
World War I, 222, 223, 227
World War II, 40, 50–51, 141–42, 154, 157, 227; Holocaust, 183, 242n9

X2 (Singer 2003), 186, 191
X-24, 197, 199, 207–8, 210

Xavier, Charles: cinema, 187, 189, 191–92, 194, 195–99, 200–201, 209, 211; comics, 180, 183, 185

X-Men: comics, 170–71, 176–85, 187, 190; Fox films, 170–71, 186–213; Marvel Cinematic Universe, 213, 215

X-Men (Fox Kids Network 1992-1997), 209

X-Men (Singer 2000), 5, 186, 202, 242n9

X-Men, The #1 (September 1963), 170

X-Men: Apocalypse (Singer 2016), 186, 202, 211, 242n10

X-Men: Days of Future Past (Singer 2014), 170, 185–87, 229, 233; 3D presentation, 191–92, 194; continuity maintenance, 209, 210–11; impact on franchise, 211–12; premise, 187; spatiotemporal malleability, 189, 191–94, 209; story settings, 188–89, 193–94, 209; superhero deaths, 208–9; Wolverine's body, 202, 203–5, 208

X-Men: Evolution (Kids' WB 2000-2003), 212

X-Men: First Class (Vaughn 2011), 186, 202, 242n9

X-Men Origins: Wolverine (Hood 2009), 186

X-Men: The Last Stand (Ratner 2006), 170, 186

Yon-Rogg, 159–60

Zod, 60, 65, 217–18, 221, 232–33

ABOUT THE AUTHOR

Photo by Melissa Hobbs

JAMES C. TAYLOR is a teaching fellow in film and television studies at the University of Warwick. He holds a BA in film studies from the University of Kent and completed his master's and PhD at the University of Warwick. James has published various book chapters and journal articles on superhero cinema, television, and comics. His research interests include adaptation, comics, Hollywood cinema, digital imaging, media franchising, and film seriality.

www.ingramcontent.com/pod-product-compliance
Lightning Source LLC
Chambersburg PA
CBHW030901280225
22693CB00011B/57